The Samaritans in the '80s

The Samaritans in the '80s

to befriend the suicidal and despairing

Edited and with an Introduction by
CHAD VARAH

Constable London

First published in Great Britain 1980
by Constable and Company Limited
10 Orange Street London WC2H 7EG

Hardback ISBN 0 09 463220 0
Paperback ISBN 0 09 463130 1
Reprinted 1982

Set in Monotype Bembo 12/13 pt
Printed in Great Britain by
St Edmundsbury Press
Bury St Edmunds, Suffolk

The extract from *The king was in his counting-house*
by James Branch Cabell is published by kind permission
of R. E. Cabell Jr.

'The men and women of Melphé, the mere run of mankind,' said the King, 'it is they whom we have to consider first, and their poor human needs. It takes so very little to content them. They need only a home and food, a little work, their mates and their children. Out of these simple things, in the ever-present black shadow of chance and of death, they create, very incredibly, their content. So for their sake, Cesario, you must now put aside Branlon, and the fine dreams of your youth, and your rights as a private person to any special happiness . . . If you do not take the throne when Lorenzo dies, then there is none to inherit . . . All would drift back . . . into the bleak bright savagery of Duke Sigismond's time: and my Melphé would be destroyed. . . .'

'I created Melphé. I cannot make phrases about it, Cesario: but in that great red and grey and green, quiet city, where now some two hundred shops have just put up their shutters for the night, and where in the plaza the town band are tuning their instruments at this very instant, there, during Sigismond's black time, were untilled fields and burned huts and frightened people living desperately upon what they could take by blind force from one another. Now, in place of those naked mudflats, at Sinapoli is a prospering seaport; and back of it are Melphé and Pania and Ferata, all blended into one kingdom . . .

'To help human beings some little way towards orderly and contented living, is that not a dream as brave and strange as is any dream of Branlon? That is what I have done, Cesario, here in my little Melphé, in my own commonplace and prosaic decreed kingdom. I have worked with what tools I might, with Holy Church and your mother's whoredoms, with Sacrobosco the assassin and with the town band . . . I have worked always in the service of my dream, of my own small, unimaginative, sane dream. It has been made tangible through my long labours. Now it is threatened . . . Cesario, my staid strong dream must not perish now that I go down, so very feebly, to my last sleep, beyond the reach of all human dreams!'

'My father,' said Cesario, 'it shall not perish! I have given men songs where you gave them sewerage . . . While my songs were but so-so, your sewers were of the first order. I must see to it that they are kept in sound condition. . . .'

The King said then: 'Pardon my loquaciousness. In one more moment I shall rest . . . The Spanish are so improvident as to raise merino wool for us, and then to buy back at our own prices, mind you, the cloths we make out of it. So their wools ought to be admitted duty free. Do you remember, Cesario, as my last word to you, now that I die, there should be no further tariff upon the Spanish wools. Then, too, in regard to the allied matter of their wines – '

With that, the old gentleman paused, as if somewhat surprised. His lips parted. You saw he was trying to moisten them, and could not quite manage it.

'But this,' he said, in aggrieved protest against the intrusiveness of death, 'this is important. In regard to the customs duties upon Spanish wines – '

He breathed sighingly, as if acquiescent, at last, in his own defeat; and his large grey head fell sideways a little, towards the left. He lifted it, though, rigidly, with an effort very painful to witness; and then lay back, prosaic and grotesque, but erect, in his tall chair, facing the sunset. . . .

Hermia slipped from off her finger the ring containing the bezoar stone. It had not ever left her finger since Cesario placed it there upon the beach at Gratignolles. To remove it was the one thing which she had refused to old Ferdinand during his lifetime. She removed it now. She gave back the ring to him who had first placed it upon her finger, reaching out to him over the dead body of her husband.

From *The king was in his counting house*, JAMES BRANCH CABELL

Foreword

The Samaritans (1965) written for our twelfth anniversary, went out of print when it was updated for our twentieth anniversary as *The Samaritans in the '70s* (1973). When revised in 1977 about one-third of the material in it was replaced or rewritten.

The Samaritans in the '80s, though it retains the same format – a long introduction by me; transcripts of talks given at our Conferences or articles written by our members; lists of Centres in the British Isles and all over the world – is a new book. Very few of the essays and transcribed addresses have been reproduced from *The Samaritans in the '70s*, except for the greater part of the section on Depression, which in my view could not be, or at any rate has not been, bettered. My introduction has been rewritten to answer the questions people still ask after reading the previous books.

To whet the appetite of readers for *Answers to suicide presented to Chad Varah by The Samaritans on the 25th anniversary of their founding* (1979) I have reproduced one article which in my view deals superlatively well with the perennial and universal problem of psychopaths.

We expect to reprint or revise several times during the '80s, so members all over the world are invited to send really outstanding expositions of some aspect of Befriending to The Editor at: The Samaritans, 39 Walbrook, London EC4N 8BP.

CHAD VARAH
London, 14 December 1979

Contents

Contents

Oh, the comfort, the inexpressible comfort, of feeling safe with a person; having neither to weigh thoughts nor measure words, but to pour them all out just as they are, chaff and grain together, knowing that a faithful hand will take and sift them, keep what is worth keeping, and then, with the breath of kindness, blow the rest away.

GEORGE ELIOT

'Never less lonely than by oneself' . . . was at first spoken by the excellent Scipio . . . His meaning no doubt was this: that he found more satisfaction to his mind, and more improvement of it by solitude than by company; and to show that he spoke not loosely or out of vanity, after he had made Rome mistress of almost the whole world, he retired himself from it by voluntary exile . . . But the greater part of men are so far from the opinion of that noble Roman, that if they chance at any time to be without company they are like a becalmed ship; they never move but by the wind of other men's breath, and have no oars of their own to steer withal. It is very fantastical and contradictory in human nature that men should love themselves above all the rest of the world and yet never endure to be with themselves. And yet our dear self is so wearisome to us that we can scarcely support its conversation for one hour together.

It is a deplorable condition this, and drives a man sometimes to painful shifts in seeking how to avoid himself.

from *Essays*, ABRAHAM COWLEY

Introduction – CHAD VARAH

The Concise Oxford Dictionary defines a Samaritan as a member of a sect living in Israel and as a member of an organisation to befriend the suicidal. *The Illustrated Oxford Dictionary* adds that this organisation was founded in 1953, and Brewer's *Dictionary of Phrase and Fable*, along with other dictionaries, mentions that it was founded by Chad Varah. This organisation has not only given the word 'Samaritan' a specialised meaning but has also, since it became nationwide in 1963, made a crucial contribution to the steady and unique reduction of the suicide rate in England and Wales.

The most humanitarian and the least 'religious' parable in the Gospel according to St Luke is the parable of the Good Samaritan. It is not, of course, as shocking to modern readers as it was to those who first heard it. The idea of a Jewish priest and a Levite being in too much of a hurry to get to their holy duties in the Temple to attend to a fellow Jew who had been beaten up and robbed, whilst a passing Samaritan was moved with compassion for a fellow-human and interrupted his own urgent business to help him, fails to stun those who today – *because* of the parable – think of 'Samaritan' as meaning a kindly and helpful chap and not as a despicable outcast near-heathen. To have the impact it had at its first telling, the characters in the story would need to be changed to (say) an Archdeacon in a mini and a Churchwarden in a Rolls speeding to the Cathedral, leaving a fellow-Englishman who had been mugged to be picked up and taken to Casualty in an old banger by a Pakistani Moslem member of the National Union of Public Employees at a time when his colleagues were picketing a Cheshire home for disabled people.

It is not only in Judeo-Christian circles that the relation between belief and conduct continues to be a live issue. In other religions there are similar controversies, and in avowedly atheistic societies there is the conflict between ideology and economic productivity. It seems eminently reasonable to teach that faith is what leads to good works and that without it these soon wither like cut flowers. It seems equally reasonable to insist on testing the reality of the alleged faith by its fruits, if any – as did the author of the parable under discussion.

The policy of The Samaritans is to seek out people of any religion or no religion who in practice are found to be humane, without enquiring what it was that made them so.

In the British Isles and in most English-speaking countries, the word 'Samaritan' is far from having the religious flavour it tends to have on the Continent of Europe. Tough characters who haven't been to Church since they were baptised, if then, will say 'Oh well, I'll be the Samaritan' if someone has to perform an unwelcome task, such as walking four miles in the rain for a can of petrol. It was common in the early 1950s for beneficent societies such as the bands of people who supplied material comforts to hospital patients to use the name 'Samaritan' in their title. It was this usage which led a national newspaper in 1953 to describe me as a Samaritan in offering my address and telephone number to potential suicides and other unhappy people, and to my transferring the term in the plural to the volunteers who gradually gathered round to help me to cope with the crowds of people who came or wrote or telephoned for help.

What made me concern myself with suicide

The question I have been asked so many times that I have become sick of hearing myself tell variants of the same story is, 'How did you come to start The Samaritans?' I should like in future to be able to refer enquirers to this book. Any who are, like myself, not very interested in the early history of the organisation, let alone scrappy reminiscences of events which helped to make me into the sort of person who would at the age of forty-two found The Samaritans, may turn to page 37.

Where does a significant event in one's life begin? Its cause was caused by an earlier experience, and this by an earlier one still. One's whole life up to the point of the vital decision must have contributed to – indeed, been essential to – that decision. Where ought one to draw the line and say '*Here* it began'? I don't know how to answer except by picking out, from the beginning, incidents which in hindsight seem relevant.

I was born in 1911 at Barton upon Humber, where the world's longest-span suspension bridge now crosses the estuary and makes it possible to get to Hull without taking the paddle steamer from New Holland or, if this was stuck in the mud or fogbound, going round by Doncaster. My father, Canon William Edward Varah, was very suitable to be the Vicar of a parish with the oldest Church in England in daily use (now closed) and two other ancient churches, for he was an outstanding authority on pre-Norman history and archaeology, and visitors came from all over the world to see the parts dating from the eighth to the eleventh centuries on the site chosen by St Chad in AD 669. My mother, Mary, whom he had married when she was twenty-one and he a bachelor of nearly fifty, was admirable in every branch of housewifery, and no impediment to childhood enjoyments ('I never know where any of them are, except at mealtimes,' she would say comfortably of the nine of us). Even the youngest, if Father was out shepherding his parishioners when visitors came to see the churches, could discourse learnedly and accurately on pilaster strip work and baluster shafts, and sometimes earn a ha'penny. We had no other pocket money, nor felt the lack of it.

Our family is English. Our surname, possibly of Ukrainian origin, is found on Yorkshire tombstones from 1537 onwards. I was the eldest of nine children. After me were three girls, who played together, and then two boys, ditto, and so on, so although I was held responsible for the younger ones, I had no playmates. There were only a few families within bicycling distance with whom we could mix socially in those days, and none had a son of my age. I wandered the countryside alone, thinking and dreaming, and I read many of the books in my father's extensive library. They were not children's books. Theology, including dusty volumes of forgotten sermons, predominated over history and archaeology and classical texts, but there were some books of science (then known as natural philosophy) which I preferred to the fiction. There were complete sets of Dickens and Scott, some of which I enjoyed, and the poets which Father liked to read aloud, particularly Tennyson. The shelf I most often went to had dozens of Dent's Everyman's Library, so I was able to read Tolstoy's *Anna Karenina*, Dostoievsky's *Letters from the Underworld* and Ibsen's plays at a tender age. I played Shylock in a scene from *The Merchant of Venice* at the age of four in my first term at the local Dame School. Lest this should sound priggish, a fellow pupil reminded me recently that I was caned nearly every day, whereas her only punishment was to hold a backboard across her shoulder-blades to encourage an erect posture.

The first act of mine which perhaps qualifies to be called Samaritan occurred early in 1917. I was, as usual in the winter, getting in my mother's way in the kitchen, where a huge coal-fired range kept the room warm. I could enjoy the smell of baking bread (my mother baked every day except Sunday) and often have my presence rewarded by a hot 'new cake' liberally spread with butter, or better still with bacon dripping from the frying pan. I was poring unenthusiastically over a tattered copy of Dr W. Smith's *First Latin Primer*, my father having one day removed my book of natural philosophy and substituted this dreary tome, saying curtly, 'Learn Latin from this – I'll correct your exercises,' when the doorbell rang. I ran to answer it with alacrity.

The visitor was a tall, pasty-faced young man in a black suit and clerical collar, who was sweating and trembling with fear and saying he had an appointment to see my father. I took a dislike to him even before he patted me on the head and called me his little man, but I nevertheless felt sorry for him, for he was clearly dreading his coming encounter with my father, a strong character who was not afraid to say what he thought and often embarrassed me (though I now admire it and sometimes do it myself) by putting into words what other people only thought but were too shy or lacking in moral courage to come out with.

It was many years before I discovered what it was the young man was frightened about. He had (I was told) been recommended by my father for free training for the ministry on condition that he served for some years in the Mission Field, and after ordination had conveniently discovered that his health would not allow him to be boiled and eaten by cannibals, so had worked safely in this country and had not repaid the cost of his training.

My father was using the dining room instead of the study to save fuel, and I led the young man into the Awful Presence, astonished that the visitor hadn't turned to stone under the glowering look he got. In an attempt to soften my father, I stayed, chattering, telling jokes and being consciously 'cute', and the visitor played up to this, praising my wit and enquiring how old I was. 'He's five,' said my father, dismissing the subject and me. 'Five and a quarter!' I cried; and that is how I know when the incident happened. I went reluctantly back to my *Latin Primer*, having failed to save the young man from the wrath he assuredly deserved.

I think it was later that same year that I had my most impressive lesson on truly Samaritan behaviour, and it came from a couple of men whom I knew to be illiterate because whenever they had 'papers to be signed' they brought them to my father and he witnessed their mark, i.e. a cross they made with a pen held ham-fistedly. I had been watching the blacksmith who was later to become the bosom friend of my brother Hugh (my own bosom friend, in my teens, was to be a greengrocer and fishmonger who also had the 'bus depot and who was known to everyone as 'Pop'), and when these two characters brought in a carthorse to be shoed they didn't notice me crouching in a corner. If I were to reproduce the dialogue in the broad Lincolnshire dialect in which it was spoken, few would understand it; and if I were to reproduce it as it is fixed in my memory, people would think I was a clever script writer for a pair of Northern comedians. I will only give the gist of it here. One of the farmhands told the other that a certain farmer had been up in his fields the previous evening and had seen a character whom I will call Asa, after the king of Israel who died of a disease of his feet, because this poor fellow had something wrong with his feet and they stank. The farmer had caught Asa 'fooking' one of his ewes. The other labourer expressed concern for the ewe, which he hoped wasn't damaged and on receiving reassurance on this point, enquired what had been the outcome. On being told that the farmer had chased Asa off instantly, the second labourer expostulated 'What? afore 'e'd done?' The first labourer agreed that this was a bit mean and a thoughtful pause then ensued. Then I heard the comments of the first two of the many Samaritans I have met in my life. One said: 'Mun be six month sin' 'is wife died.' The other said, 'An' the pore boogger won't nivver git another – not wi' them feet.' It was sheep and barley land up on the wolds, and one had the impression that they would have kept *cave* for him as long as he didn't 'damage' any ewe.

I was lucky to grow up in what were then the Parts of Lindsey, among those earthy, kindly, stubborn, morbid, loyal people, who always wanted to know what was going on, but then kept it to themselves. During my adolescence they knew a good deal of what I got up to, but none of them ever told my father. Forty years later, when I was the subject of 'This Is Your Life', they grumbled that there did ought to have been someone from Barton to say ' 'E wur a rum lad.' No details, of course.

Probably the best thing that happened to me in my childhood was suffering from an unidentified stomach ailment which caused me to be in a children's hospital in Hull for many months and after that to have a long period of convalescence at home. During all this time I read and read and do not ever remember being bored or lonely. Visitors were, in fact, an interruption of my reading. At the age of twelve I was confirmed by Bishop J. E. Hine, a tall man with a mass of white hair and a white beard who had five doctorates but had spent his life loving and serving the simple people of Central Africa until the time came for him to come home and help in the diocese of Lincoln. He had never married, and lived with two sisters, and 'adopted' three clergymen's sons to spend their holidays with him. I was fortunate to be one of these. He, too, played an important part in the genesis of The Samaritans, without either of us being aware of it. I was staying with him one day in the Subdeanery in the Minster yard at Lincoln when he called me to his study and said, 'You are twelve, are you not?'

'Nearly thirteen!' I boasted.

'I don't suppose either of your parents has ever told you anything about the subject of sex?' he enquired.

'Certainly not', I replied, 'and there hasn't been much about it in any of my books, except the Bible, but I have watched horses and dogs, and I realised how we come into the world when I saw piglets being born, on Uncle Charlie's farm.'

'It's time you knew the facts,' he decided. 'I shall sit here at my desk, and you can sit behind me in that easy chair and you may take the cat upon your lap.'

He then gave me a most lucid account of the process of conception and reproduction, and as I listened and stroked the cat a great many things fell into place. After what may have been as much as an hour he said, 'Now, have you any questions?'

'Er – I don't think so, my Lord,' I said, 'you have made everything very clear.'

'How many times have I told you not to call me "my Lord" except on arriving and departing?' he enquired testily. 'If you have questions, put them now, for we shall not speak of this matter again.'

I thought very carefully for some minutes, feeling that courtesy demanded at least one question. Then I asked: 'Since Bartholin's glands lubricate only the vulva, how does there come to be lubrication deep inside the vagina?'

There was a long pause. Then the Bishop said: 'That is a very shrewd question. I do not know the answer. You will not think me boastful if I state that that means the answer is not known. Have you any other questions?'

'No, thank you.'

'Then I suggest you run three times around the Minster Yard,' prescribed the Bishop.

When I had done so, I felt a tremendous intellectual satisfaction and a sense of 'knowledge is power'. It was good to *know*, and not to have to guess or to be exposed to old wives' tales.

It was a particular relief to know, and to be able to tell other boys (who wouldn't always believe it) that masturbation is a normal part of adolescence, does no harm whatsoever, and should not be confessed as a sin.

At the age of thirteen and a half I went to my public school, Worksop, situated in that part of Sherwood Forest called The Dukeries. We could wander around Clumber estate, but never go into the town.

I found the work effortless and fascinating, the textbooks of those times being easy reading compared with what I had been accustomed to, and my insatiable curiosity about natural science could be satisfied at last. I was soon top of my form, then promoted to higher forms, and after getting nine credits in the School Certificate was allowed to take the Higher in one year instead of two, and work for an Oxford scholarship.

It was not a happy school. Most of the boys looked forward to the end of term, but it was the first place where I had companions of my own age so I dreaded the end of term and looked forward to the beginning of each new one. During term time we never saw any girls, and 'romantic friendships' between big and little boys were common. I made bets with myself on which boys were 'really' homosexual, and in later years was able to confirm several of these assessments.

I was still listed as below par medically and was not allowed to take part in games, but cross-country running had escaped mention. To please the rugger master who had made me, 'a dirty swot', a prefect, I ran every day, going harder whenever it hurt, and astonished everyone including myself by winning my colours.

In 1930, thanks to an eccentric master who took four of us up to Finals standard in calculus, I won an Exhibition in Natural Science at Keble College, Oxford, and was able to study atomic physics under Professor Soddy, discoverer of isotopes. The work I had done at school got me through the first part of my degree, in Chemistry. Then I switched to Philosophy, Politics and Economics for Finals, as the Faculty in which an ingenious undergraduate might be able to obtain an Honours degree without working, and thus be able to enjoy Oxford, whose social life in those days was exciting and stimulating. It was there that I began to be cosmopolitan: I was secretary of the Russian and Slavonic Clubs and founder and President of the Scandinavian Club and most of my friends were foreigners.

When I came down from Oxford, I didn't know what I wanted to do with my life. I worked for a few weeks at a Rudolf Steiner home for handicapped children. I taught English Literature at a college for foreigners, and made more foreign friends. Then I did some research into Humberside clay for a brickyard, and when that was successfully concluded I did some freelance writing, my first acceptance being from *Punch*; but it looked to my father as though I was wasting my time. Bishop Hine invited me to go and stay with him, and was as direct as usual.

'Why don't you go to Lincoln Theological College?' he asked. 'It would please your father, and you enjoy community life, and one can never know too much, and at the end of the course you don't need to be ordained if by then you don't feel that it is your vocation.'

It seemed to me eminently reasonable, and I agreed. At Lincoln, I was immensely influenced by the Sub-Warden, Michael Ramsey, later Archbishop of Canterbury, and such a staff as no Theological College has ever had before or since; but at the end of the course I had no desire to be ordained. I was convinced of the truth of the Christian faith, and I did not wish to be a professional exponent of it. I did not want to be on the other side of that great divide which separates the clergy from the laity and in those days caused people to treat a man in a clerical collar as though he were their maiden aunt. So I went to tell Bishop Hine, now living in a smaller house in the Minster Yard, of my decision. His surviving sister told me that he was ill in bed and unlikely to recover. However, he recognised me when I went in, and I told him why I thought I ought not to be ordained. He said nothing. I then told him again, and again he said nothing. The third time, it began to sound unconvincing even to me and I petered out. Then he opened his eyes briefly and uttered his verdict, the one word 'Scruples'. This is a technical theological term for the sort of rationalisation one employs to get out of doing one's plain duty by pretending it is against one's conscience. I felt the word was appropriate. I said: 'You are right, as usual. Well, I will be ordained.'

He made no response, so I kissed his forehead (the first time I had ever done such a thing) and crept out. His sister went in and turned on the service on the radio.

'Switch it off,' he commanded; and died. Whenever anyone asks me why such an unconventional character as myself decided to become a priest, I shrug my shoulders, but I tell myself, 'What choice did I have? Press-ganged into it by a saint on his deathbed!'

It was a proud day for my father when I read the Gospel at my ordination in Lincoln Minster where he himself had read it at his ordination so many years before.

My first job, on arriving in my new parish, was to take a funeral, because my Vicar had influenza. Accustomed to loud sports jackets and Oxford bags, I felt somewhat conspicuous dressed in black from my skullcap to my shoes, with only my clerical collar and a glimpse of my white surplice where my ankle length cloak parted in front, to relieve the black. It was pouring with rain as the cheerful little undertaker and I left the cemetery chapel and led the coffin, followed by the mourners, to the distant grave. I asked why we were going right over there, and he explained that that was the unconsecrated ground and that the girl for whom I had just said the Order for the Burial of a Child, as she was only fourteen, had to be buried there because she had committed suicide.

'Suicide?' I exclaimed. 'Why? At that age!'

'Well, Sir,' said the undertaker, 'we don't usually know, do we? As it happens, however, in this case we have a hint, because my girl used to play with her, and she says that when her periods started, like, this kid didn't know what it was, because no one hadn't never said nothing to her, and there wasn't no one she could ask, so she thought it was VD. Of course, she wouldn't know what VD was, either, but she'd have an idea it was shameful.'

We paced for a while in silence. Then he said, 'If this is your first time, Sir, I'd better show you the ropes. Don't ever turn your head to me as we talk, nor I won't to you, and if you laughs, do it quiet, so the mourners don't notice nothing.'

'I'm not laughing,' I said.

'Well,' he said, 'It's no good getting morbid.'

'Morbid?' I snapped. 'Do you know what the word "morbid" *means*? It means "of or pertaining to death". If a funeral isn't morbid, kindly tell me what is!'

I was still upset about the child's suicide – the undertaker and I had many a joke at subsequent funerals, talking out of the sides of our mouths like stage villains, but on this occasion he said no more until we got to the grave, when he asked 'Will you bless it, or leave it?'

'I'll bless it,' I said – which, as a mere deacon, I was not entitled to do. I blessed the grave, conducted the committal, and then stayed and looked down at that narrow coffin and said silently, 'Little girl, I never knew you, but you have changed my life. I promise you, I will teach youngsters about sex, as I was taught when I was younger than you are now, even if I get labelled a dirty old man at the age of twenty-four.'

I had the opportunity to begin to keep that vow that very evening, for there was a meeting of the Church Youth Club. Not surprisingly, some of the boys tried to embarrass the new young curate by shouting out improper remarks. I had been warned that the drill was to pretend not to hear, but I seized the opportunity to reply, taking every observation seriously and answering the implied question within it. Before long, many of the youth club members had put down their billiards cues and pingpong bats and gathered round to listen. It became well known that at my youth club you could ask any question and get a truthful answer. The impromptu talks about some aspects of human sexuality didn't happen every time we met nor did they always last long, but sometimes if the members were in the mood, a discussion would continue for twenty minutes or more.

It will be noticed that it was not suicide, but the ignorance of sex that had caused that girl's death, which I had taken up and begun to tackle. This was in 1935: it wasn't until 1953 that I turned my attention directly to the problem of suicide.

My next concern was to try to instruct those who were likely to become parents before they had any children, so that *their* children would have their questions about sex answered truthfully from the very beginning. A year later when I was ordained priest and could take weddings (which a deacon can't do because he can't give the Blessing) I began to insist that young couples wishing to be married should come for a prior talk with me in the course of which I gave them the information I thought they ought to have, about the sexual relationship we call marriage. Such 'pastoral preparation for marriage', which is now commonplace, was hardly heard of in those days, and I expected some opposition. Instead, I found couples who were going to be married in other churches coming and demanding one of my 'little talks' and at times I had half a dozen couples in my landlady's sitting room. People who had already been married but encountered sexual difficulties began to hear on the grapevine about my frankness and lack of embarrassment, and so by about 1937 I was doing marriage guidance long before the formation of the Marriage Guidance Council.

There is nothing much to explain the movement of my mind towards the idea of The Samaritans during the next ten years, which covers the period of the Second World War. I was curate of Putney, London, when war broke out and at the end of my time there got married and went to Barrow-in-Furness and two years later to my first benefice, Holy Trinity, Blackburn, where my daughter and my triplet sons were born. I did, of course, continue my teaching about sex. It was at Blackburn that I made a survey of the young couples who came to me for instruction, and discovered over a period of several years that three out of every five of the males had no idea whatever of the function of the clitoris, and more surprisingly two out of five of the females were in the same situation. Even those who *did* know that there was such an organ were almost all unaware of its importance in the sexual relationship in marriage, and most of those ladies who knew from their own masturbation what kind of stimulation was necessary to procure an orgasm, did not connect this up with their failure to reach a climax during sexual intercourse with a husband who did no caressing at all of the clitoris before, during or after the act. There has subsequently been a considerable improvement in this regard, but there is still a long way to go before men become the kind of lovers most women need.

Whilst in Blackburn I edited the diocesan magazine and called a conference of such editors from all over the country and thus made friends with Marcus Morris, who at that time was Vicar of St James, Birkdale, Southport, and publishing the most go-ahead parish magazine in the country, *Anvil.* He was working on a project for a strip cartoon magazine of very high quality and serious purpose, along with a brilliant young artist, Frank Hampson, whom he had discovered in Southport. When I moved to London to be Vicar of St Paul, Clapham Junction, I was able to be a London base for this project and eventually *Eagle* was born (soon followed by *Girl*) and was the publishing success of the century. Marcus Morris then employed me first as scientific and astronautic consultant to Dan Dare, to make sure nothing scientifically ridiculous was done by our space hero; and secondly as a reader of the manuscripts sent in. I also wrote a text serial before it was discovered that I have a freakish 3D visual imagination in colour, and am able to write visualised scripts from which an artist can do successful strip cartoon stories. The importance of this in the preparation for The Samaritans is obvious: leading a double life, half as a parson in Battersea and half as a writer in Fleet Street, I became friendly with many people in the newspaper world. This not only meant that when I wanted to write articles on the subject of human sexual behaviour I was able to find a ready market, but also that when as a result of the response to these articles the idea came to me that there ought to be an emergency telephone number and address for potential suicides to turn to, I already had numerous contacts in the media.

By using my benefice income to pay my secretary, and by working on scripts until the wee small hours, it was possible for me to make a success of my parish, building up the congregation from eight to well over a hundred and twenty; regularly visit the patients in St John's Hospital, Battersea; and run a Youth Club which was open to any youngsters in the neighbourhood whether they attended church or not.

Several of the brethren were horrified at my idea of having a secretary instead of a curate, and may have thought this an affectation, but in fact those who had a curate were tied to their desks while their curate did pastoral work, whereas I tied my secretary to my desk and did my own pastoral work.

How The Samaritans began

In the summer of 1953, I wrote an article for a magazine which was the most explicitly permissive article on sex written by that date by a clergyman, and based not upon a lowering of Christian standards but a raising of them from Pharisaic 'letter of the law' morality to a Spirit-directed application of the One Law of Love by each individual in every situation he encountered. I was in a tiny minority in those days. It has since enlarged, but the legalistic judaisers are on the rampage and are as much of a nuisance to true disciples at the present day as they were long ago to St Paul. Some of them have at times managed to diddle their way into The Samaritans where they would make clients feel guilty and thus more likely to commit suicide until exposed and expelled.

If I could find the article now and reread it, I expect it would seem cautious rather than audacious. It defended masturbation and homosexual partnerships on theological grounds, but (if I remember rightly) did not state plainly that the teens are a time for gradual learning about sex or that whilst adultery is in most cases unloving to the neglected spouse, there are cases where it is loving behaviour and only the parties concerned can rightly judge this. The contention that the One Law of Love applies to sexual activity was what shocked the puritans and attracted those who were worried about their own sexual situation.

It is a common fault to apply today's standards to historical characters, expecting them to act on information they didn't have in a climate of opinion that didn't exist – hence the injustice done to St Paul, whose general line makes it clear that if he'd known as much as (say) I do about human sexuality, he would have chosen his words more carefully in denouncing child prostitution in Corinth in such a way that they couldn't be twisted by the malevolent into a condemnation of loving homosexual partnerships. But he couldn't possibly have known. And even twenty-five years ago, it would have been what we now call 'counter-productive' if I had *then* written the articles I have written more recently e.g. in *Forum* magazine. However much 'permissiveness' may be attacked by the bullies who favour 'repressiveness', the former has come to exist in some measure in Britain in a way it didn't when I first advocated it.

Just as 'the permissive society' is (too optimistically) taken for granted, so The Samaritans are now a familiar part of British life.

Many readers will have been born into a world in which The Samaritans already exist and indeed are known to practically everybody and increasingly taken for granted. They may wonder what people did in the days before you could pick up a telephone or drop in at a not too distant Centre and find someone willing to listen to your troubles. The short answer is, they suffered; and, in many more cases than at present, they killed themselves. The amazingly rapid spread of The Samaritans came about precisely because the need already existed, but little provision was made to meet it until I had the idea of providing a place to which people could telephone or come or write in order to find what *Reader's Digest* called, in the title of an article about my work in May 1960: 'Love from a Stranger'. There were plenty of hospitals and doctors and caseworkers and clergymen, all of them offering some kind of specialist help, but it was difficult for a lonely, anxious or depressed person to find someone trustworthy to unburden to and talk things over with, before making up his/her mind whether expert help was needed and acceptable or not.

I am often asked whether I thought of The Samaritans because of having been suicidal myself. The answer is 'no'; and though there had been two or three occasions when if The Samaritans had existed I might well have rung them up about some worry, it wasn't this that I had in mind when I conceived the idea. From the very beginning it was suicide that I wanted to tackle, having read somewhere in the summer of 1953 that there were three suicides a day in Greater London, I asked myself what these victims were supposed to do when they found themselves on the verge of taking their own lives. What would have been the proper course of action for them, if they were not willing to lose control of the situation as they thought they would do if they put themselves in the hands of a psychiatrist? It struck me that suicide is undeniably an emergency. I therefore looked at my telephone, on which was announced: EMERGENCY and under that 'Dial 999 Fire Police Ambulance'.

It occurred to me that the Fire Brigade might be useful if one were teetering on a ledge and uncertain whether one wanted to jump, but presumably there would be no telephone instrument on the ledge. To call the Police at that time (we didn't get the law under which suicide was a felony changed until 1961) would have been unwise, and to call an Ambulance might have seemed premature – jumping the gun, so to speak. There ought, I thought, to be a 999 for potential suicides. It was as simple as that. Well, someone had to think of it. The answer wasn't difficult when you asked the right question. Logically, the next question was, What would you do if someone who was on the verge of committing suicide, or even had suicide in mind as a more remote possibility, were to ring up? What sort of person should answer, and how should he/she answer?

I had some idea about this because at about the same period I had, as a result of my being accepted for many years as an authority on sexual problems, combined with my contacts in Fleet Street, had the opportunity to write the 'permissive' article to which I have already referred. Hundreds of people who had read it contacted me to discuss their problems, and I found to my astonishment I was able to help even those of them who because of their anxiety and depression were suicidal. I was astonished because until then I had supposed that suicidal people were all mentally ill and therefore needed a doctor. I did not then know that the majority of those who kill themselves are emotionally disturbed rather than ill in a psychiatric sense, though a sizeable minority do benefit from psychiatric treatment, and for most of these nothing else will do.

Trying to meet the need of those who telephoned me or wrote to me or asked to meet me, I did not then realise that I was adjusting the nature of my counselling to each individual and in some cases my activity would more properly be described by a word which in those days did not exist in this sense, namely 'befriending'. I cannot claim that I thought of befriending before starting The Samaritans, although without realising it I had been practising it upon occasion. What I thought must be offered was counselling by someone who though not a doctor was still a professional. Like the man who discovered to his surprise that he had been talking prose, it was only after I had observed the volunteers 'befriending' that I realised that I had myself sometimes done it, though not so well. The original idea therefore was to have a sort of 999 for suicidal people, at an address to which those who wished could come or to which they could write, and thus make contact with someone who would receive them kindly and listen to their troubles and then give them non-directive counselling. I knew this person couldn't be me. I had neither the time nor sufficient qualifications. I had a more than full-time job which was just beginning to show results for all the work I had put in, and I had no experience of counselling on other than sexual or theological problems. The kind of enterprise I envisaged would be suitable only for the incumbent of a down-town church such as is to be found in most of our big cities and of which there were forty in the square mile of the City of London. I did not, however, mention this to anyone.

That summer I took my family to Knokke on the Belgian coast for a holiday, as one got a house in exchange for doing duty at the English Church there. Whilst there I received a cable from the Worshipful Company of Grocers inviting me to apply for the living of St Stephen Walbrook in the City of London. I didn't know then and I have never discovered since how they heard of me, but I knew they hadn't heard of my idea, and as I was not keen to leave my exciting parish and embark on this untried and possibly perilous scheme, I decided that I would accept the invitation to meet the Court of the Company, and then queer my own pitch by telling them the crazy antics I should get up to if they were foolish enough to appoint me.

At the interview, these successful and intelligent men asked some very searching questions, and when I retired to allow them to discuss me, I felt I had sounded like a charlatan. I was therefore astonished to be called back and informed that they were going to appoint me because they wanted done what I proposed to do, and thought the experiment worth trying. At that time, and subsequently, it has been a great encouragement and comfort to me to know that a body of men of this calibre was willing to be so enterprising in connexion with the most important Church in their gift. It was on the point of becoming the Lord Mayor's parish church and is generally recognised as the finest built by Sir Christopher Wren, who lived just opposite. It is listed by Sir Niklaus Pevsner as one of the ten most important buildings in England, and Canova told Lord Burlington there was nothing finer in Rome. When I first entered St Stephen Walbrook I fell in love with it and have remained so ever since.

It had been damaged by incendiary bombs during the blitz and part of the dome (the first built in England) came down in flames. The restoration by Gilbert Meadon had just been completed. Men were still at work on the bomb-damaged vestries, and the telephone which was destined to become famous and which had been reconnected by the contractors was hidden under a pile of rubble. The story of my using it to dial the operator and ask if the number could be changed to MANsion House 9000 or 9999 is well known and I can assure readers it is not apocryphal. The operator *did* get me to wipe the dust off the dial to see what number I was calling from, and I did find that it was MAN 9000 already.

I persuaded a former secretary of mine, Vivien Prosser, to return from Paris where she was working in order to help me to launch my scheme. My appointment was to start on 1st November, and I was determined to advertise the service for potential suicides to start on 2nd November. My connexions with

Fleet Street were an immense advantage at this point. The only way you can tell the potential suicide that you are in business to help him or her is to tell everyone, and if you haven't much money, the only way you can tell everyone is through the good offices of the press. . . . I toured the pubs of Fleet Street and found many pressmen willing to regard my plans as a human interest story: I suppose it could be said that for the price of a few dozen whiskies I received millions of pounds worth of free publicity, not only at the beginning but regularly thereafter. Without the help of the press, and later of radio and television, the enormous success of The Samaritans would not have been possible.

The first telephone calls

The first telephone call I took on MAN 9000 was from a lady faced with eviction who was going to kill her four children and then put her head in the gas oven. I did what Samaritans are not now allowed to do, namely left my post and went to the lady's flat, leaving Vivien to cope. This must have been when she took what *she* remembers as the first call and describes in her account in *Answers to Suicide*.

What seems most significant now about those early days is that instead of asking what it was that I wanted to give, I asked what it was that the clients needed to receive. It is obvious that the phenomenal growth of The Samaritans is due to the fact that it meets a widespread need which was not previously being met. My enterprise was thus in the nature of an experiment, and we learnt from the first clients what they do and do not find helpful. We also, sadly, learnt what sort of people are unhelpable, at least by us; and what sorts we ought not to spend our time on if we are to be reasonably unencumbered to help those for whom the organisation exists. In my opinion, we shall do well always to be guided by the principle we adopted in those early days, of making decisions on the basis of a statement beginning with the words, 'The needs of the client dictate that . . .'.

It was clear to us within the first few months that the needs of the client dictated that those who wanted our help should be free to telephone, or to come, or to write, or to ask us (if we had someone to hold the fort) to come to them; that they should be free to choose whether to give their name and address or whether to be anonymous; that they should know that in no circumstances would we betray their confidence, even if they had committed some crime; and that by confiding in us they would not lose their freedom to make their own decisions, including the freedom to commit suicide. Our relaxed and permissive attitude was made clear in the publicity, and potential clients realised that they had nothing whatever to lose by getting in touch with us.

When I say 'with us', I am not referring only to myself and Vivien, for within a very few weeks volunteers came along and offered their help. I can shorten a long story by saying that the most obviously unsuitable as well as the apparently suitable came to offer their services, and the real difficulty was in deciding which among the latter were really helpful to the clients. It was easy to fend off the cranks and do-gooders and Lady Bountifuls and religious maniacs and political fanatics and people with panaceas. It was more difficult to distinguish between those whose excellent qualities made them suitable for what we subsequently dubbed 'befriending' and those whose different excellent qualities made them suitable only for a quasi-parental taking-charge-of-the-situation which was incompatible with befriending.

What was done in those days largely by intuition and trial and error is now fairly well codified and systematic. Selection remains the key to the success of a Samaritan Branch. If the volunteers selected are truly Samaritan types, then they will begin to benefit the clients even before they have had very much instruction and experience – indeed, a lot of experience may make a volunteer less effective than he/she was when still new, anxious, convinced of inadequacy and starry-eyed.

The first volunteers joined in order to help *me*. They were very humble about the contribution they might make, thinking of themselves as running errands and achieving the height of responsibility in chatting with a client, impatient with a long wait, to keep him/her ticking over until the Big Event, i.e. an encounter with me. Their faith in me was touching. They expected me always to know the answer and to work miracles. For their sakes I didn't let on how inadequate *I* felt very often. I suppose it was only fair that I got my own back by trusting *them* with things they themselves felt totally inadequate to cope with. Perhaps we were all of us right to trust one another and support one another and to have confidence in one another.

As the number of clients grew it was totally impracticable for me to see everybody, and the problem solved itself, because those who got tired of waiting to see me 'made do' with a volunteer who, in fact, gave them far better attention than I could possibly have given. To say this is not mock modesty. The volunteers had nothing whatever to do or think about except befriend the person they happened to be with, whereas I had at all times many preoccupations. Furthermore, they had no temptation to engage in counselling for which they were not qualified, and therefore could only do that which we discovered is the best thing in the first instance in all cases, namely *befriend*. Only about one client in eight required counselling or referral to some expert in addition to befriending, and I and one or two others whom I gradually trained were able to see all of these. It was clear by 2nd February 1954 that befriending by the volunteers was what we were offering and what people were coming for, and on that date I handed over 'my' ministry to the suicidal to the volunteers, to The Samaritans. Before that, it was usual for me to take emergency calls, even in the middle of an interview with someone else. After that date, I made it clear that never again should I be the one to pick up the emergency telephone, or to say 'Come in' when someone knocked at the door. I did remain the one who opened all letters, but sometimes managed to pass one to a volunteer or to my secretary to answer.

Just listening

It was astonishing to businessmen, housewives, bus drivers, typists and the like to discover that they could be rescuers – that they could actually save lives, just like those highly trained people they had always admired and secretly envied, such as brain surgeons, helicopter pilots and pit or mountain rescue squads.

The Samaritans went to their appointment with a client who had an appointment with death as unobtrusively as possible with no sirens shrieking, and their efforts were almost always rewarded with success.

I studied as carefully and scientifically as possible what the volunteers actually did. At first sight, it appeared that they did practically nothing, but on closer observation it was clear that their listening was active and positive although they said little. They had the gift of enabling the client to see his situation more clearly and calmly, and of encouraging him to make his own decision on what he wanted to do about it rather than to try to decide for him.

I don't know whether I learnt this from them or whether I was able to perceive it because it was something I myself did whenever it appeared the right thing. I remember clearly one of the most instructive occasions when I thought I was going to have a counselling interview and in fact found myself befriending.

A lady came to see me whose story was so incoherent that the volunteers had thought she might be crazy and had passed her on to me. She told me her story five times. During the whole of her recital, I said nothing, except for encouraging noises, but my mind was very active and I gave her my total attention. At the end of the interview, I was most grateful to her, because I had learnt something of immense importance. I had discovered the answer to the question, Why did she have to tell her story five times? The answer was, that that was precisely the number of times she needed to tell it. Any more would have been too many and fewer would have been too few. The first time, the story was chaotic; the second time, it was much longer and slightly more in order, though still jumping about. The third time a number of irrelevancies were omitted, but a number of possibly relevant details previously forgotten were put in. The fourth time she succeeded in making the kind of précis of essentials of the story in chronological order which I had made in my own mind after her first telling. The fifth time she was considering on the basis of this précis what her reactions were and advising herself what to do.

Some people can only think aloud, and she was obviously encouraged by my patient attention and my nods of approval, so she thanked me warmly for giving her 'the best advice she had ever had' and departed with an air of determination. So the answer to the question, Why did she have to tell it five times? is simple. Five was precisely the number of times she needed to go over it in order to get it straight and decide for herself what she wanted to do. It was a great lesson for me, once I had analysed the reason. It should be noticed that before analysing the reason why it was necessary for her to tell the story five times, I permitted her to do so. In that, I was being a befriender – and it is important to note that all Samaritans, whether they knew or considered the reason for her telling the story five times, would have given her the same courteous attention as I did, because that is their way.

Befriending the paranoid

The best Samaritans not only have this gracious attitude towards the clients, but also seem to have a natural intuition which enables them to steer clear of errors that other well meaning people fall into and in certain cases make the situation worse. An example of this that I can think of comes from the very early days when I had even more to learn than I have now. Going home on the train, as I did whenever I didn't sleep at the office for a late appointment or an early one the next day, I pondered on the question, How could we best help people in a paranoid state, suffering from delusions of persecution? We had had several such cases in a single month, and it appeared that our psychiatric consultants did not usually manage to cure this condition. Quite a lot of these people had been in psychiatric hospitals and had been discharged, uncured, incurable, and believed to be harmless to others, though sometimes a little alarming because of wild speech and accusations. As usual, once I had grasped that befriending often works miracles when nothing else will do, I asked myself how one could *befriend* such a person? I combined this with a second principle, which is to look into myself and the crazy aspects of my own nature to try to gain some insight into the kind of person I was thinking about. I was aware that without being paranoid in the psychotic sense, like many merely neurotic people I do have my paranoid moments when I imagine conspiracies which don't exist or that people are thinking or saying something which in fact they are not. This doesn't happen as often now as it used to, but I am glad that I was then able to recognise that even those in a genuinely paranoid psychotic state – which means that they didn't have the insight into it that I had brought to my occasional touches of it – are not mad all the way through all the time. Once I had realised that the sufferer from this particular form of madness is able to do quite a number of sane things, like the rest of us, I realised that there are areas of the personality which are sane, and areas which are not. This led me to wonder whether by paying enormous attention to the sane areas and encouraging them, and paying no attention whatever to the insane ones, one could cause the latter to wither or even die from inanition; and even if not that, at least one could form some sort of relationship with the sufferer, who must be very lonely. A person is bound to be lonely if he or she is suspicious and full of accusations and talks in a crazy way, because people tend to avoid such characters. They find them embarrassing even if they are not nervous of them.

Once I realised that the life of the person with paranoid delusions must be very lonely, I realised that they were right to come to The Samaritans, and that if befrienders were properly instructed, they could make the lives of the sufferers much less miserable; and since there was no way of guaranteeing which volunteer would be on duty when such a person came in, it was necessary to instruct everybody. I therefore called a meeting of all the members, and told them how very fortunate they were that their Boss had applied the Great Brain to a question which had been troubling some of them, namely how to befriend paranoid people, and I told them my solution. More particularly, I said that they must not be squeamish about changing the subject abruptly or even rudely: they should never take any notice of a mad remark but simply reply about something that that person was able to treat sanely. So however long the person went on, reverting to the mad remarks, the Samaritan befriender must ignore the remark and talk about something sane.

I had just finished saying this, when a lady came in who had not untypically got on a 'bus going in the opposite direction to the one which would have brought her to the hall where the meeting was being held, and it was particularly sad that she missed my talk, because she was, in fact, befriending a very seriously paranoid person, who suffered from the delusion that the woman next door was stealing her hot water. No, not going into the house with a bucket and pinching it, but 'magicking' it away. The poor lady would put a lot of coal on the fire (this was before we were a smokeless zone) and heat up the back boiler and hear the water bubbling in the tank, and then when she went to enjoy wallowing in a hot bath the water would be stone cold, because 'that woman' next door had stolen her hot water. I was going to take this as a practical example, saying that any attempt to argue rationally against such a conviction would merely deepen and extend the delusional system, and one mustn't do it. If, for instance, one said 'But she couldn't do that without the aid of a plumber to fix up the piping', the lady would be forced to defend her beliefs with the greatest possible ingenuity, by saying there *was* a plumber in the plot, and that this woman was no better than she should be and the plumber took advantage thereof. And if you were foolish enough to go on to suggest that it would need a plasterer to make good after the plumber had been at work, the imagination boggles at the relationship the plasterer would have had with either or both of the first two oppressors. If you were stupid enough to go on, you could have the poor lady paranoid about half the neighbourhood, instead of only about the woman next door.

So when her befriender came late, I was forced to revise my teaching method and decided to ask her to explain what she did in the course of her befriending, so that I could point out the errors.

'Oh,' she replied, 'she is a very nice lady – I quite enjoy spending time with her.'

'Have you', I enquired, 'noticed anything peculiar about her conversation or – or anything?'

'Oh, well,' she admitted, 'she does have some rather funny ideas, but that doesn't stop her from being a very nice lady.'

'What sort of funny ideas, sweetie?' I persisted.

'Well, Rector, I thought you knew,' she replied. 'She has this idea that the woman next door is stealing her hot water.'

So now came the $64,000 question. 'And what do you do,' I enquired, 'when she says things of that kind?'

'Oh,' replied the volunteer innocently, 'I don't take any notice of remarks like that. It wouldn't be kind, would it? I just change the subject.'

'In what sort of way?'

'Well,' she said, 'I might say, "Shall we go and make some jam? I found a rather good recipe in a magazine last week." Or I might say, "I wonder whether you'll give me some help with my knitting, dear?" She's a marvel at knitting, and can even do Fair Isle while talking with someone or listening to the radio. I have to confess I sometimes get my knitting in a mess simply to give her the chance of straightening it out.'

I turned to the class and said, 'I hope you notice that the two possible approaches to this question, the clever one which was mine, and the intuitive one, which you have just had displayed to you, both lead to the same conclusion. I really believe that we Samaritans can make an important contribution, not perhaps to the cure, but certainly to alleviation, of the paranoid state. It isn't possible to deal correctly with every client on the basis of what is called common sense, but if you have *uncommon* sense, sanctified common sense, with natural graciousness and respect for the client, you will seldom make the situation worse by responding inappropriately, and you *may* improve it more than anyone else in the world.'

Selection of volunteers

During the early years of our existence, we became more and more convinced that befriending was the only method of help by which our service would stand or fall. This meant that selection was more important than instruction, though obviously people who were rightly selected ought to be well instructed once they had been recruited. This is one of the main differences between The Samaritans and other organisations which have sprung up in imitation of only a part of what we pioneered. It must be a befriender who first encounters the client, and any expert who is later involved must be so with the consent and preferably at the request of the client. Those organisations which have a counsellor or even a psychiatrist responding to the first approach, have, of course, a perfect right to do this, and we mustn't predict that the results will be bad. Clearly, if the nature of the service is honestly explained, those who get in touch with it will be ready to accept the kind of help that is offered. We Samaritans are, however, convinced that unless it is made clear that what is offered *in the first instance* is simply a fellow human being who will listen and accept and sympathise as a friend, a very large number of potential clients will not make an approach at all. It has to be remembered that in many countries there is a good medical and hospital service, and people who wish for medical attention before anything else, having already decided that that is what they need, or having been persuaded to this by their family or friends, can go directly for it. So our attitude is, not that organisations working on different lines ought not to exist, but that there ought to be – and we are determined that there shall be – a branch of The Samaritans offering befriending in every sizeable centre of population throughout the world.

Religious or non-religious?

As for the services which are based on a Church or group of Churches, we similarly recognise their right to exist, but maintain that they do not meet the need of the suicidal population in most countries, even if they resist the temptation to evangelise, which is difficult for some of their members because it comes to them so naturally they don't know when they're doing it. 'Of course I didn't push religion down his throat – I only told him Jesus loves him, and I assure you he was quite pleased. He only rang off because someone else was waiting for the 'phone box.' Even in what are called Christian countries the majority of the population is alienated from the Church or considers it irrelevant.

A Church connexion therefore arouses suspicion and is likely to repel rather than to attract callers. I have known several examples of Church-based emergency centres where the volunteers have been humble enough to learn from the clients, or from us, or from both, and to have begun to do their 'counselling' in such a client-centred way that we would be inclined to call it befriending. The complaint of these volunteers is that they seldom have the opportunity of applying this method, which they know we have found so successful in the British Isles, to people who are in immediate danger of suicide, because the proportion of such people who will get in touch with their service is very small indeed.

Suicide is our business

I have often been accused by representatives (officials, not working volunteers) of church-based organisations in Europe, North America and Australia of prejudice against church-based services. If the word 'prejudice' means that I believe there is an *a priori* case against church-based services, then the accusation is just, but if the suggestion is that I am against the participation of church people who are willing to abandon all thought of evangelisation, I can only reply that I am myself such a person.

Many church-based services are staffed by dedicated people who are doing their best to provide the kind of service the clients want, and between them and the Samaritans they meet at conferences there often seems to be an easy camaraderie and mutual respect. There is, however, always the danger that someone in a position of authority in the church who has not learned to transform his or her thinking about modes of help as a result of years of dialogue with the clients, may influence the whole character of the service in an unhelpful way. An example from the Antipodes is a centre whose church authorities sacked one Director, and later turned down a candidate for a subsequent vacancy, for being Samaritan-minded rather than evangelistic.

How bad it can get is illustrated by the following account which I wrote down immediately after it was told to me by a trustworthy friend.

A Swedish-speaking Samaritan whom we will call Britta, at a

time when we had no Branches in Sweden, offered her services to Kyrkans Jourtjänst, roughly meaning Church on Call, in her town. It was at that time a sort of Flying Squad and general dogsbody to Jourhavande Präst (the priest on duty – a different one each night) who could be reached by dialling the general emergency number and asking for him rather than for the police or an ambulance. The few volunteers tended to gather round the colour television handing round their hip flasks, and it was not clear how they had been chosen, let alone why. The priest on duty was supposed to occupy a room with a bunk in the same premises, but at least nine times out of ten he wasn't willing to leave the comfort of his home, even though he was on duty only once a month, so the operator transferred calls to his home (or, if he hadn't even remembered to stay in, to some other priest who might or might not be grateful). If the priest, who had quite likely had no instruction in how to deal with crisis situations on the telephone and had possibly been over-persuaded to put himself down for one night a month, thought that the caller ought to be seen face to face, or didn't see how he himself could cope, he would promise the caller a visitor and then ring the volunteers and tell them the name and address.

Britta found herself on duty with a nice young man who seemed to have had no instruction but had his car with him. When the priest on duty called to say one of them must go at once to an urgent case, Britta asked what sort of problem it was, and was told it was a serious religious difficulty. She could not quite see how such a difficulty could require a home visit in the wee small hours, nor why it was up her street rather than the priest's, but assumed he wanted to get to sleep. Her young companion was unwilling to go alone, and she didn't drive, so she told the priest that until one of them got back, it would be no use him ringing again.

When they arrived at the address, a woman who was roaring drunk came out, pointed to Britta and said, 'You're no good to me, hop it,' and beckoned to the by now alarmed young man and said, 'You'll do nicely, come with me'.

After waiting around for some time, Britta managed to get a

taxi back to the centre, and rang the priest on duty to say that she was back and that he had described as a serious religious difficulty needing immediate attention a case of a sex-mad woman who was not merely tipsy but rip-roaring drunk.

Meanwhile, back at the ranch, so to speak, her nice young fellow-volunteer decided to make his escape at the moment when the woman requested him to undo her bra. No sooner had he got back, considerably shaken, and been calmed down by Britta, than the phone rang. It was the lady they had visited, who had become less aggressive but more maudlin, apologising to Britta for telling her so rudely to hop it, and enquiring with squiffy familiarity, female to female, what the priest looked like. Britta was able to reply truthfully that she hadn't the slightest idea, as he was miles away in his own home and she had never seen him and never expected to do so.

It wasn't long before Britta found better uses for her spare time.

It is, of course, important to make it clear in one's publicity that one is in the business of suicide prevention – if indeed this is true: not all 'emergency services' *do* consider themselves suicide prevention centres. We Samaritans have from the very beginning made it clear that suicide was our primary concern even though we were interested in long-term as well as short-term dangers, and our headed paper reads: THE SAMARITANS To Befriend the Suicidal and Despairing. Although suicide is not such a taboo word as it was when The Samaritans began, when it was almost as unspeakable as (say) masturbation – and both words are more freely used nowadays, partly because of our influence – it was important to make it clear to potential suicides who might be shy of mentioning that they had such a 'wicked' thing in their minds, that we existed primarily for them. If they came to us, they would have come to the Right Shop.

This reminds me of an incident in 1955 which strengthened my conviction that we must always mention the then taboo word suicide. I was in Boots the Chemists buying some razor blades when a nervous little character who had been skulking around for some time was eventually nobbled by the portly and pompous male assistant on the counter near me. The little man whispered something to this gent, who thereupon boomed out in a voice which must have been audible down by St Paul's, 'Boots, sir, does not purvey contraceptive appliances!' (It didn't then: it does now.) The poor little man shrivelled, and slunk out, hotly pursued by me, ever eager to be helpful. I caught him up. He gave a squeal of dismay, and I said 'It's all right, old chap, I just wanted to take you to a shop where I know they have what you want.' He tried to get away, but I had hold of his sleeve and was stronger and bigger than he. I didn't realise until afterwards that I had been to a clerical meeting and was wearing a clerical collar – the poor little man must have been shattered to find himself rebuked by a pompous shop assistant then chased by a mad parson. However, I took him along to a little shop which used to be in Queen Victoria Street, but isn't any longer, and said to him 'Now you wait here and I will get what you want for you.' When I was sure he wouldn't run away, leaving me with unwanted merchandise, I marched into the shop where there were two languid damsels in attendance, one of them re-arranging things on a shelf, and the other sitting down painting her nails. I addressed myself to the seated one, saying 'A packet of Durex Gossamer, please – 3*s* 9*d* isn't it?' The other one came down the ladder and put the packet into a little bag, handed it to me and took my money without ceasing her conversation with the nail painter. When I came out of the shop and handed the packet to the little man, he was gazing and pointing at a sign in the window which said in large letters DUREX. 'Why,' he exclaimed, 'it *says* that they sell them! It says so plainly! I'll always come here for them! – By the way, how much do I owe you, your Reverence?' 'Nothing,' I said. 'You have taught me a lesson worth far more than 3*s* 9*d*. It must always say in *our* shop window that SUICIDE is our business.'

In those days, everybody thought if you talked about suicide it would 'put the idea in people's minds'. The general public still believes an enormous number of fallacies about suicide but we are gradually getting it across that talking about it doesn't 'put the idea in people's heads', but if the idea is *already* in people's heads, it gets it out – through their mouths and into our sympathetic ears, so that something can be done to help.

Another popular fallacy is that those who talk about it don't do it. The truth of the matter is, that of those who have done it and are now dead, 70% talked about it and no one paid sufficient attention.

Early struggles

By the time our second branch was founded, in Scotland's capital, in 1959, our basic principles were already clear, though not set down in the form of the Twenty Principles (see page 77). The late Rev Professor James Blackie felt that the idea of one supreme director of a branch was too Anglican a concept for Scotland, which was accustomed to more sharing of responsibility. Something of this still remains in the Committee-and-Chairman control of some of our Scottish branches, and now that we no longer rely on Meenisters, the time is surely overdue to drop this awkward difference. But there was no difference whatever about the sort of persons we wanted as volunteers, nor the befriending they would give, nor their being selected solely on the basis of their human qualities and aptitude, and their dedication to the concept of befriending.

The late Christopher Pepys (then Rector of Liverpool, later Bishop of Buckingham) naturally had no penchant for a group of 'elders', but organised our third Centre in the British Isles on similar lines to mine in London with himself as a very amiable supremo.

It might appear that The Samaritans was in those early days a more religious organisation than it is now, but this was not so. We were always open to people of any religion or no religion, and evangelisation of the clients (or indeed of one another) was strictly forbidden. The apparent link with Christian churches simply reflected the fact that at first, before we became well known and attracted some financial support, the way I had begun was the easiest way for others to begin: if you were a clergyman or minister, you were accustomed to be a leader of people whose acceptance of your leadership was freely chosen, and you had premises of some sort, even if a bit off-putting, in areas of big cities where office accommodation would have been prohibitive. It is difficult to see what occupation other than the minority of parsons then free of ecclesiasticism could have supplied the type of leader who was largely his own boss, had experience of inspiring and organising adults, was non-medical, and had well-placed if not very well-adapted premises. This was strikingly illustrated when Glasgow, Stanmore (which folded when the Vicar moved to Chelsea) and Aberdeen were followed by Manchester as our seventh Centre (we cannot speak of 'Branch' before 1963 when we became a Company Limited by Guarantee). All sorts of people were advertising their telephone numbers, and it was not until the late Rev Basil Higginson (later General Secretary of the Association) took matters firmly in hand and used rooms at his own Church as a base, that a service following a similar pattern to that of London was able to be given. The penalty of the pioneer is that he is by definition ahead. He has to be patient with people who need a little time to catch up, but can be maddened by those who want to repeat all his wrong turnings or dead ends, or who persist in trying to persuade everyone to go in a different direction. Leaders have cause to be grateful for Samaritan types who aren't too proud to follow, and get on with the job.

I should not now wish to live again through the trials and struggles of those early years. I had not only had an idea, 'made a breakthrough' and worked all hours to put the theory into practice, but in the first fifty of the volunteers I had 'seen the future and it worked', and therefore could not but be impatient with those who wanted to modify the tried and tested methods because of their whims or prejudices or failure to see the objective clearly.

The lack of a single organisation and the impossibility of my closely supervising the development of other Centres than London led to a chaotic variety of customs and terminology, some more permissible than others, and my attempts to secure agreement on such matters as selection, supervision, nomenclature and report forms in order that we might offer recognisably the same service to clients in all our Centres provoked disproportionately passionate resistance and resentment. This was doubtless partly due to my own . . . pig-headed self-will? refusing to be 'disobedient to the heavenly vision?' . . . let us settle for the neutral noun 'character'; and partly to the fact that it wasn't always the most Samaritan types who got elected to Committees or who held forth about the superiority of 'what we do in *our* Centre' and how they were 'not going to be dictated to by London' (i.e. by me). Such attitudes die hard: the reference to 'dictation by London' was heard as recently as 1979, when I hadn't been Chairman of the Samaritans Inc. for twelve years, or much concerned with the work in the British Isles for five, and when HQ, which was never in London anyway, was at Slough, and any dictation was done by the representatives of all the Branches in the Council of Management. I try to be thankful that the exasperating muddle-headed people in our organisation as well as the sweetly-reasonable near-saints are usually able to submerge their egos when befriending clients.

Those who shared the vision predominated, or we could not have succeeded in laying such good foundations for the Association which on 11th April 1963 linked our twenty-one centres in the UK and four in Asia and Africa into what was called for short 'The Samaritans Inc.', registered under the Companies Act and in 1964 with the Charity Commissioners. After four years as Chairman, I had a friendly tip from our Psychiatric Consultant Dr Richard Fox, whose services to our movement have been invaluable, that the negative side of the ambivalence even such a hand-picked organisation as ours had towards its leader would be much reduced if that leader were not the Founder. I was happy to hand over (at Cardiff – we had now spread to Wales) to the late Rev Dr William Thomson, who headed an ecumenical team in charge of our intrepid Branch in Belfast and set a pattern of wise leadership which has been faithfully followed.

The London Branch was still operating only from the vestries and rooms up the tower, which were somewhat inaccessible. In that year, someone gave me some new (well, less threadbare) linoleum for my study. I was taking up the old stuff in my study when

I found a trap door which, when opened, showed a sort of well or pit about eight feet deep with mud at the bottom. I lowered myself gingerly into the well, and found from near the bottom of it a tunnel about eighteen inches high running eastwards. I crawled with difficulty along it and was soon in complete blackness and could recognise human bones and decayed coffin wood only by the feel. Eventually I came to a point where my hands went over an edge into a void, and when I shouted at it, I got an echo which indicated that this was quite an extensive vault. As I did not care to dive head first into it, I went back to the original pit and turned round and re-entered the tunnel backwards, so that I could hang over the edge at the end by my hands. When I did this, my feet were not touching the floor, and I thought it prudent to scramble up again and come back with someone else and a rope. However, it proved not to be possible to scramble back, so hoping there was not a well 200 feet deep below me, which even without crocodiles would have been alarming, I let go – and fell about four inches. Then I flicked on my cigarette lighter (it was about three or four years before I gave up smoking) and found myself in an almost disused burial vault. There were three or four mouldering coffins near me, and I managed to pile one on top of another to climb back to civilisation. It was this space, which unfortunately extended only under the vestries and the very west end of the church, which was imaginatively converted by Donald Armstrong Smith, at the cost of the Worshipful Company of Grocers, to make the present premises of The Samaritans, still called 'Grocers' Gift' and admirably adapted for their purpose.

Expansion

With 'Bill' in the Chair, I, having accepted Permanent Life Membership of the Council of Management but not having sought to be on its Executive Committee, was free to give any of my time and energy that was not exhausted by being Director of the London Branch, to the extension of Samaritan methods and principles to the world outside the British Isles, and particularly at that time to Europe.

I ought not to have been surprised that the difficulties I had had in getting the basic principles of The Samaritans accepted and formalised by our Centres in England, Scotland, the Channel Islands, Hong Kong, Rhodesia, India and Pakistan (all in a sense part of the English-speaking world) paled into insignificance when compared with the ideological conflicts between The Samaritans and most of the emergency services on the Continent of Europe.

The earliest Centres there were in West Berlin, where it was at first medically-theologically orientated but then split into two, the second part being staffed largely by volunteers; Hälsingborg, Sweden, which remained a one-man-show served by a priest who described himself in English as The Suicide Pastor; and Zürich, where three devoted evangelists attended an elaborate switchboard enabling them to transfer calls to any of thirty 'experts'. Except for Telefonseelsorge Berlin, any resemblance to The Samaritans was imaginary, but the work begun by a Protestant Pastor in Paris, S. O. S. l'Amitié par Téléphone, came closer, except for its heavy dependence on full-time professionals and the fact of working from a secret address by telephone or letter only (still the policy of most French *postes*). In September 1960, by the generosity of a French businessman, M. Georges Lillaz, a conference was held at Château de Bossey near Geneva, attended by about thirty delegates from *postes* in Western Europe, including six from The Samaritans. A Centre d'Information des Services de Secours d'Urgence par Téléphone was set up.

Later the same month, Professor Erwin Ringel held an almost exclusively medical conference on suicide in Vienna, the first conference of what was to become the International Association for Suicide Prevention (IASP). I attended both these conferences, and have attended all but one of the subsequent conferences of the International Information Centre, which at first were held every two years and then every three; and all but two of the conferences of IASP, now held every other year. In 1965 I became an individual member of IASP to prepare for affiliating The Samaritans corporately, as Dr Ringel wished to widen it into a multidisciplinary organisation.

Our association with IASP has been a happy one, and at Ottawa in 1979 Dr Richard Fox, its British representative, was elected a Vice-President to represent The Samaritans.

The International Information Centre, with its secretariat in Geneva, held its third conference at Christ Church Oxford in 1964. As Chairman of the organisation in the host country I presided and was elected President of the International Information Centre. After a very unhappy three years, during which I was usually in a minority of one on the Committee, I was glad to be replaced at Brussels in 1967 by Father Rémi Mens. The Information Centre was then renamed the International Federation of Telephone Emergency Services (IFOTES). At the time of the setting up of the 'federation', Branches of The Samaritans outnumbered all other *postes* in it, but the voting in the General Assembly was deliberately arranged so as to put The Samaritans always in a minority by the simple expedient of rigging the franchise to the disadvantage of any country with a large number of *postes*. Countries with only one *poste* had three votes; countries with three *postes* had five votes; with ten, seven votes; with fifty or more (which was our state at the time) nine votes. With a hundred or more *postes*, which was soon to be our situation, we should have eleven votes. It didn't really matter, because it soon became evident that the Protestant minister in Geneva who had been appointed Secretary was interpreting the wishes of all except The Samaritans accurately when he made nationalism the policy. No country's organisation would feel bound by any decision of the General Assembly if it did not wish to be. The universality of the method of The Samaritans, which had already spread to all the continents except the Americas without any serious modifications, was thus prevented from being recognised.

Befriending was not adopted by the organisations set up in the different countries of Europe, except for Anonymowy Przyjaciel in Gda sk, Poland. It was assumed that no one could know how best to organise a service for potential suicides in any country except people who were not only nationals of that country but also happened to be first in the field. Samaritans know that human beings are much the same everywhere, and although there are some peculiarities arising out of certain exotic cultures, such as the horrifying number of young Indian married women driven to suicide by their mothers-in-law, the vast majority of the situations encountered by our Branches are the same everywhere, and the method of befriending is equally effective everywhere. They also know that this work attracts many who are unsuitable for it. The Samaritans find themselves able to accept only one in three or more of those who apply, and would not expect good results from a service operated and controlled by persons not selected.

The reason why we have so few Branches on the Continent of Europe is that our Council of Management made a decision to remain in IFOTES and have the possibility of commending befriending to our continental colleagues instead of setting up our own Branches. It is impossible to estimate whether the clients will benefit more in the long run than if we had withdrawn from IFOTES and set up Branches wherever we could. The question would be academic but for the fact that in many parts of the world exclusively Christian centres are spreading faster than centres of Samaritan befriending, and we cannot evade the duty of thinking out our policy in these places.

By our twenty-first anniversary in 1974 we had so many Branches in the United Kingdom and the Republic of Ireland that meetings of the Council of Management were crowded with their representatives. There was no room for representatives of our Branches outside the British Isles, and no time to add the business of the 'Overseas Committee' to the agendas – business which the majority of those present would not have the local knowledge to debate. Delegates from most of our Branches in other continents met at St Stephen Walbrook in London and at the annual Conference in Manchester and decided unanimously that they wanted their own sister organisation, parallel to The Samaritans Inc. and based on the Twenty Principles, but independent and autonomous. After some hesitation, this was accepted at the Council of Management held on the actual twenty-first anniversary. At this meeting I was allowed to relinquish the position of Director of the London Branch to the Rev John Eldrid, and was recognised as Chairman of Befrienders International, The Samaritans Worldwide, to which I had been elected by the delegates. They had also elected a representative for each Continent, and since I, as representing Europe, was Chairman, Professor Tadeusz Kielanowski of Poland was elected as additional representative for Europe on the Intercontinental Committee.

This development not only put our work in the other continents on a firmer basis but also opened up Europe, for Befrienders International made it clear that it was not a member of IFOTES so there was nothing to prevent us from setting up a befriending service in any country where we could find nationals who were suitable and willing. A start was made in Gothenburg, Sweden, in 1975, under the name 'Någon att tala med – Samaritans', on the initiative of Fru Greta Meyersberg. It quickly appeared that volunteers of the right calibre did, as might have been expected, exist in Sweden, and when found were indistinguishable from Samaritans anywhere else in the world. The difficulty in enlisting male volunteers was somewhat greater than in most countries because of a tradition that 'charitable work' was women's work, but this is gradually being broken down. Once established, the Gothenburg Branch was quickly able to make good relationships with other services in the city, run by the Church and by the Red Cross. If this could be achieved in Sweden, it can be achieved anywhere.

The aim of the Samaritans

Reduction of the number of suicides has always been our objective. The success or otherwise of our work is to be judged solely on whether it does or does not reduce the number of suicides in the areas in which we operate. If we are not saving lives, we are failing; and it is no good giving us pats on the back for doing something else. To decrease human misery is undoubtedly a worthy endeavour, and we may be thankful for the activities in this regard of such diverse professions as comedian, restauranteur, prostitute, hairdresser, and health visitor; but *our* task is to decrease human misery in those who might, unless this were achieved, be more likely to die by their own hands. Obviously, like any other specialists, we cannot hope to be so fortunate as to encounter only those who come clearly within the realm of our specialisation. We can, however, fashion our image and publicity in such a way as to attract the highest possible proportion of potential suicides, and the lowest possible proportion of those who are not by any stretch of the imagination likely to fall into this category. Furthermore, we can firmly decline to accept any other criterion of the success of our work than the saving of those who would otherwise have killed themselves, so that when we are praised for other socially useful things we are alleged to have done, we can make it clear that this is a mere bye-product, however welcome, and not an indicator of our effectiveness in the task to which we have committed ourselves. In the same way, if the quality of befriending offered by a particular Branch were poor, it would be no satisfaction to us to be told that the Branch had excellent consultants or good relationships with the medical profession, so that clients needing an expert received excellent counselling or psychiatric treatment.

In the late 'Seventies, desperate attempts were made by people whose names were more than sufficiently publicised in repeated press handouts at the time to 'prove' that the fall in suicides in Britain since 1963, unique in the world, is totally unconnected with the existence, also unique, in the same country and from the same date, of a nationwide organisation, universally known and respected and trusted, which invites suicidal people to seek their help at any hour of the day or night. Even as a clergyman, let alone as a scientist, I am not credulous enough to believe that an organisation which has over 20,000 volunteers manning 170 Centres with 1¼ million contacts a year, listening patiently and sympathetically each year to the troubles of a quarter of a million *new* 'clients', makes no difference whatever to the incidence of suicide. It should be remembered that the people thus given encouragement, moral support, and (where desired) referral to medical or other experts for further help, in conditions of total acceptance and confidentiality, have been sampled by researchers and have been found to be as 'lethal' as mental hospital patients, i.e. enormously above the national average.

Some professionals are apparently unable to bear the thought that non-professionals, however numerous, well chosen and carefully supervised, can achieve anything worth while in the field of suicide prevention. In effect, they ask the general public to believe that a graph which shows the number of Samaritan Branches, clients and volunteers steadily increasing, and at the same time the number of suicidal deaths decreasing in proportion, so that an X is formed on the graph, is pure coincidence. It would be interesting to make an investigation of the motives of those who persistently attempt to discredit and discourage Samaritans. They can hardly wish the number of suicides to increase, though if they are successful in their attempts to reduce confidence *in* The Samaritans by the potential clients and *of* the Samaritan volunteers, this would be the obvious result. Everyone knows The Samaritans would never go on strike, so the best proof of all of their effectiveness, namely the catastrophic results of a sudden cessation of their activities, can safely be ruled out. Evidence of a similar kind, though less dramatic and impressive, is to be found in an examination of those countries which are comparable to the British Isles in being Western-style industrial democracies, with excellent medical facilities, particularly casualty and resuscitation services and intensive care. Their standards of diagnosis and treatment are at least equal to what is found in the British Isles, but they either have no Samaritans at all, or the Samaritans are recently established and have not yet become widespread and widely used. In these countries, the suicide rate has remained steady or has risen.

Our denigrators, eccentric though their ideas of plausibility seem to me to be, have confined themselves to denying the effectiveness in suicide prevention of anything that The Samaritans or others are doing. They have not at the time of writing gone to the lengths of making any positive suggestions as to what might usefully be done; though they boast that they can work out on the basis of tendentiously-chosen social factors what the suicide rate of a particular country must be now and predict whether it will increase or decrease in the future. This would be more impressive but for the fact that some calculations of the *present* situation are wildly out: e.g. Hungary should have increased its suicide by 9%, the same as Switzerland, but in fact it went up by 48%. With these researchers, we go back to Durkheim's views of 1897, when study of the phenomenon of suicide led to the depressing conclusion arrived at that there was no way its incidence could be changed by trying to do so. The rate would go up in times of social disorganisation and down in time of war, and nothing else would prevent the steady rise which we now attribute to increasing urbanisation. Durkheim, genius though he was, could not be expected to envisage in his day such creatures as Samaritans, let alone their numbers and activity and widespread acceptance. He was rather in the position of a man who, if he had thought about it at all, would have 'known' that it would be impossible to recruit billions of little people with tiny syringes to draw infinitesimal drops of nectar from trillions of flowers in order to make for mankind a sweet viscous substance called honey. If he *had* thought of it, he would have 'known' that it would cost a million pounds a pound. We who can all afford to have it on our breakfast tables must not sneer at the fellow who was handicapped by never having encountered or heard of bees.

It may be that statisticians don't like interferences with the natural course of events which introduce an unpredictable human factor into their impersonal calculations. Nevertheless, in the mid 'Sixties, when it was still possible to find sizeable towns which not only didn't yet have a Branch of The Samaritans but also were not particularly well catered for by the Branch in the next nearest town, a study was made by Dr Christopher Bagley of fifteen towns which did have, and fifteen comparable towns which did not at that time have, a Branch of The Samaritans. He found that the suicide rate of the latter was about 26% higher than that of the former. Certain criticisms of this study led him to repeat it with more safeguards, with a similar result. The attacks continued, however, and when replication was no longer possible because 'control' towns free of Samaritan beneficence were no longer to be found, he ceased to stand by his study; but the verdict of statisticians we have requested to examine the matter is that the study was a reliable one.

Once The Samaritans had become sufficiently well known for people to seek the help of their nearest Branch even if it was a good many miles away, so that meaningful repetition of Bagley's study was no longer possible, our denigrators attempted to repeat it and have found (as we could have predicted they would) only a little difference between those towns which have their own Branch of The Samaritans and those which make use of the services of the Branch in a neighbouring town. There is no way in which this comparison can any longer be made meaningfully in the British Isles. There are parts of the world in which such an experiment will be possible in a year or two, and I very much hope it will be undertaken.

An interesting statistic comes from Perth, Western Australia, where the inhabitants like to boast that their next nearest town is in Antarctica. There, they told me, the suicide rate during the five years preceding the foundation of a Branch of The Samaritans, and the subsequent five years, showed a reduction in the suicide rate in the second five years of 15%.

The denigrators have changed their minds on one factor: looking around for something, anything, other than the work of The Samaritans to which to attribute the fall in deaths by suicide in the British Isles, they had picked in the mid 'Seventies on the change from coal gas to North Sea gas, i.e. from a lethal gas containing carbon monoxide to a non-lethal gas consisting largely of methane. This never made much sense, because the decline in the suicide rate began before the change had started, and the changeover took a very long time before it was anywhere near complete. By 1979, the denigrators had abandoned the natural gas theory, because they had found no significant difference between towns which were still on coal gas and those that had changed to natural gas. I confidently predict that when their 1979 theory is proved to be equally groundless, they will find a different 'explanation' for what we may hope will be a continuing decline in the suicide rate.

The highest-risk age group

There is one distressingly valid criticism of the scope of our work up till now. This is that we still find great difficulty with the highest-risk age-group, namely the over sixty-fives. For a long time most of our clients were between fifteen and fifty-five, and we made special efforts to extend the range downwards and upwards. The best publicity we have ever had, a series of eleven fifty-minute dramas based on the work of the London Branch and titled 'The Befrienders', was televised on BBC 1 at a peak viewing hour on a Saturday. This meant that a great many children became aware of our work in a way that appealed to them, and since then (1972) there has been a considerable increase in the number of child clients approaching us. In an attempt to get elderly people into contact with us we reduced the stringency of our rule forbidding volunteers to act on third party tip-offs, by providing that if these came from a reputable person such as a Health Visitor in relation to an elderly person who through being bedridden or housebound was unable to get in touch on his or her own account, we would be willing to send someone round to make a discreet enquiry. Clearly, we must continue to look for ways whereby a greater proportion of the elderly, in and out of hospital, may receive the benefit of Samaritan befriending when they are depressed.

Another direction in which we must seek improvement is at the younger end of the scale, in relation to parasuicides. In the 'Eighties we need to do two things in this regard: first, to find ways of inducing young people to get in touch with us *instead of* making an act of self-injury; and secondly, to find ways of making it more likely that those who have been admitted to hospital after a suicidal act which did not prove fatal will, on discharge, wish to come to us for help.

Our most obvious objective must be to increase our total number of clients to such a point that we are seeing most of the people at risk, instead of (apparently) only about a third of them.

I have referred above to countries with few or no Branches of

The Samaritans. The reader may wonder perhaps about those countries in which there exist organisations offering what they tend to call 'emergency telephone counselling'. Do the activities of these organisations make any difference to the suicide rate in their areas? The answer is, that in no country except those of the British Isles do we find a dramatic decrease in the number of suicides. This is not to suggest that these organisations do not prevent any suicides at all. In our own early days, we knew for certain that we were preventing a certain number of suicides, but this number was not sufficient, at a time when we were befriending only a few tens of thousands of clients, to make a noticeable difference to the number of reported suicides.

It is probably necessary to 'process' at least 10% of a population at risk before looking for any statistical proof of success showing up clearly despite adventitious changes.

The Samaritans would not expect a great deal of success from any organisation which did not work in accordance with the Twenty Principles. In particular, they would consider that an organisation was unlikely to be very effective if it presented to the general public an 'ecclesiastical' image, or a professional one, or was not particularly well known at all; if what it offered was referral or counselling rather than befriending; if it restricted the clients to certain hours on certain days rather than being available all the time; or if it insisted on dealing with people only on the telephone; or did not guarantee confidentiality.

The worldwide spread of The Samaritans

Is it going to be possible to spread our work throughout the world?

The continents for which I have been responsible since 2nd November 1974 divide neatly into two categories. In Europe (excluding the British Isles), North America and Australasia, Branches of The Samaritans are outnumbered by Branches of other organisations. These are mostly restricted to Christian participation, except in Eastern Europe, where they tend to be based on psychiatric hospitals and the work of professionals.

Three continents are largely virgin territory: Africa, where only in the Republic of South Africa are there services other than those of The Samaritans; Central and South America, where The Samaritans have work in progress or in preparation in every country, with particular success in Brazil, and where only Lima and Buenos Aires have non-Samaritan services; and Asia, where the greater part of the enormous populations have no service whatever, and where the number of Centres belonging to Befrienders International is about the same as the number not, or not yet, belonging.

The strategy for these two divisions of the world must obviously be different. In the second group, we must make every effort to establish Branches on sound lines before any organisation offering a less effective service can complicate the issue. In the case of the continents in which there is already a multiplicity of services of different kinds, with varying degrees of effectiveness, the question arises whether it will be necessary in every centre of population to start *ab initio*, or whether in some it may be possible to persuade an existing service that the method pioneered by The Samaritans is the one most likely to meet the needs of the clients in that area.

The three 'western' continents present us with very different problems. The simplest case is that of Australia, where The Samaritans in the west and north and Life Line in the east and south are very far removed from one another, and in any case many of the Life Line Branches seem to be developing in a Samaritan direction. There is nothing to prevent Befrienders International from starting Branches in those few cities where the exclusively Christian nature of the existing service makes it unacceptable to the majority of the population.

The really complicated cases are Europe and North America. In the latter, Mexico is virgin territory and we have preparatory work going on there. Canada has a national organisation to correlate the work of its many and varied crisis centres, some of them started originally by us.

Europe, as has already been seen, is more or less covered by organisations which are more or less homogeneous in each country concerned, though IFOTES has lately begun to accept more than one organisation in a country.

In the United States there has been a tremendous proliferation of telephone emergency services of every conceivable and inconceivable kind. Although it appears that the majority of these services are funded by the community rather than church-based, the fact that most of them do not belong to any wider association means that there is no outside check on the maintenance of standards and in some areas, because of the way 'hot lines' are born and die, no guarantee of continued existence. The American Association for Suicidology (AAS) sets a high standard for its members and organises useful annual conferences, in which, now that we have Branches in the USA, The Samaritans are always represented. I was most touched and honoured to be given the AAS's Louis I. Dublin Award in 1974, especially as Dr Dublin, whom I knew, was one of the first writers on suicide to praise the basis of The Samaritans.

I do not think it is possible to prophesy how the situation in Europe and the USA will develop. We have no ambition other than to serve the clients by the method we have proved to be the one they need. We can do this only if we are able to ensure that the Twenty Principles are observed, with no departure from them except what is permitted by the organisation as not being inconsistent with the spirit of the whole. Far from wishing to produce an impressive list of Branches, good, bad and indifferent, that 'belong' to us, we have been crossing off the list centres from which we have no recent news of an acceptable service being offered, or whose fidelity to our principles we have reason to doubt. When a centre is set up under our auspices by nationals of the country concerned who are themselves Samaritans who have been through the selection procedure, we are as sure as we can ever be that what is set up will be recognisably a Branch of Befrienders International.

What about those cases where, without any formal connexion with us, a Centre, or a national organisation with several Centres, seeks so far as we can judge to work along Samaritan lines, and has good relationships and much exchange of information with us, but is not affiliated to any international organisation (as in the case of Inochi No Denwa in Japan) or is at present affiliated to another organisation (as in the case of Taiwan, Republic of China)? What would be the advantage, if any, to them and their clients, of affiliation to Befrienders International? Are there any disadvantages in having close and friendly contact without such affiliation?

It may not make a great difference in practice unless and until something goes wrong: if, for example, a fanatical minority were to capture control of a Centre, or a maverick become director of it. Even this could be dealt with if the Centre is not independent and isolated but is one of a group united in a national association. We see the value of such an association very clearly in the case of The Samaritans of Hong Kong and of Rhodesia, the first two countries to have their own National Committee to take responsibility for supervising all their Branches and deciding where to open new ones. It no longer requires authorisation from me as Chairman of Befrienders International or from the appropriate continental representative to open or close Branches or to appoint or dismiss Directors. Perhaps the most that one can say about Centres not formally affiliated is that it would be a pity if there were people in many parts of the world working along Samaritan lines who did not participate in the making of policy at global level.

Befrienders International is on the look-out for opportunities to start Branches wherever suitable and willing nationals are to be found, unless it is clear that this would detract from a really good service being given to the clients by an existing organisation there.

Meanwhile, The Samaritans Inc. (i.e. in the British Isles) continue at the time of writing to participate in the International Committee of IFOTES and in the excellent Congresses organised every three years, and continue to commend the method of befriending as the right one if suicide prevention is seriously intended, rather than merely generalised help offered to people with every possible kind of difficulty. This leads us directly to the subject of publicity.

Publicity

It is obvious that an organisation existing to cater for a small proportion of the population, consisting of people whose identities are not known, can communicate with its potential clients only by making the fullest possible use of the media: press, radio, television, advertising, posters, and such things as slogans on T-shirts worn on sponsored walks. By informing everybody, repeatedly, about the nature and purpose of the service offered, it may be hoped that those who need to avail themselves of it will become aware of it. There are, of course, exceptions to this: the isolated and elderly may be too depressed to listen to the radio or read the newspaper or may live without these, so other means have to be found of communicating with this category of people who may need our help.

However it is not merely our existence but our terms of reference which need to be publicised. It makes all the difference to the kind of people who get into contact with us whether we have in our publicity accurately conveyed what we do and what we regretfully cannot undertake. The Branch in Birmingham, England's second biggest city, was slow in getting off the ground because of the conviction of the person who first attempted to start it that suicide must not be mentioned or even specialised in, but that 'personal help' should be offered in a general way. 'Ring us if you have a problem' produced many requests for money, accommodation, jobs and information, including such matters of life and death as why did the preacher in the cathedral have to have a poker carried in front of him on his way to the pulpit – but no suicidal people whatsoever. The disillusionment caused by this false start delayed the opening of an effective service considerably.

Our Branches must be clear what they exist for and what they do not exist for, and having set our own house in order, we must then make it unmistakable in our publicity what it is that we are offering and express it in such a way as to discourage as far as possible people wasting their time and ours by coming to the wrong shop. Of course, human nature leads people who urgently want some kind of help to see a possibility of getting it where none exists. If a charity is set up to help residents of Pimlico of Irish origin and Roman Catholic faith with the school fees of their daughters, it will inevitably be approached by people who are not of Irish origin and do not live in Pimlico and have no daughters but require help in paying off their rent arrears. We must therefore not be surprised that, when an organisation offers help without making such stringent restrictions, large numbers of people should consider it worth a try. If there is a discrepancy between what the Branch says it does and what it does in practice, this will become known on the grapevine, and the latter will be believed and acted upon if it is to someone's advantage. For instance, it is no good stating clearly in a press handout that The Samaritans do not give money, as is the policy in the British Isles, if there are cases where some sentimental volunteer organises a whip round for a tramp, who proceeds to tell all his colleagues, who come swarming to this honey pot and are justifiably annoyed when turned away empty-handed. It is bound to sound hard hearted to those who cannot concentrate to say that even giving the assembly of tramps a hot drink before sending them away would run the risk of a genuine client taking one look and turning tail, certain that he had come to the wrong shop and that all the talk about suicide prevention was eyewash.

We have been amazingly fortunate in the sustained interest shown by the press in our operation. The mere fact that 'ordinary' people are selected and instructed and go on duty in rotation day and night, day and night, all through the year, and where this is necessary, dash out in the wee small hours to the scene of human tragedy, is regarded by them as having perennial human interest, and quite rightly. But reporters cannot be blamed – indeed, it is part of their professional competence – if they try to obtain information which other reporters have not published. We must not blame them for trying to obtain a fascinating case history of Miss Mavis Muddle, aged 19, of 3 Gasworks Road, Runcorn, but we must explain good temperedly that confidentiality is the most important thing we offer and that people would not come to us if we shouted their secrets from the house tops, and that it would not solve the problem to re-name her Doreen Bloggs, because people nervous about the skeletons in their cupboards would either be sure that it was her real name however much we said it was not, or else would recognise themselves as having been publicised under a pseudonym and would believe that all their friends would recognise them too.

It requires thought and ingenuity to help a reporter write a story which is in accordance with our principles and likely to attract clients of the kind we are seeking, and that is why it is important that every Branch have a publicity committee or at least a publicity officer, to give careful study to all the forms of publicity open to the Branch and the best way to exploit them for the benefit of the clients. One thing that cannot be tolerated is volunteers giving interviews without any authorisation or briefing from the branch: all enquiries from the press or other media should be referred to the Director or the person nominated by him or her for this purpose.

Whoever is appointed to take responsibility for the Branch's publicity must learn how to be interviewed, which is a skill that has to be acquired and improved by experience. A publicity officer must know exactly what he or she wants to say: what are the most important points to be got across, and how to present these to a reporter possibly unfamiliar with the basis and nature of our work in such a way that no misconceptions inadvertently creep in. Setting the scene and conveying the gist of what is to be stressed needs to be done as briefly and lucidly as possible, so as to allow the maximum possible time for the person doing the interview to ask questions. Any questions which cannot be answered should not be evaded, but the reasons why the answer cannot be given should be courteously explained. An offer should be made to have a look at the copy when written, or to have it read over the telephone, in order to correct any factual errors, but this offer will not always be accepted and if it is declined for what seem adequate reasons, it should be accepted that our giving of an interview does not entitle us to censor the copy in any way. A good reporter wishes to do an accurate story and is grateful for help in this regard, which is a very different matter from an attempt to interfere with his or her expression of opinion. I can hardly remember a single occasion when a reporter has taken advantage of the offer to 'vet' his or her copy where I have not found several errors of fact, and sometimes very many. It is usually the fault of the interviewee for pouring out words more rapidly than the reporter can get them down into a note-book, if not using a tape recorder. A considerate interviewee keeps an eye on the ballpoint as well as his or her mind on the point.

I myself have never refused to give an interview, nor unduly delayed it, to someone who wanted to write an article for a newspaper or magazine, or to make a tape recording for broadcasting. Even when it has seemed likely that the person asking on the telephone and mentioning the name of some important journal is not in fact a member of the staff nor has even been commissioned to write for it, but is a freelance writer hoping to place the article there, I have still been willing to give an interview on request, sometimes even over the telephone. The benefits of this policy have, I believe, been enormous. Amongst other things, I have in recent years met journalists in important positions to whom, when they were young and inexperienced and not always used to being treated with courtesy, I was as helpful as I could be; and this is remembered with gratitude. I can remember only three occasions in a quarter of a century on which confidence reposed in a newspaper reporter was misplaced and led to my feeling very badly let down. As for broadcasting, the treatment of our Silver Jubilee by Radio 4 compels me to advise representatives of The Samaritans giving interviews to representatives of the BBC to take the precaution of making their own tape recording of any conversation about agreed conditions, and to secure in writing any undertaking given.

The well known saying 'There is no such thing as bad publicity' may well be applicable to commercial enterprises, because any mention of the company is likely to be beneficial in the long run, even if it is unflattering. For one thing, it gives the opportunity for a reply. But a Charity like The Samaritans cannot do its work effectively unless those who might make use of its services have a good impression of it and have confidence in its reliability. Any suggestion that it is not reliable and does not conduct itself in an efficient way is likely to reduce the number of desperate people availing themselves of its services, and therefore is indirectly likely to cost lives. In a situation like this, we dare not allow the confidence of potential clients to be undermined without protest.

Another large institution which must come in for some criticism is British Rail. Its appropriate official does not permit us to display posters advertising our service and making mention of the word 'suicide'. It is common ground among 99.99% of psychiatrists working in the field of suicide prevention that to mention the word 'suicide', far from 'putting the idea into people's heads', assures suicidal people that if they were to come to The Samaritans they would be received without surprise or disapproval. That a railwayman should be able to put his opinion before that of the experts in a matter of life and death is ludicrous.

The freedom to choose

There is a matter of policy which deserves mention because it must have a profound effect on the nature of the publicity we receive. Are we to be known to the general public as an organisation which respects the right of a caller who expresses the intention on the telephone of killing himself or reveals that he has already done something which will shortly lead to his death, to the point that we allow him to die without any intervention by us of a kind which he has expressly refused to agree to? Or are we to be known as an organisation which is so determined to save lives that in such circumstances it would trace calls and send ambulances or police cars round to prevent the person who wanted to commit suicide from doing so? In this dilemma our policy is different from that of our colleagues in suicide prevention centres in California and in some other parts of the United States. They say that it would be irresponsible to know that a person was in danger of death by suicide and not take effective action to prevent that person's death if any possibility of doing so could be found. We, on the other hand, take the view that we should only have to force suicide prevention on an unwilling client once, and for this to be wildly publicised as it inevitably would be, to destroy the confidence that clients have in us and to reduce gradually to zero the number of persons in such a situation who would venture to telephone us. However, without making any judgment on our American colleagues, who have the responsibility of making their own policy for their own clientele and who are in a better position than we are to judge the reaction of potential clients in their area, we have to say we could not possibly bring ourselves to believe such action to be justifiable in the British Isles or in any other culture in which we find ourselves operating. The difference is, that we have publicised ourselves as offering disinterested help to those who approach us, whilst still leaving the client in charge of his own destiny, so that he has nothing whatever to lose through ringing The Samaritans. He retains his freedom to say that he is grateful for the befriending he has received, but it has not made any difference and he is still of a mind to kill himself and is now going to break contact and follow that course.

According to our beliefs, the right thing for a Samaritan volunteer who receives a call on the telephone from a client who says either that he is intending to kill himself or that he has already done some act of self-injury which will fairly shortly lead to his death, and who refuses to give his name, address and telephone number and who does not agree to any face to face intervention by or organised by The Samaritans, is to accept the conditions laid down by the client, and regretfully to recognise that there is no feasible alternative to this. Any attempt to impose *our* conditions can only have the result of causing the client to hang up and leave us in a situation of being unable to resume contact with him. We must face the fact that any telephone caller has us at his mercy, in that if we do not know his telephone number we have no way of resuming contact with him if he decides to hang up on us; and even if we *do* know his telephone number, we have no guarantee that he will answer if we call.

We often explain to new volunteers that 'the client is the boss', and whether we like it or not, this is most certainly the case where the clients approach us by telephone, and not in a face to face encounter. Clearly, if a person on Flying Squad goes to meet a client at some agreed place in the middle of the night, and then is asked to stop on a high bridge, and the client gets out and expresses the intention of jumping over to his death, there is every excuse for the volunteer to intervene physically, and to take the view that if the client did not wish him to do so, he would have terminated the encounter, waited until the Samaritan had driven off, and *then* jumped. The fact is that people do not commit suicide in the presence of another person, though they may make suicidal gestures, for some appeal or manipulative reason. It is a different pattern when, because the contact is only by telephone, the client knows for certain that intervention is just not possible, except by his call being traced and police or ambulance being sent. It is our firm conviction that our constituents know perfectly well that we do not force our attentions upon those who have explicitly refused them, and that our publicity has in effect promised that we will not trace calls unless, in most exceptional circumstances, we have very good grounds for supposing that that client wants us to do so and hopes we will do so.

I had an example of this in the 1950s when a client ringing from a telephone kiosk on the Embankment, after having swallowed a large quantity of tablets, had refused to give his whereabouts until he was already beginning to find it difficult to stand up or speak. Then, at the fifty-ninth minute of the eleventh hour, he expressed a desire to be rescued and slumped down unconscious in the kiosk, and in answer to my enquiry as to where the box was situated, all I heard was the clang-clang of the instrument swinging like a pendulum. It was clear to me that he wished me to trace the call, and I did so, and went and lifted him out of the box myself and took him in the taxi to the nearest casualty department and waited until he had been pumped out. I was able to make arrangements to see him the following day and in the meantime he was able to say that he was glad to be alive.

However, there is a different answer to the question: what

should a volunteer do in a somewhat similar situation, where right up to the moment of not being able to answer, the client has quite firmly forbidden any intervention? Suppose the conversation had not merely *begun* with the statement that he didn't want to be saved from death, but as he didn't want to be alone when he died he wanted to have someone to talk to whilst he was dying; but also *continued* to hold to that position right to the end? Hard though it is to be faithful to our principles and promises in such a situation, I am quite clear that this is what we must do, and that any suffering and grief involved are simply part of being a member of a disciplined organisation which exists to bear part of the sufferings of those who are in a suicidal state. We never promised the volunteers a rose garden. We have never pretended that Samaritan work is easy and painless. It is a dreadful thing to suffer the anxiety of talking with a person whose death by his own hand is approaching ever closer and closer, and not being permitted to do the very thing for which the organisation exists, and save that person's life. It is hard to resist the temptation to go rabbiting on about how the volunteer wishes to do something to prevent the person's death, instead of acceding to the request made by the client simply to talk to him whilst he dies. Any nagging about what the *volunteer* wants is not only a failure in befriending, a form of un-Samaritan self-centredness, but is also likely to result only in the client breaking contact and dying alone.

There is no guarantee that when the volunteer *does* accept the conditions laid down, and bears the distress occasioned by having to talk about everything and anything except what the volunteer wants to talk about, it will lead to a situation where the client relents and allows us to rescue him. But although there is no guarantee of this, there is a very good chance of it, and when I asked at a conference of 300 Samaritans how many of them had been in this situation, eleven put up their hands, making twelve with myself, and a further enquiry showed that in seven of those cases, only when it was becoming fairly chancy, did the client relent and give his name and address and permission to come to him. In the other five cases, contact was broken without the volunteer knowing the outcome, but in at least one of those cases the volunteer concerned was fairly certain that the client did die. Discussion of this dilemma was publicised in the press and on the radio in a way that, though quite legitimate, led inattentive people to suppose that we were quite content to talk to people who were about to die by suicide without making any attempt at intervention. It needs to be made clear to volunteers that in obeying the rules of the organisation they are not merely avoiding counter-productive action which would deter such clients from ringing us, but are also behaving in the way most likely to save a life in the end, even though this happy outcome cannot be guaranteed.

Importance of loyalty

Samaritan procedures are not arbitrarily imposed from on high. They represent the experience of a quarter of a century and a distillation of the wisdom of a very great number of volunteers who have consulted with their leaders and with one another at seminars, schools, and regional and national conferences. There should be very good reasons indeed for departing from anything enjoined by this corpus of wisdom and experience. That same humility which is the chief common characteristic of Samaritans is a safeguard against the pride which leads a person to suppose that his unconsidered opinions are of more value than the carefully considered conclusions of the organisation to which he has promised his loyalty.

Loyalty is always important, but it is going to be even more important in the '80s than it was in the '50s, '60s and '70s, because the organisation is now in danger of being part of 'the Establishment', and in any case is greatly respected and has an enormous influence. Those who are in the position of speaking on behalf of The Samaritans will find increasingly that their words carry great weight, and it is therefore going to be increasingly important that no one presumes to speak for The Samaritans who has not been elected or appointed to that task, and that Samaritan volunteers who want to express disagreement with the official line should be encouraged to do so provided they do it in

Samaritan circles and not in public. Apart from our *raison d'être*, namely befriending as the answer to suicide, there are no sacred cows, and there is nothing in our ways of working which cannot be modified if it can be shown to be in the interest of clients that such modification be made.

We have always said that The Samaritans is more like an organism than an organisation, and it is constantly growing and developing, and must be ready for any changes which are clearly proved to be necessary to adapt to the changing needs of the changing years. No change could possibly be as dramatic as that which took place in the first few months of our existence, when we ceased to be an organisation offering non-medical but still professional counselling to suicidal and despairing people, and instead became an organisation of volunteers offering befriending – a therapeutic method so unheard of that it has constantly needed definition and explanation, and even after a quarter of a century is still, quite rightly, a subject of immense study and discussion within our movement.

We believe that a person so lonely, confused, agitated, anxious or depressed that (even though like all pre-suicidal people he will be ambivalent) he is turning very much in the direction of some suicidal act, needs more than anything else in the world to find a friend of the kind Samaritan volunteers try to be. Obviously some suicidal people will turn to their families and some to their doctor or clergyman or other person they trust, and we can only rejoice if those who need *medical* help are willing to accept it without having first been wheedled into it by a befriender. But those of the people at risk who do not go to their doctor or turn to somebody in their own circle are not going to be helped by being offered, in the first instance, anything other than that befriending which, it has been proved, can by itself save lives, and where it is not enough by itself, can lead the client to more appropriate forms of help.

What the client needs and what the Samaritan is in a position to offer is fortunately the same thing. Anyone who can say 'I am a psychiatrist', 'I am a counsellor', 'I am a psychotherapist', 'I am a social worker', can be very proud if they are dedicated representatives of their chosen profession. It is much less impressive to say to a suicidal client when asked what you are, 'I'm just someone who wants to be a friend to you, if you'll let me'. Much less impressive, that is, to any innocent bystander.

The client, however, is likely to say, 'But that's just exactly what I need – a friend whom I can trust.' To be the best friend anyone ever had in a desperate situation is a modest ambition. For about 25,000 Samaritan volunteers around the world it is enough.

Suicides and Samaritan Branches 1959 - 1978

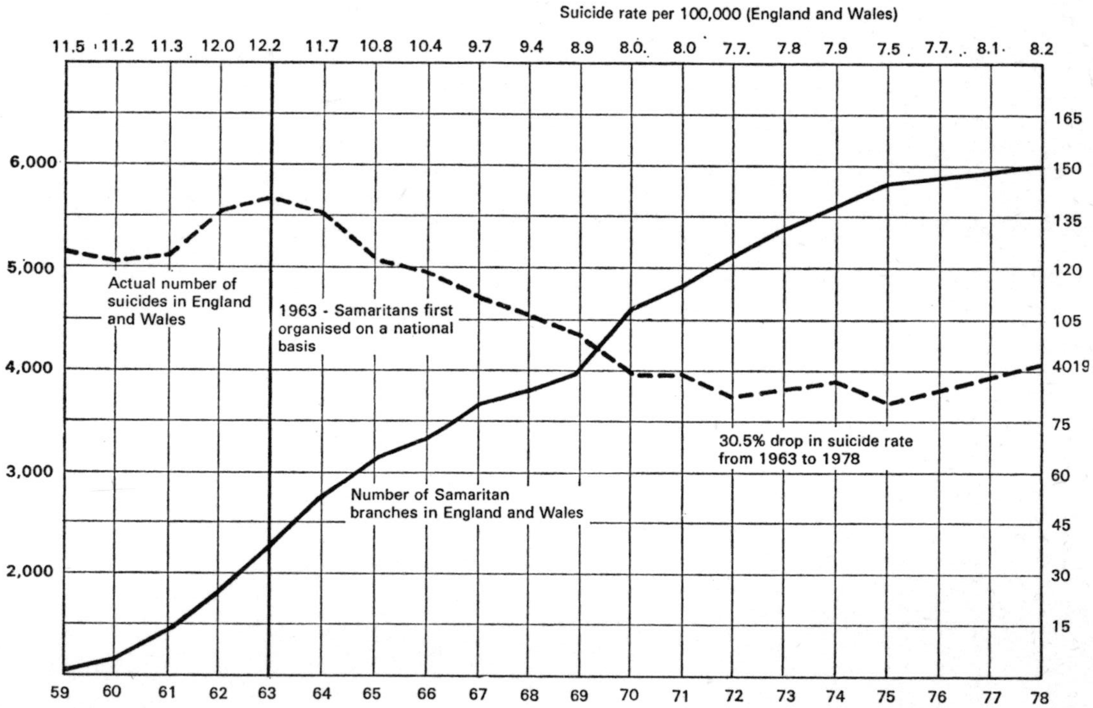

Year	*1974*	*1975*	*1976*	*1977*	*1978*
New callers	192,284	204,978	209,518	229,970	250,740
Samaritans	18,022	18,539	19,294	19,801	20,131
Suicides (England & Wales)	3,891	3,689	3,813	3,976	4,019

The Twenty Principles of The Samaritans

Originally formulated and later revised by Chad Varah. Further revised by him at the request of the Council of Management, approved by its Executive Committee and ratified by the Council on 21st March 1973.

1. The Samaritans are a world-wide fellowship of volunteers dedicated to the prevention of suicide and the alleviation of the loneliness and depression that may lead to it, by making their befriending immediately available at any hour of the day or night to those who feel they have no one else to turn to in their distress.

2. The befriending which the volunteer offers to the caller is the personal concern of a compassionate fellow human being who, like the Samaritan in the parable, seeks simply to love him as a friend in his time of deepest need.

3. The volunteers are carefully selected for their personal qualities and natural aptitude for the work, without regard to their creed, colour, politics, age, sex or status.

4. The volunteers in each Centre recognised as a Branch of The Samaritans work under the supervision of a Director (or Chairman) and other Leaders, who are advised by Consultants with medical or other professional qualifications, so that the highest standards of caring may be achieved. Consultants may also assist in the selection and preparation of volunteers and give help to clients.

5. In countries where the telephone is generally available, an easily remembered telephone number is advertised by each Branch, in addition to its address, to enable swift (and if the caller

desires, anonymous) contact to be made with the minimum of effort on the part of the caller.

6. The Samaritans receive callers in person at their Centre, and invite telephone callers who seem likely to benefit to meet a Samaritan face to face. Callers are free if they wish to have contact only by telephone or by letter.

7. The Samaritans' primary and overriding concern is for those who seem to be in immediate danger of taking their own lives.

8. Samaritans engage in long-term as well as short-term prevention of suicide by befriending despairing and lonely people who do not seem to be suicidal at the time when they seek help, or who seem unlikely for conscientious or other reasons ever to commit suicide.

9. If a caller is concerned about another person, The Samaritans try to support him in his anxiety and to suggest ways of obtaining help for his friend. The Samaritans do not intrude upon persons who have not sought their help directly, unless an identified responsible person informs them of the need of someone who is too young or old or ill to ask in person, in which case they may make a tentative offer of help.

10. The Samaritans do not permit their immediate availability in cases of a suicidal emergency to be impeded by attention to cases of long-term chronic inadequacy, though callers in this category may be accepted as clients during a crisis.

11. The Samaritans do not flatter themselves that what they have to offer will be helpful to every caller. Those in charge of each Branch are responsible for using their human resources to the best advantage, and protecting them from being wasted by the grossly psychopathic or any others not capable of benefiting from befriending.

12. The Samaritans' service is non-medical. Callers requesting medical treatment may be helped to obtain this, and each Branch has at least one medical consultant, usually a psychiatrist, to advise those in charge of the Branch about such cases.

13. The Samaritans are not a trained case-work agency, and volunteers are not permitted to attempt to do for a client in an

amateur way what social workers are trained to do with professional competence.

14. The Samaritans are not a social welfare agency. They refer those who request material aid to the appropriate welfare services, except in countries which lack these.

15. The Samaritans are not a Christian organisation, except in the origin of the concept. Volunteers, whatever their original beliefs, are strictly forbidden to make any attempt to convert the callers or to exploit a caller's distress by using the opportunity to witness to the volunteer's beliefs. Callers spontaneously requesting spiritual help of a particular kind are referred, with their permission, to a representative of the appropriate body, who may or may not be a member of the organisation.

16. Volunteers are normally known to callers only by their Christian names or forenames and their volunteer's identification number, unless continued befriending by a chosen volunteer is arranged, when one of the persons in charge of the Branch decides what other information may be given to the client concerned and whether hospitality may be offered by the volunteer in his or her home.

17. The fact that a person has sought the help of The Samaritans, and everything he has confided in them, is confidential within the organisation. All communications from callers which could reasonably be regarded as of a highly secret nature, and those relating to criminal acts, are received in the strictest confidence and are revealed neither to any person outside the organisation without the callers' express permission, nor to persons within the organisation who are not involved, except the Director. Volunteers are not permitted to accept confidences if a condition is made that not even the Director should be informed of them.

18. The caller remains at all times in charge of his own destiny and is free to reject the help that is offered and to break contact without fear of being sought out against his will, even if it is felt certain that he intends to take his own life or to commit some other act which The Samaritans would deprecate. A volunteer in contact (whether by telephone or face to face) with a caller

judged to be in some danger of suicide is encouraged to seek the caller's permission for a discreet approach to be made to him subsequently to ask how he is, and to record the fact if permission is granted. In such cases 'follow up' is clearly not against the client's will.

19. The various Branches of The Samaritans are banded together in a legally constituted Association whose Council of Management represents all the Branches and reserves to itself the appointment of the person in charge of each Branch, responsible for seeing that the above-mentioned principles are observed.

20. Only the Council may authorise departures from these principles, for instance by permitting new Branches to offer a limited service for a period; and only the Council may from time to time revise these principles.

On the 21st anniversary of the founding of The Samaritans, 2nd November 1974, the Council of Management agreed to the unanimous request of the delegates of the 'overseas' Branches who had met in London six weeks earlier, that Branches of The Samaritans outside the British Isles should no longer be under the Overseas Committee of The Samaritans Inc., but should be an independent sister organisation to be known as Befrienders International (The Samaritans Worldwide) with Chad Varah as Founder President, bound by the first eighteen of the above Twenty Principles. The last two have been rewritten as follows:

19. The various Branches of Befrienders International (The Samaritans Worldwide) are banded together in such manners as are agreeable to the laws of the countries in which they work and are entitled to be represented on their national, regional or Continental council and to vote for the representative of the appropriate Continent on the Intercontinental Committee, registered as a charitable Association under Swiss law, responsible for the good order of the whole organisation, and its faithfulness to these principles.

20. Only the Intercontinental Committee may authorise departures from these principles or undertake revision of them if this should be necessary.

The Twenty Principles may be summarised as follows: A branch of The Samaritans is one which people who are now (7) or will possibly be later (8) in a suicidal crisis or worried about someone who is (9) may approach for help, by telephone (5) at any time, or by a face-to-face meeting at the Centre or elsewhere, or by letter (6), and thus make contact with a Samaritan, a Befriender (1) i.e. one of a team of volunteers selected for aptitude for the work (3), and instructed in it, and supervised (4) by professionals of whom the chief is the Director appointed by the Council of Management in the British Isles (or approved by Befrienders International elsewhere) (19). The client encounters the personal concern of a fellow human being (2) known only by a first name (16) who will keep the confidence of the client (17) and will not contact him/her without permission (18) nor regard him/her as a case for medical care (12), casework (13), or social welfare (14) unless at his/her request; and will not thrust any religion or ideology at him/her (15), but will try to befriend unless the person seems to be unbefriendable (11) or to require indefinite help to the detriment of the organisation's readiness for crisis (10).

It is hoped that the above summary will be useful in enabling members of Branches of The Samaritans anywhere in the world to assess whether their Branch is working strictly in accordance with the Twenty Principles. It will also enable Branches of other organisations considering the possibility of applying for affiliation to Befrienders International (The Samaritans Worldwide) to assess what changes in their attitudes and procedures would be necessary for them to be recognised.

Crisis – GEORGE SPAUL

The Samaritans is one of the very few organisations able to deal with personal crises at the time of occurrence. Numerous organisations deal very effectively with special kinds of crisis, but the Samaritans offer a crisis service – which in availability and organisation is exactly what is required. Those who are professionally associated with the organisation work with it to increase the effectiveness of the advantages it has.

There are three types of crisis:

1. Biological
2. Environmental
3. Adventitious

These classes are not clearly differentiated and often examples are mixed, but for clarity let us say:

1. *Biological crises* are inevitable in the nature of man:
Growth crises – e.g. weaning and puberty
Illness in general (none of us can hope to escape illness)
Loss of function through age
Pregnancy and childbirth

Biological crises because inevitable *should* be prepared for through an enlightened education which would reduce their impact, making the successful resolution almost universal.

2. *Environmental crises* are not quite so inevitable. In this group the whole area of personal relations is involved in the production of crisis:

Bereavement
Marriage
Retirement
Migration

In this class there is often an element of personal choice, and always a relationship involved. It is the area with which psychiatrists and Samaritans are most involved.

3. *Adventitious crises* are basically due to unlucky chance:
Injury
Unemployment
Disasters – flood, fire, earthquake, famine, etc.

Crisis resolution

The process of *crisis resolution* has been studied in detail, particularly in terms of disaster and migration, but the work done in these circumstances is also applicable to the more individual crises with which we more commonly deal.

Clinically there is one characteristic of the whole period of crisis resolution and it is so important that almost all writers and original researchers comment on it. It is the *openness of the personality* at these times. There are fewer defences (in psychological terms) and the personality is vulnerable from without. Intervention can be effective which is quite impossible at other times.

I speak of the whole personality – not just of the cluster of ideas or feelings involved in the actual events of crisis.

However, there is a very special responsibility about our intervention in a crisis – intervention *must* be restricted to relevant matters. It is possible to convert or unconvert a person much more easily during crisis resolution because the general defences of the personality are low. It is not accidental that 'brain washing' techniques have as their basis the artificial production of crises.

We have a special responsibility not to impose our brand of political, religious, psychiatric or sociological dogmatism on our clients when they come to us for quite other reasons.

To return to *crisis resolution* – there seem to be *three phases* involved in the resolution of crisis:

1. Physical and mental *turmoil*
   Aimless activity or immobilisation
   Disorganisation of some degree – often great

2. *Painful preoccupation* with the past

In psychiatric terms the person may *regress* to infantile or childhood methods of dealing with the world and with oneself. These methods include dependency, alcoholism, depression or withdrawal. If he finds these old methods either not workable in terms of a solution, or not acceptable in terms of his self-esteem, he may then go on to the third phase.

3. *Remobilisation*, activity, adjustment

To simplify:
Pain, digestion, action or
shock, grief, action

It appears to be established that missing any of these phases leads to non-resolution, i.e. injury on a more or less permanent scale.

Problems are less painful than crises; they involve no disorganisation. No new solution (in terms of the personality) has to be found – it is merely a matter of sorting out already acquired functions and selecting an appropriate one.

Crisis presents pain and disorganisation and its resolution demands a change in the view of, or a readaptation to, the world, or the person – or both.

We have to allow clients *time* to get through the phases. Aid can only be effective in the second or third phase. We may need to protect the client during phase one.

Ego growth (increase in 'self-ness') can only occur during crisis resolution. A crisis successfully met leaves the person larger, more efficient, more capable than before – and permanently so. This underlies the necessity for the *solution to be found by the client*, not by the counsellor. If we ignore this: 1. We deny the client the possibility of growth. 2. We court dependency – non-resolution and regression to 'Daddy make it better'. It also explains why only *listening* is necessary on so many occasions, and why Samaritan volunteers are so valuable in this work.

Depression – CHARLES BAGG*

Depression is a many headed monster. We shall consider two of the forms in which it occurs.

Endogenous depression

The first depressive syndrome (i.e. collection of symptoms) that I will mention is ENDOGENOUS DEPRESSION. 'Endogenous' means generated from within, not as a result of external misfortune.

The practical implication of this is that if you have got somebody with an endogenous depression, *don't think that you are going to make it better by tinkering about with the environment*, or *even by befriending them, except as the most effective means of getting them to the doctor*. It is a condition which is not primarily and predominantly due to external factors, and it is not going to be remedied by external factors. If you fail to recognise that, and try to do your stuff on behalf of the patient, sooner or later you are going to put your foot in it, and there may be a very tragic outcome. This I have seen happen, not with Samaritans but in other circumstances.

The answer, when you have diagnosed an endogenous depression, is to get it off your hands. Now by that I don't mean jettison the patient in an unkind way, but seek professional advice, and don't try to cope with the situation yourself. If you do and thereby fail to ameliorate the condition, the patient may commit suicide. Not everyone with endogenous depression will commit suicide – most of them don't, but it is a condition in which suicide is a known risk.

There are other unfortunate sequels – there will be a great deal

* From a talk given at The Samaritans' National Conference 1969.

of unhappiness that the individual will suffer, quite unnecessarily, because this condition is eminently curable. The unhappiness will be both for the individual patient and for the family. There will often be misunderstanding by the family, and when the family finally recognise with hindsight that the condition was in fact an illness, they will reproach themselves accordingly.

Loss of employment is another risk. The incompetence that this illness creates in individuals is liable to give them a reputation that they may not be able to live down, even after recovery, and they may, in fact, lose their jobs. Another thing that tends to happen is *marital disturbance*, and even, occasionally, a marital break-up. The depressed patient becomes very unattractive, and the marital partner, not understanding the reality of the situation, may construe the change as a loss of affection, and may go and seek affection elsewhere. For all these reasons it is important that this condition is diagnosed in the very *early stages*.

Usually when a patient comes to a GP, and still more to a psychiatrist, things have gone manifestly awry. Before that stage has arrived, any of these circumstances that I have just named may have developed, including suicide. *They may commit suicide before they ever get to the doctor*. Furthermore, anybody except a half-wit can diagnose endogenous depression in its advanced stages, in its clear cut form. To spot it in its incipient stages is a very different matter, and this is just the point at which you are likely to come in.

Endogenous depression comes on for no apparent reason, or if there is an alleged reason, that reason is in fact more apparent than real. Sometimes, I must admit, this illness does seem to have been genuinely precipitated by some factor, but this factor is only something that has just been the last straw, it is not the essence of the condition.

The symptoms of this condition are, first *a decline in interest and initiative and emotional response*. Matters which had previously been of interest to the patient cease to form the centre of his attention. Work or domestic duties are liable to tail off. A degree of incompetence, which may not be recognised as pathological at that stage, begins to assert itself. The patient begins to spoil his daily work, not necessarily very grossly, but to people who are working closely with him it becomes apparent. Often people cover up for him, because he is usually a very nice person who has always been very conscientious.

Since this illness tends on the whole to come on the basis of a conscientious personality, the sufferer tends, with commendable stoicism, to struggle against the illness. In the early stages he often succeeds, and this obscures from the bystanders the fact that there is an illness at all. The patient will feel different, he will feel this coming on, but you may not notice it very much.

Another feature is *indecisiveness*. The person who previously had been at least capable of taking firm decisions – though he often tends to have been the sort of personality that rather laboriously weighs the pros and cons – will become indecisive. This, of course, is a thing that often gets under the skin of people working with him, and gets under the skin of the marital partner; and to the misfortune of his illness is added the misfortune of recriminations.

All these things are part and parcel of 'Psychomotor retardation' – which is exactly what it says – slowing up of the psychological processes and movement. In the extreme stage of this condition I have seen people so frozen that they have been brought into hospital on a stretcher in a condition that is known as depressive stupor – they just can't move. It is seldom that one gets to that stage, but in a moderately severe case they often present a picture rather like a film in slow motion – with droopy stance, depressive facial expression, and slowing of mental functions. This is very distressing to them, and they find that they have to make a conscious intentional effort to drag out of themselves thoughts which, before they became ill, would arise perfectly spontaneously. Their concentration tails off, they will tell you that they read the paper and at the end of it they don't know a word of what is in it. As the condition gathers momentum, they can no longer overcome the disabling influence of these symptoms and they are laid low by the illness; at that point they go to the doctor – if they haven't committed suicide before.

All these symptoms, characteristic of the early stages of the illness, may very well occur without the patient spontaneously informing you of the facts. He is not the sort of person, normally, and still less when he is ill, who wears his heart on his sleeve, and he just won't tell you these things. So *ask him* whether he is getting indecisive, ask him whether he is losing interest; if once you suspect the diagnosis don't just leave him to tell you, because he may very well not do so, and you will have missed the significance of the whole thing.

There are certain qualities of thought which are extremely characteristic of this condition and the cardinal feature, I would say, is *self-reproach*. He will blame himself, quite irrationally, for things which superficially might have a basis in reason, but which in fact are rooted in illness. This is where your skill in distinguishing between the two has to come into play – he will accuse himself irrationally of things, and in the gross degree of the illness the patient will say something which is so clearly delusional that nobody could possibly fail to recognise that he is in fact ill.

A delusion by definition is a false belief that is not amenable to reason. It is not founded in logic and it can't be dispelled by logic. So that if you try to use a logical approach, which would seem on the face of it the sensible thing to do, you are going to do no good at all, you are going to make things worse. Another delusion that is common in greater or lesser degree in this condition, is the *delusion of futility*. He feels, in the extreme anyway, that everything is utterly black, there is no hope, there is no salvation. Again, if you don't recognise the essentially morbid origin of this, you are liable to try to talk him out of it.

There may be delusions of *hypochondriasis* – that is to say, believing that there is bodily disease when in fact none exists. Such delusions are very characteristic of the depression of middle life and the senile period. They are very characteristic indeed of the menopausal depression, the involutional depressions (what used to be termed involutional melancholia), which occur in middle-aged women at the change of life.

Involutional melancholia is characterised typically by very bizarre hypochondriacal delusions, for example, a lady with agitated depression, who believed that her gullet stopped 'here' – I don't know what she thought happened to the food after that. This was one of the hypochondriacal delusions of involutional melancholia.

A further example, particularly characteristic in the senile period, is delusions of *poverty*. One has seen people, who are unquestionably well off who believe absolutely that they are financially ruined.

Loss of appetite is another very characteristic depressive symptom. They go off their food, or, even if they don't actually reduce the intake, they don't enjoy their food as they did. So this condition, anorexia, is very characteristic indeed of depressive illness.

Associated with this is loss of *sexual appetite*, loss of sexual interest, sexual capacity, sexual enjoyment, and of course this symptom tends, as you can imagine, to feed into the depressive tendency to self-reproach. They tend to feel that they are letting their marital partners down, and the marital partner may in fact feel rejected.

One more symptom that you really need to commit to memory is *insomnia*. This doesn't mean that because we sleep badly we have got depression, but there is a certain pattern to this insomnia which is characteristic of depressives. They wake during the small hours of the morning, only to be tormented with this ceaseless round of delusionally coloured unconstructive ruminations, as a result of which in the small hours of the morning they may get up and go downstairs and 'take a bottle', and that's the end of that.

Diurnal variation means that they are typically worse first thing in the morning. As the day goes on the condition improves.

There are certain phases in which *suicide* is a particularly high risk. Paradoxically, it is not so much when they are utterly immobilised by depression that the risk is highest, but when they are *going into the depression* – that is when you may come into it – and when they are *coming out of it*. When the depression is maximal, they are so retarded as to be incapable of the initiative, mental and physical, to make a suicide attempt. But give them three or four electric treatments, for example, and they are comparatively better, but they are still deluded and wretched; they are capable by then of taking the suicidal action, and this is the time when it is likely to happen. Also, when they are first going into the depression, particularly if they are receiving any form of anti-depressant treatment as out-patients, and are not under immediate observation in hospital – this is the time when you need to be particularly vigilant.

One feature of unmixed depression is that it can be satisfactorily cured, dispelled. I still never cease to wonder at the metamorphosis that one produces over three or four weeks or less in these cases. It is a condition, most often, from which they completely recover. The immediate outlook is very good, and there is no residual defect, but it is an illness which tends to recur. (So if you know of anyone who has had such an attack, just keep on the look-out for recurrence, and nip it in the bud.)

The person who becomes depressed is often an *obsessive personality*. Many of us are normally obsessive about details, about order, about tidiness, but an obsessional personality may develop a psychosis in which the person loses touch with reality and suffers from delusions – he does not understand that he is ill, but believes that he is guilty, useless or unclean.

Features of endogenous depression

These are psychomotor retardation, indecisiveness, self-reproach, the sense of futility, hypochondriasis, delusions of poverty, loss of appetites, the pattern of insomnia, diurnal variation; and the dangerous phases, going into the depression and partial recovery.

Reactive depression

By contrast, reactive depression is explicable and comprehensible in terms of the circumstances that preceded its onset. That is to say, if someone suddenly loses all their stocks and shares, they may go into a reactive depression. The condition subsides when these precipitating circumstances are resolved.

If, on the other hand, it so happened that an endogenous depression followed, perhaps precipitated by a financial disaster, it would not make one scrap of difference if I won all the football pools.

So you can spot the reactive depression, partly by a process of exclusion. You don't typically find it preceded by an obsessional personality, you don't find the diurnal variation, you don't find many of the other symptoms of endogenous depression; and they are not concerned primarily and predominantly and fundamentally with self-reproach, futility, hypochondriasis, etc. – they are preoccupied with whatever misfortune brought on this state. They are not typically retarded in the way that the endogenous depressive is. Indeed, if you have a co-existing element of hysteria in the condition, as you fairly frequently do, you will find that there is a flamboyant display of grief quite often.

There is no denying that they are depressed, but it is a different quality, it has a different essential origin, different management, and a different outcome.

The content of the reactive depression does not spread into the irrational ideas which characterise the endogenous depressive. In the reactive depression, when once you are satisfied that this is what you are dealing with, don't be afraid of helping them in their crisis, by befriending plus, if necessary, referral.

After-treatment for depression – W. Linford Rees

Severe depression is treatable with drugs. There are ways, however, in which Samaritans can help the sufferer. They can befriend, show interest, and give support. This is helpful in all types of depression, but in severe cases may not produce much in the way of improvement. Nevertheless it is important and appreciated by the patient.

For the patient who has undergone treatment and is discharged home, it is often a critical time when commonsense and enlightened help with the patient and with his relations is so important. One has to try and live in the boots of one and the shoes of the other. Consider the patient first – he may still have some residue of his illness, he may have some feelings of inferiority and alienation as a result of his hospitalisation. He may have practical problems with re-employment. Consider the family, with their complex attitudes towards the patient's recent illness – there is bound to be some apprehensiveness and concern for his future, some exasperation, perhaps, with any residual symptoms. Befriending by Samaritans can provide invaluable help in one of the most distressing and incapacitating illnesses which afflict mankind.

The incurable case – P. W. W. Leach

As in other fields of medicine, psychiatry is still frequently faced with the incurable and untreatable problem. Depression is no exception in this field. There are some forms even of endogenous depression that do not fully recover after the most skilful and generous use of physical methods. This may be because of an underlying and insidious organic change such as cerebral arterio-sclerosis, or it may be because of an admixture of some other mental disorder such as schizophrenia or hysteria, or it may be some as yet undiscovered biochemical abnormality. And then again with the reactive and neurotic forms of depression one must accept that there *are* insoluble practical problems in life which even the most devoted doctors or social workers are unable to ameliorate. The aim must then be to support the patient with the shared knowledge of their difficulties, as is achieved by Samaritan befriending. It cannot be pretended that the depression is being alleviated but the life of the sufferer is being made more supportable.

'Masked' depression – William Sargant

Why is it that so many people, having consulted their general practitioners and even psychiatrists, almost straight away go off and still kill themselves? The answer, or a very large part of it, lies in the existence of large numbers of states of '*masked*' *depression*, which need special psychological training and skills to recognise. Doctors, whatever their philosophical viewpoint, do not in practice stand aside and let patients kill themselves, if it can be avoided. Yet thousands and thousands do either attempt or succeed in doing so each year, often with the very drugs prescribed by their doctor.

Let us get down to the basics of this problem. Around one-third of the patients coming to St Thomas's, for instance, for various tests, X-rays and other physical examinations, are people of often sterling worth, who have worked regularly, supported families and relatives, helped others and been, in all respects, model citizens. Then gradually, or suddenly, they start to feel a variety of pains, sometimes in the head, or in the back of the neck. They may also complain of dryness of the mouth and throat. Their chest or heart may pain them periodically, or their stomach starts to get a vague tense and uneasy feeling. Constipation can be a major worry, or faulty eyesight, not helped by glasses.

Along with the development of these physical symptoms and abnormal feelings, they may start to experience intolerable anxiety for no known reason. Perhaps they have been through a period of stress which is now passing. They also start to become very tired for no known reason, or they may start waking early and regularly for the first time in their life. Some alternatively sleep deeply all night and still feel just as abnormally tired the following day, when they try to do their normal work. For many, jobs that were easy for them for years start to become difficult. Making decisions over simple matters also worries them. They become more irritable with people they really love, and later they may start to blame themselves for the most foolish things, and search their past lives for causes for self-blame.

When asked whether, in fact, they are depressed, they will generally say they are more tense and anxious. And they almost invariably attribute their increased anxiety to the recent onset of the physical symptoms, of which they are now complaining, and what these symptoms may portend, such as brain tumour, stomach cancers, coronary heart disease and the like. And it is then, to find out about these symptoms in somebody usually so well, that the patient is sent for special tests to a teaching hospital or elsewhere.

It is now that a mistake can be made by general practitioners, physicians and psychiatrists alike. This is to examine the patient very carefully, perhaps do all sorts of tests and X-rays and then tell him that he is normal and there is nothing very much the matter with him. Perhaps, even worse, is to say it is 'all nerves', which means nothing serious to too many doctors and patients, and to simply prescribe sedatives.

What is such a man or woman then to do?

They begin to think the only thing they can do, as they become more and more incapacitated and yet supposedly medically quite well, is to put themselves out of the way, to stop, by committing suicide, being a 'medically well' total burden to their family and themselves. How many patients, with a missed depressive illness, have gone to their death with their doctor's supposedly heartening reassurance in their ears, that there is nothing the matter with them that a bit of will-power won't put right?

Clinical treatment of depression – William Sargant

1. *Drug treatment*

In recent years, psychiatry and general medicine have become equipped with two groups of powerful and effective drugs, almost specific in certain states of depression and anxiety. If general practitioners could learn their skilled use and not be too worried by side effects that happen with all powerful and effective drugs in medicine as a whole, they could themselves cope with around 75% of the anxiety states and depressions in persons of adequate personality, without any need to refer them for specialised psychotherapy and psychiatric treatment. Several practitioners have already found this out, having taken the trouble to learn about them.

Drug manufacturers tend to claim that their particular anti-depressant drug covers the whole group of depressed patients, and muddle doctors up a lot with their excessive claims. There is a tendency to rush from one new anti-depressant to the next new one, although they may be the same group of drugs under different trade names. The two main groups of drugs must be discussed since too many people think they overlap where a few patients made worse by one are made better by the other and vice versa. The MAOIs (Monamine Oxidase Inhibitor drugs) are extremely valuable in states of anxiety and reactive depression in patients, who may have been ill for years, but are still fighting their symptoms. They are particularly valuable in phobic anxiety states, where people get panicky at going into the street, attending church or cinema, and going in trains, etc. These people are also depressed and can be suicidal in their despair about their restricted life. The MAOIs are also valuable in fatigue states, where people sleep deeply all night, and wake up just as tired in the morning, as opposed to those who wake up early in an extremely agitated state. Unfortunately, the MAOIs require certain dietary restrictions, and severe headaches when the wrong foodstuffs are taken frighten some doctors and patients off them. Nevertheless, unless they are fully used in states of depression, large numbers of people will remain ill, and possibly suicidal, since the MAOI responding depressions and anxiety states do badly with the other group of anti-depressants called the *tricyclics.* These are much more useful in patients who are retarded and slow with early waking and guilt. In fact, the 'masked' depressions often do best with the MAOIs, and the obvious melancholias with the tricyclics. And there are other neurotic depressions, who do best of all when both groups are combined. This is now quite safe if certain precautions are taken.

People have such silly attitudes to mental illness and drugs. Few would think it wrong to take insulin for diabetes or Vit. B12 for pernicious anaemia – both killing diseases. Yet some baulk at using drugs in depressive illnesses, which can be just as lethal, judging by the 50,000 to 80,000 suicidal attempts each year. One of the important things about the anti-depressants is that there is no need to increase the dose despite years on them. And please do not encourage patients to try to 'get down to the root' of their problems, when they are depressed. Lots of depressive illnesses are inherited, run in families, occur for no known reason, and respond to drugs: we do not yet know why. Such a position is common in medicine, where we do not know even how aspirin works. *Psychological probing can be very dangerous in depression.* Wait until the patient is much better with drugs or other treatment, and then see if he can be further helped psychotherapeutically without risk of precipitating a suicide attempt by trying to uncover material the patient just cannot cope with. ECT is a much older treatment than the new drugs. But there are still many suicidal depressives who will quickly get well with it, even when the drugs have failed to help.

2. *Electrical treatment – P. W. W. Leach*

The sheet-anchor in serious *endogenous illness* is *electroplexy* (electrical treatment). This entails the passage of a measured amount of current for a measured time through the frontal region of the brain while the patient is asleep with short-acting anaesthetic and muscle-relaxants given by the vein. One treatment lasts about three minutes and the patient is awake and up and about again in half an hour. Out-patients are able to return home and resume work on the same morning. About six treatments given twice weekly are sufficient. There are no ill-effects other than muzziness or headache for a period after each treatment and minor disturbances of memory lasting for a few weeks after a course of treatment.

Causes of psychiatric disorder – Kenneth Rawnsley

Psychiatric disorder is not uniformly distributed throughout the population. It occurs in pockets. It occurs in certain sections of society more than in others. It appears to be more prevalent in some conditions in women than in men. It is certainly more frequent in the elderly than it is in younger categories and it may be possible in time to throw some light on to problems of causation, because this is a field where we are at the present time sorely in need of information. We know a certain amount about the cause of mental disorder. We know also how very ignorant we are on this matter. And we have to use all kinds of methods to forward this aim of discovering the causes of psychiatric illness: the clinical method, the bedside method, methods derived from the basic sciences, chemistry, physics, physiology and so on. The epidemiological method is one of these tools which we have and which we can use for this purpose, because if we can find certain sections of society, certain kinds of people, groups of people who have high rates for specific mental disorders and, conversely, if we find people who have low rates for these conditions, we may be able to derive clues about the causal factors operative. For example, it has been known for many years now that the prevalence of the psychiatric disorder schizophrenia, which is a serious condition, is highest in the unskilled section of society, what the Registrar-General calls 'Social Class V' – far higher in the members of Social Class V than it is among other social categories of the population. At first it was thought that this might indicate that something about the way of life in Social Class V was productive of schizophrenia. We now know that it is more likely that the high prevalence of schizophrenia in Social Class V is a consequence of the disease rather than a cause, because if you develop schizophrenia you may become socially less competent, you may lose your job, which may be a skilled job, and you may slide down the social scale. By the time you enter a psychiatric hospital, or by the time you become a declared case as it were, your social position may be that of an unskilled worker and therefore this produces an apparently high prevalence in Social Class V. This is an example of the difficulties which the method presents, the problems of interpretation which one has to cope with in using this method, and there are many such problems to be met and sorted out before we can really gain the maximum use from this method of enquiry.

Social pressures towards suicide – Ivor Mills

Everyone must pay homage to the new god which is called *efficiency*. More money must be earned by more work until everyone is pushed to the very limit of his tolerance. . . .

Workers pushed to the limit of their tolerance no longer conform to the principles of economic theory; they are no longer reasonable. When they strike, they are not crying for help: they are telling you that the conditions of life are intolerable. From animal studies we know that when the breakdown of social order begins it may progress with fantastic speed. We are witnessing today the early stages of the breakdown of civilisation in the most highly developed countries. It is the result of too many people and too great a drive to reach too much affluence, in short, too much competition. If life is to be made more tolerable we must have a dramatic reduction in the population: we must reduce considerably the competition in schools, colleges and universities: we must include some degree of inefficiency in every job carried out by a man or woman: we must be content with less affluence.

Potential suicides – George Day

Most suicide risks are among ordinary people with no mental illness – ordinary, everyday people stricken with worry, dispirited by disaster, beaten down by their personal problems. To enumerate some of the misfortunes that can dispirit us: bereavement, loss of security, loss of job, redundancy, loss of social status; the failures: matrimonial failure, failure to get expected promotion, failure to pass examinations; and the *fear* of failure, because the students take their overdoses *before* the exams which they dread, not usually after them. Nagging anxieties that can't be relieved, about one's health, about the health of one's loved ones, and – loneliness.

These life situations are situations in which the victim may feel a bit shamefaced, a bit to blame, so he doesn't want to advertise them to anyone he knows, certainly not to his family, nor to his doctor, nor his priest. He's bursting to get it off his chest, discuss it with somebody. But it must be somebody he doesn't know, whose confidentiality he can trust, and whom he need never see again if and when he gets through his trouble.

The majority of suicides are not mentally ill – Richard Fox

Assessment of the suicidal episode requires careful consideration of the act itself and of the life situation in which the act took place: of the state of affairs to which the suicidal episode appeared, at that time, to be the answer. Usually the wrong answer. Many would say that it is always the wrong answer though one does from time to time find situations in which one has to admit that in all logic suicide just does make sense and in which one might oneself very well choose suicide; underlining a point which is often forgotten, that not every suicidal person is mentally ill. It is easy to assume that anyone who feels like ending it all must be *ipso facto* insane, but this is an immature view, reflecting personal anxieties about death, and not one which fits the facts. Clear evidence of psychotic disorder is only found in about one-third of cases of successful suicide, and of less significant mental instability in a further one-third, though these figures are often disputed.

Suicidal survivor – LYNNE ROSS

I would like you to think of me not as a Samaritan but as a potential client. I have been ill recently and I don't feel terribly confident. I don't intend this to be a comical type of case history, I want it to be my story from my point of view. Of course, you could call it 'That Was My Life That Was', or something like that. My reason for telling you this is to let fellow-Samaritans have a little more insight into illness from a client's point of view. It is very difficult for someone who is not experienced in clinical depression to understand just what it feels like and why depressed people attempt suicide. I know from personal experience when I was only fifteen what I now know to be depression. My last two years at school were very unhappy ones for me, but no one realised that anything was wrong, least of all myself. I sensibly entered the nursing profession and enjoyed my work but found it very difficult to make friends. Responsibility on night duty for very ill patients worried me excessively until, in my second year, I became ill. Nothing dramatic happened: I simply woke up one evening, in the night nurses' home, knowing that I could not go on duty that night. I didn't know why, and I wasn't able to tell the Assistant Matron why, so I was sent home and told to contact my GP. After five weeks at home, he decided to refer me to a psychiatrist and I was admitted to the psychiatric ward of a general mental hospital.

At this point, I feel I should perhaps enlarge upon what it feels like to be depressed. Having suffered recurrent bouts of depression for years now, I know when a bad spell is coming on. My mind begins to slow down. I have to make a conscious effort to make decisions, even unimportant ones, such as what shall I wear tomorrow, when shall I do my shopping, or shall I leave it till later, I don't know. I can remember on some occasions taking a couple of hours to make a simple decision. It is very difficult to be sociable, to converse with people. I find that my mind goes blank and I can't contribute anything to a conversation. It's almost like a thick blanket descending on top of you, cutting out light and deadening the feelings. At these times I want to be on my own, away from other people's depression. I have found from my own experience that this is the best way that I can cope. I shut myself away until I come out of a black spell of depression.

For approximately five years I was in a psychiatric hospital. My first stay lasted for four months and I returned to work after that after having been treated with anti-depressant drugs and the treatment called electro-convulsive therapy. Unfortunately for me, I was sent to a small hospital for pre-convalescent patients, where there was an acute shortage of trained staff. Responsibility was thrust upon me, and although I enjoyed it at first, it began to prey on my mind.

Because I had been sleeping very badly, my doctor had prescribed sleeping tablets which were barbiturates. At that time, it was about twelve years ago, barbiturates were quite freely prescribed for sleeplessness. I became more and more depressed, and began to feel there was only one way out, and that was death. After all, I did not ask to be brought into this world, why should I be denied the right to go out of it when I wanted to? I know now, looking back, that I wasn't thinking logically or rationally or I could never have come to these conclusions. I had ceased to feel anything emotionally. When you're really at rock bottom, nothing means anything to you: parents, family, religious belief, etc. Absolutely nothing. You can see only one end, and there is no alternative, none. You cease to have any thoughts about the traumatic effect any suicidal attempt on your part will have on your family and your friends. Two of my friends have committed suicide and I have seen what their parents have gone through. The first time I tried to commit suicide I took an overdose of barbiturates, but I was found, I am not sure when, or how long after I took them. I woke up in hospital.

Fortunately, I have a good deal of insight into my illness, so that when a really bad spell comes on as it did recently, I know where to get help when it is needed. It is possible to reach a point when you once more cease to think rationally and are not really responsible for your actions. Knowing that you are on the brink of this is really frightening and it is often at this time one experiences the intense loneliness of depression. Not many people seem to know about this.

You can be surrounded by people, people like yourself, who may be trying their level best to communicate with you, and you to communicate with them, but you are so totally and utterly alone that it is like being imprisoned inside a glass cage.

At this point, I make an earnest plea to any Samaritan coming in contact with someone who is depressed, please, please keep trying to get through. We want to talk out our innermost thoughts and fears, but are unable to. Only someone like a Samaritan who has both the time and the patience can fill the gap left by the professionals, who are very busy people and really can't give as much time as obviously they would like to. Samaritans can listen and really help at this point. It is not too difficult to actually talk, but it is almost impossible to put the thoughts into suitable words. The sheer frustration of this simply adds to the misery of depression.

I have tried to take my own life on several occasions. Looking back objectively, I can honestly say that two of those attempts were in deadly earnest. Only timely and unexpected intervention saved me. On other occasions, I was badly depressed and desperately needed someone to give me the time. Not having this help, I took the only way out I could. Therefore, by encouraging a depressed client to talk, I firmly believe that it may help to prevent a suicide attempt if the client is suicidal. At this point, I would say that if I had gone to the Samaritans and if I had been asked if I was thinking about suicide, I would have been very glad to have been asked, because I don't think I would have brought up the subject myself. If my story has helped, perhaps even non-Samaritans, to understand depression a little better, it will have served its purpose. You, in your turn, may be able to help someone like me.

Thanks mainly to excellent psychiatric treatment and the support and encouragement of my wonderful family, I have survived to tell the tale. I still require treatment in the form of a drug which helps to minimise the severity of depressive spells and lessen the frequency. I would liken it to a diabetic requiring insulin. During the past year, I have survived the break-up of my marriage and just by pure coincidence, today happens to be my fifth wedding anniversary and although I have been forced to take a course of anti-depressant drugs again recently – I am still taking them – I am determined not to give in, and I am determined to make a completely new life for myself. Towards that end, in a few weeks' time, I start a university degree course at the ripe old age of forty-two.

None of this would have been possible without the help of so many people. I would particularly like to point out the care and concern of my colleagues, at the Dundee branch of The Samaritans, which has done so much to help me during my years as a member of the Movement. Samaritans don't only help clients, they also care very much for each other. I would like to thank you all.

Danger signs of acute suicide risk

1. Client withdrawn, cannot relate to you. Medical aid needed.
2. Family history of suicide.
3. Earlier attempts at suicide.
4. Definite idea of how suicide would be committed. The tidying up of affairs indicates suicide is being planned.
5. Anxious tone to depressive picture.
6. Dependence on alcohol or drugs.
7. Some painful physical illness and long sleep disturbance.
8. Feeling of uselessness. In elderly, lack of acceptance of retirement.
9. Isolation, loneliness and uprooting.
10. The possibility of having to live with few human contacts.
11. Lack of a philosophy of life such as a comforting type of religious faith.
12. Financial worries.
13. Within the period of the rise and fall in mood, the most dangerous time is often when the client appears better. Now he has enough energy to kill himself.

Assessing suicide risk – ROY VINING

The Samaritans' response to a suicidal caller must be proportionate to his danger, so careful enquiry into his suicidal feelings and intentions is essential if fatal errors are to be avoided.

The caller may mention suicidal feelings himself, or hint at them – 'I can't go on', 'I wish I was out of this mess', 'No way out' or the like: hints need to be followed up at once by asking the client what he means, lest he feel the subject is taboo. If he provides no such opening, then the Samaritan must ask, either gradually – 'Do you feel life isn't worth living?' – 'Have you ever felt like ending it all?' – or straight out: 'Have you turned to The Samaritans because you feel suicidal?'

If the caller does feel suicidal, there are three essentials to be found out:

1. Is there a *suicide plan*? If so, what is it, when, and perhaps where?
2. Are the *means* available?
3. Has any *previous* suicidal act been made, or started? If so, what, and when? To what extent did the caller intend to die?

These form a quite natural sequence and need not seem like a questionnaire.

The suicide plan

The suicide plan and its intended timing are the main indicators of the immediate risk. Alongside the plan and any history of previous suicidal acts, the caller's story may have revealed other risk factors which should be taken into account: if a person is old, ill, addicted, depressive, isolated or rejected, or devoid of hope, these things (listed here in order of growing importance) will increase the risk – they are the things which place the caller 'in a high risk group'.

Lethality scoring

Lethality scoring offers a convenient summary of what we need to know, and by assigning numerical weightings to the risk factors provides a rough measure of a client's danger in a form that is easy to use and remember. Many Branches are using it in their instruction of new volunteers.

LETHALITY SCORING TABLE

Start on left by scoring the Suicide Plan (chief indicator of immediate risk), then add points for anything relevant on the right (mostly long-term factors).

SUICIDE RISK	**Score	OTHER FACTORS		Add to score
Imminent sudden death	8	Previous suicidal acts	up to	4
Imminent slow method suicide	7	Absence of hope; loss of faith		3*
Planning sudden death	6	Recent broken relationship		3
Planning slow method suicide	5	Isolation; Rejection		3*
Planning a suicide gamble	4	Depressive illness (endogenous)		2
Planning a suicide gesture	3	Dependence on alcohol or drugs		2
Definite suicidal thoughts, no plan	2	Possession of means of suicide		2
Toying vaguely with idea of suicide	1	Putting affairs in order		2
No suicidal thoughts	0	Over 60; Male; Ill; Chronic pain		1*

**Score one figure from this side. *Score everything that applies.

ASK ABOUT SUICIDE RISK IN *EVERY* CASE AND AT *EVERY* CONTACT!

Examples

1. A widower aged sixty-seven with painful arthritis, living alone in a twelfth floor flat, who took an overdose last year (intending to die and prevented by an unexpected visitor), has made a new will and intends to jump from his balcony. For planning sudden death he scores 6 (8 if he means to do it immediately). Then add 4 for his previous overdose, 3 for his hopelessness, 3 for his isolation, 2 for the twelfth floor (he has the means for his plan), 2 for the new will (putting his affairs in order), plus 1 for age *and* 1 because he's male *and* 1 for his pain. So he scores 23 or 25, and we'll try not to let him out of our sight till he feels differently.

2. A girl who openly took eight aspirins during a row with her boy friend and threatens to do it again unless he sees her more often, scores 3 for planning a suicide gesture, plus 0 or 1 for the previous gesture. Having heard her out fully we could let her go.

Study of such examples, and intermediate ones, suggests that a lethality score of over 20 requires that we stay with the caller till the risk declines. 14 or over requires us to arrange another contact very soon; 6 or over should make us seek another contact less urgently; below that it's probably fair enough to invite the caller to contact us again if he/she wishes (unless there are separate reasons for keeping in positive touch).

The relation of response to risk can be summarised thus:

LETHALITY SCORE	LEVEL OF RISK	LEVEL OF RESPONSE
	Attempt in progress	Arrange treatment if caller willing
7 or 8 on left or total of 20+	On the brink	Stay with caller
14 to 19	High risk	*Fix* another contact *very* soon
6 to 13	Moderate risk	*Fix* another contact
1 to 5	Slight risk	Hear client out and let go (unless other reasons for further contact)
0 on the left	No suicidal thoughts	

When lethality scoring was first introduced at a Leaders' School at Swanwick, Derbyshire, some anxiety was expressed that the spontaneity of the 'befriending response' of the Samaritan volunteer might be impaired by attention to lethality calculations. This must certainly be avoided by so familiarising the applicants in the Preparation Classes with the procedure that it becomes second nature. The most relaxed possible conversation with a caller seriously at risk should in any case provide information which will enable a Director or Leader to score his/her lethality.

Keep on asking

Since suicide risk fluctuates we must never fall into the trap of regarding our original assessment as permanently valid (whether expressed as a number or not). On the contrary, we must be alert for changes – especially upswings that can result in death; and this means that we must *keep on asking*, and make a fresh assessment at every encounter.

One further warning: failure to find out everything relevant will result in too low a score and a false sense of security. This is not a fault of the lethality scoring system – it is a fact of life that however lethality is assessed, if it isn't done properly the danger will be underestimated and clients put at risk.

Summary

Never ignore possible suicide hints.

Assess the risk by asking in detail about suicidal feelings, *every* time.

Match The Samaritans' response to the client's danger.

To whom shall I speak today?
  I am laden with misery
  through lack of an intimate . . .
Death is in my sight today
  like the clearing of the sky,
  like a man attracted thereby to
  what he knows not.

Death is in my sight today,
  like the longing of a man to see home
  when he has spent many years held in captivity.

A dispute over suicide, Egypt, before 2000 BC, ANON

Talking down suicides – RICHARD FOX*

Twenty-five years ago, the Rev Chad Varah answered the emergency phone in his office at St Stephen's Church, in the City of London, for the first time. Ten years later, the figures for suicide reached their peak in Britain and declined from then on, by a remarkable 38% to an all time low in 1975. England and Wales in rates per hundred thousand population, had a drop of 12.2 down to 7.5 and, in whole numbers, from around 5,800 down to around 3,800.

This staggering number of 2,000 deaths a year *less* must surely be one of the most striking post-war social phenomena because (a) the economic climate with strikes, unstable government and falling currency would lead any social scientist to predict that suicide ought to have gone up and (b) the only other country in Europe to register a decline was Greece, with most countries recording a pronounced rise.

The Grecian situation in the early 1970s was more than likely a matter of government policy, such as the ban on the recording of crime and suicide in Russia during the Stalinist days. The Colonels probably did not want people to know too much of what was actually happening.

What appears to have been agreed, however, by every statistician who has looked at the data, is that the suicide decline here is a genuine one, no kind of statistical artefact, and no greater hiding away of suicides in accidental or open verdicts than is usually the case – very possibly the reverse. So, why us?

At a conference in London on 12th October, 1978, Dr Peter Sainsbury reported on research he had done for the World Health

* This article first appeared in *Community Care*, 1st November 1978.

Organisation in which he had studied every interesting variable he could, except, unfortunately, suicide prevention services. The results seemed rather underwhelming. The numbers of births to women aged under twenty or over thirty were the strongest predictor of the suicide rise. Affluence, as judged by the number of television sets contributed substantially, which seems very odd in our local context: I make around two hundred home visits a year and have yet to find the most squalid council house without one, although, of course, whether they have licences is altogether another matter!

High unemployment appeared to predict a low increase in suicide, which contrasts very curiously with a strong correlation between high unemployment and suicide both here and the USA during the 1930s. Our peak here was in 1931, that in the USA 1935.

The switch from coal gas to safe gas, Dr Sainsbury discounted completely because the Dutch suicide rate had continued to rise during the time they went over to North Sea gas and, one might add, that Dr Jean-Pierre Soubrier is observing the French situation where, as district after district is switching to the new gas, people turn to overdosing and the suicide rate remains stable.

If we take Durkheim's 1897 finding that suicide rates reflect in a subtle way the quality of life in any given community, this is just what one would expect to happen. There was a rise in overdose deaths in the 1950s in both sexes in the United Kingdom, the curve flattened out in 1963 and neither it nor any other method has changed significantly in order to fill the gap left by the absent coal gas suicides.

Whatever else you care to speculate about, such as the welfare state which they seem to do better in Scandinavia, intensive care, which they do everywhere, the switch from lethal barbiturates to very non-lethal benzodiazepines to treat insomnia, or whatever, it is hard to see that our situation is different from other countries. The drop has been steepest in the more suicide prone elderly and it is interesting that some other countries have had a drop in the elderly too, but unfortunately, more than compensated for a rise in the young. Maybe it is more respectable to be old nowadays? Maybe services for the old are better, who knows?

Our young people, depending on which years you compare with which, can be described as slightly more suicidal than they were, but the change is very slight. On the medical scene, the only significant change through the 1960s seems to me the explosion of psychiatric teaching in medical schools, but if we are going to say that our suicide has dropped because our doctors are getting better, it ought to follow that German, etc., suicide has risen because their doctors are getting worse, and, anyhow, no treatment for depression has ever been shown to influence suicide rates.

The universal introduction of electric shock treatment, by common consent the most rapid and predictable treatment for the severer forms of depression which become suicidal, at a time when the suicide figures were steadily rising after the war, made no perceptible dent in the curves.

There is an academic dispute going on just now about whether a Samaritan branch in any particular locality can be shown to exert a suicide preventive effect. Dr Christopher Bagley in 1968, compared fifteen towns with Samaritan branches with fifteen that did not have them and concluded that there was a significant preventive effect. Dr Brian Barraclough and his colleagues have just published a study which they say shows that there is no effect. The jury is still out. However, Chad Varah, as soon as his service became known, received calls from literally all over the country, so the relevance of this debate is uncertain.

Also, looking at figures when you do not know actually what is going on in a town is grossly misleading. Thus, an article discounting the influence of the Samaritans in the suicide decline in Brighton because there was not a branch there, was written without the author considering the generalised effect of a national organisation and the fact that Eastbourne branch publicised its existence in Brighton and had an active nucleus of volunteers in that town, carrying out befriending.

A mystery, but a very important mystery, because if we knew what it was we were doing, we could presumably be doing it better and other countries could do it too, with incalculable saving of life, distressed survivors, loss of people in key positions, police time and so on. In terms of impact on survivors, suicidal death does appear to be the most disastrous death there is with the possible exception of the very much rarer deaths by murder.

Is it too naïve to suggest that an organisation advertising itself to the suicidal and despairing might have something to do with it? Clearly, this suggestion has raised the antibody levels among threatened professionals who cannot conceive that a bunch of amateur do-gooders could possibly achieve what they, as fully qualified whatever they are, had failed to do. One leading suicide researcher set out from a position of absolute faith that Samaritans could not possibly lower the suicide rate, and that was that. Hurray for scientific objectivity. However, Samaritans do offer a new form of caring, a new parameter, if you like, in the giving of help, so let us look at what has happened.

Twenty-five years ago, Chad Varah had in his mind a counselling service directed particularly at the sexually ignorant and distressed, a concern initiated when as a young curate, he conducted the funeral of a fourteen-year-old girl who had killed herself because she was convinced her first period was venereal disease. His service was used more, however, by people with other forms of distress and also by people offering to give a hand. After a while he noticed that many who came got what they wanted by chatting to a volunteer over a cup of tea and went away without bothering to see him. Thus was born the concept of *befriending*, i.e., the giving of ordinary human friendship by an ordinary person who cared, to someone whose life was in a mess.

That suicide correlates highly with loneliness, isolation, 'anomie', lack of a significant other, or however you like to phrase it, is quite clear. We know that 30 to 40% of callers to Samaritans admit to active suicidal thoughts. Is the entry into their life of a new, rather special and very unthreatening friend likely to make them more or less suicidal? Experienced Samaritans have no doubt which and there are few who cannot tell tales of clients who, without their befriender, would in their minds have certainly committed suicide. But, then, it is possible that they might not and things like this are difficult to prove.

Chad Varah realised very early on that people did not just get unhappy during the daytime and individual case studies amply confirm that there is for many people a 'critical period' during which they are accessible to help and that this critical period can be very short. He had to have volunteers available twenty-four hours a day, seven days a week and that practice is now accepted by crisis services the world over. The Good Samaritan of the parable did what was needed immediately and did not content himself with giving the man set upon by thieves an appointment for the Jerusalem County Hospital for Friday fortnight at 2 p.m. There is reason to suppose, incidentally, that both psychiatric referral and admission to a psychiatric ward may sometimes *increase* suicidal hazard.

Samaritan branch number two opened in Edinburgh in 1959 and growth built up from there. The creation of a national organisation with a central secretariat and the imposition of standards in 1963, coincided with the suicide peak. There were, at that time, about 21 branches. There are currently 173 branches of which 159 offer the full 24 hours' service, including five in the Republic of Ireland and growth over the last four to five years has been slow. New branches are mostly in fairly small areas and the number of volunteers has stuck at something over 20,000.

New ways of bringing a service to sparsely populated areas are being explored but it looks as though saturation point has probably been reached both in the size of the service and in those amongst us who are willing to use it. The numbers of new callers rose steeply through the 1960s, the rise being a remarkably consistent 30%, but after reaching around 200,000 in 1972 the rise became much smaller and seems to have stabilised at about 230,000 new callers every year. Adding old callers from previous years, the Samaritans are probably in contact with about one person in every 150 every year and there are well over a million total contacts. It could be that this flattening out in Samaritan work is associated with the slight rise in suicide in 1976 and 1977 before the fall resumed in 1978. (These figures were updated in 1979. Ed.)

Another thing worth looking at is the public's awareness of the service. In 1975 National Opinion Polls (NOP) surveyed over 2000 people at random, recording that 92% said they had heard of The Samaritans. The great majority had the right idea about Samaritans being a distress and suicide prevention service and the idea of absolute confidentiality had evidently got through. If you go to a professional agency in a crisis, and the first things they seem to be interested in are your name, address, date of birth, next of kin and religion, that can be a bit off-putting. The Samaritan at the point of first contact does not care too much about all that and gets straight into the problem. Confidentiality within the Samaritans is probably tighter than in any organisation outside the priesthood. An army combat unit, all blacked up, arrived at a Northern Irish branch demanding to go over the records for IRA suspects. They went away disappointed.

Another message that had apparently got through to the public was that The Samaritans, despite the name which some journalists coined very early on and which stuck, are in no way a religious organisation. As a name, it still causes problems overseas, but I suspect that if NOP had asked what came into mind when you mention the word 'Samaritans', I doubt if many would mention the New Testament. We found that the more knowledge respondents had of the organisation, the more favourably they looked on it. Asked if they would contact the Samaritans at a time of personal need, one third said yes and another third couldn't make up its mind. Thirty admitted to actually having contacted the Samaritans and of these twenty said they had been helped.

Other countries also use the publicised twenty-four hour telephone, with almost all of them copied from Samaritans. Without going into vast details, it can be categorically stated that nowhere in the world is there a suicide prevention organisation remotely offering the kind of population saturation The Samaritans have achieved. Los Angeles, the greatest urban sprawl in the world, has one suicide prevention centre (and its main interest is research). Greater London has fourteen Samaritan branches.

Very few European centres allow face-to-face encounters. All the Samaritan branches are drop-in, usually from before breakfast to after closing time. Some European services are heavily church-orientated, and I have heard of none that operate the flying squad principle of a rota of volunteers with transport, who are willing at any time to go out and deal with a crisis on the spot. We can, thus, identify Samaritans internationally as a unique, intervening variable and to discount this as a factor in the suicide decline seems rather stupid.

We have to face the problem that, while actual suicide has declined, suicide attempts or what are increasingly described as 'parasuicides' have increased dramatically and seem still to be increasing, though there is the suggestion that a limit has been reached. The term 'attempted suicide' was misleading in that it covered a vast range of behaviour from the person who goes in front of a tube train or shoots the front of his head off and somehow survives, to the other extreme, the girl who takes five aspirin and calls the doctor because she wants her boyfriend back. These are different, albeit overlapping groups, with a preponderance of middle aged or old men among the suicides and an overwhelming preponderance of young harrassed women among the parasuicides, almost all of which are nowadays by overdose.

We have an overdose epidemic and apart from telling doctors to be less liberal in their prescribing, no one seems to know what to do about it. This is not really surprising because, though one can discern certain patterns (e.g., the planned versus the impulsive attempt), there are as many causes of both suicide and parasuicide as there are unhappy people who set out to injure themselves. It is a complicated and fascinating field for study.

What is clear is that only a small percentage of parasuicides have been in contact with the Samaritans. As a group they are less likely to know about Samaritans than the general population and, also, any Samaritan branch will tell you of people who have the overdose there already but have decided to ring the Samaritans first. For the ones who don't ring, the answer seems to be that they acted impulsively in, e.g., a marital blow-up and that the thought of contacting anybody at all, just never entered their minds. The 'cry for help' element in most overdoses is less demanding in ringing your doctor or The Samaritans than the swallowing of half a bottle of tablets most certainly is (and it is fascinating how often it is *only* half the tablets that are swallowed!). As a form of dramatic, non verbal communication, a call to the Samaritans is not in the same league as the overdose. However, it is worth noting that 1.5% of clients, i.e., around 3,500 people, rang Samaritans in 1976 actually during or after an act of self-injury.

I speculate that the organisation is suicide preventive in three ways: first, just by being there. The very existence of a well known and respected organisation which says 'don't do it, we care, contact us', has an influence on people who never contact it. Patients not infrequently tell me that though they have never actually rung Samaritans, they have got a cutting from the local paper with the emergency 'phone number tucked away in their wallet 'just in case'. This factor would be hard to measure.

Secondly, The Samaritans prevent suicide because of the effectiveness of the actual work they do in *befriending* the vast numbers of clients who seek their help in varying degrees of desperation and with varying needs, but all requiring an unhurried, unstructured encounter with a concerned, utterly trustworthy person who will listen to them and accept them.

Thirdly, with a turnover of volunteers averaging 20–30% per year, it can be calculated that there are approximately 75,000 people in the community who have had on average three to four years' experience of Samaritan work, which is, if nothing else, learning about how to be with and care for other people when they are in a mess. To what extent, one speculates, does this ex-Samaritan 'leaven' influence the kind of society we live in? If we are to take into account Durkheim's view already quoted, one must conclude that the existence of the organisation has in some way altered the quality of life in Britain; and if we think suicide is a bad thing, to have altered it for the better.

Helping people in anxiety – H. J. WALTON

A person in adulthood feels 'good' to the extent that his relations with his parents were satisfactory. A person who had bad relations with a parent will be prone, throughout life, to experience spells of 'bad' feelings: self-criticism, inferiority, depression or anxiety. In this sense the exact nature of a person's associations with his parents remain embedded in him and are a source of feeling states which can occur to him throughout adulthood.

The people we see in crisis, therefore, talk to us about their present social relationships, their own family members, and at length also about relationships they had with their parents.

A person communicates with other people by means of speech. He communicates with himself by thinking. Thought is internal behaviour. In an interview we enable the person we are helping to give us access to his internal behaviour, by asking him to tell us about his thoughts.

In our attempt to understand behaviour through talking to a person, a double task faces us. We have to understand the person in the first place, and then we have to comprehend the situation in which he finds himself. When his crisis is the result of external difficulties or pressure, we can talk of *press*, as when someone loses an important person through death. When the crisis is the result of internal pressures inside the troubled individual, we can speak of *stress*. Such internal stress can be produced by thoughts in a person's mind, by feelings such as anger or resentment, or by impulses such as sexual urges which trouble the person but which he cannot allow full expression.

A useful way of looking at people in crisis may be by assuming that when they contact us they are disturbed by painful inner tension: they suffer from anxiety which has reached an insupportable level. Anxiety is caused by the human environment. It is a mood of fear which puts out of action a whole range of normal skills and functions. An anxious person does not attend adequately to his environment, does not notice things, makes errors, is forgetful. Generally, anxiety serves to disorganise ordinary behaviour.

Anxiety can increase in intensity to produce a state of terror. If a person is appropriately predisposed, there is a wide range of life events which can precipitate a state of anxiety.

Being rejected by another person is one: as when an employee is told that his work is not good enough, or a husband tells his wife that her housekeeping does not satisfy his expectations. (Perhaps his standards are over-conscientious, ingrained in him by an excessively perfectionist mother when he was young.)

The other person may precipitate anxiety in our client or patient by more clear-cut aggression or hostility, making threats which endanger the security of the person who consults us. It can be, however, that there is no other person prominently implicated; instead it may be a person's own thoughts which precipitate anxiety in him: a mother suffering from fearfulness that she is not good enough to care for her child and will inadvertently perpetrate some harmful or even fatal accident. Thoughts connected with sex are often extremely distressing to people, and if we get from them details about their past lives, it is clear how the conflict state about sex arose. They need to express their responses of loving and physical tenderness, but there are forbidding images or memories lodged in their minds which forbid such natural expressions of love.

We arrive at mature forms of sexuality only in adulthood, passing through phases which society considers abnormal, indeed will not recognise as customary or common at certain stages of life. We forget the devious paths by which adolescents arrive at mature sexuality.

The person who contacts us will usually be in a state of excessive anxiety. This is a painful inner state, a pervasive sensation of fear which is uncomfortable and in extreme cases may be intolerable. Anxiety is so distressing a state that, when it is severe, the sufferer will seek to reduce the painful tension, sometimes in ways which lead him to suffer great harm.

There are various kinds of anxiety, with three main types. The importance of distinguishing the type of anxiety lies in the fact that for each type a different kind of approach is required.

A person may have extreme, massive anxiety because he fears he will be suddenly isolated, or because he is suddenly overwhelmed with self-reproach or self-loathing, or because he dreads that some harm is about to befall him in relation to his body.

The first type of anxiety, the dread of isolation, occurs when a person is suddenly deprived of the support of another person upon whom he had been more deeply dependent than perhaps he knew. He may lose the protecting person through death; a woman may lose the husband on whom she is emotionally dependent because he leaves her for another woman; a person may never have married in order to retain the protectiveness of a parent, and be precipitated into an anxiety attack if the parent withdraws affection or support.

This type of separation anxiety has been studied in small children who are taken from parents when admitted to hospital; but you can also see very similar reactions in adults, say in a woman whose husband leaves on a business trip overseas, or in someone whose more emotionally robust marriage partner becomes ill.

The second type of anxiety, the anxiety of self-disgust, is different. Healthy people have a reasonable appreciation of their own attainments; they tell themselves that, considering the obstacles they have encountered, they have acquitted themselves fairly adequately. But the anxiety which comes from an unhealthy conscience leads a person to think that he has failed, that he betrayed all the trust reposed in him, that he is a disgrace to those who had believed in him. This type of anxiety leads the person to say to whoever is approached for help: 'Please don't let my mother or father hear of this.' Such a person will figuratively beat his head, overcome with self-hatred and abnegation. They may say that they deserve only condemnation or punishment. Some may actually punish themselves, taking their chastisement in their own hands. These people are flayed by their consciences. Psychologically they have, as part of their minds, attitudes of self-disgust. These attitudes are seen by psychiatrists as stemming from hatred or criticism or rejection experienced during growing up. Disliked by a parent, they have come to carry for ever, as part of their mentality, the inner reflection of what was once directed upon them from the censorious parent. Now it has become a part of the self. Any criticism they evoke, a failure of their efforts, or even a reproof uttered by someone in the heat of anger, suddenly lights up their own stores of self-criticism.

Only someone who has experienced the horror of being alone in a state of terror while the full light of consciousness plays relentlessly over all the weakness, failures, omissions and faults, can understand the fear which may be felt by somebody who regards himself as beyond contempt. Often such a person, when seeking help, is in an extreme dread that he has failed, that he is an outcast and will be despised if only people knew.

We recognise that when a person seeks our help for anxiety of this self-despising variety we will probably find in his life history a parent who was not able to feel appropriate affection for him. This parent is then retained in his mind throughout life as a sort of inner assailant, who can undermine him, bring him down, humiliate him. His precarious self-esteem drops to an agitatingly low level when in addition he encounters criticism or rejection in his current experience with other people.

The third type of anxiety, dread of physical damage, may be illustrated by its expression in a young man: 'Lately I go to bed many nights haunted by the fear that I won't wake up the following morning. I can assure you this fear of dying is torture to go through.'

The person is suddenly struck with terrible certainty by a fear that his heart is diseased, or that he has a cancer. People anxious in this way, overcome by a fear of some serious physical affliction, are likely to seek medical reassurance directly, so they are more prone to have their first recourse to doctors than to any other sort of helping person.

To give first aid to people with these varying types of anxiety calls for very different responses in the helping person. The individual with separation anxiety needs substitute company from a friend or a relative, or hospital care. The person with conscience anxiety, convinced of his worthlessness, needs a personal response which will revive his self-esteem. To protect and provide comfort and care for him, as advocated for the earlier type of separation anxiety, may only convince him of his worthlessness. The person with the third type of anxiety, fear of bodily dissolution, usually needs medical attention as a first step, before tracing out with him what the roots of his physical panic were.

While we may approve of the wisdom of those in trouble who seek help, they themselves may consider their help-seeking despicable. Jerome Frank has demonstrated that one of the changes occurring in people who are successfully treated by psychiatrists is their greater effectiveness in getting help for themselves when they feel troubled. Some people approaching us will show, as part of their personality disturbance which has not yet been improved by treatment, a great hesitancy in asking for help. Many of our clients or patients will reach us only when the extremity of their distress has pushed them over this inner barrier against asking for aid. They will often be ashamed and apologetic at this weakness, as they see it, this lapse into open admission of lack of independence. Many will not come to see us until their distress has driven them to contemplate suicide.

Coping with clients under 16 – JOHN ELDRID

There has been a marked increase in the number of very young clients (fifteen years and under) contacting The Samaritans. Whilst it is an important principle of our work that we regard all clients as human beings irrespective of age or problem, it is useful to recognise that clients vary considerably in their approach, and our reactions vary according to what is presented.

When a fourteen-year-old rings up for the first time he or she may present what may appear to be a trivial problem about which to ring The Samaritans. He or she may complain of being afraid to go to school because of bullying or it may be that the parents do not like children staying out late. He or she may make the approach amidst giggles and laughing. It may be a general kind of enquiry about finding a club or information about knowing when you are pregnant or how to get an abortion. How do we react? We must treat the call very seriously because the giggling approach is more likely to be a cover-up for shyness. The worry about other girls or boys is likely to be only the tip of the iceberg. Samaritans must recognise that teenagers do not find it easy to be articulate about their problems, so they will have a struggle to verbalise their feelings and worries. Older people, particularly in their late twenties to fifties, do not on the whole find it so difficult to speak of their troubles, but from the fourteen-year-old we can expect initially the rather typical problems of anxiety about parents not understanding and so on, yet once you get the confidence of the girl or boy you may discover they are frequently away from school presenting false absentee notes, and that they are terrified to speak to their parents. You may be surprised to learn he or she would like to make a go of it at school and longs for someone with whom their problems can be discussed. In addition to the worry about bullies at school you may discover the parents are fighting most of the time or a break-up of the marriage is imminent – or conversely the parents may get on well, but because they are so anxious to see Johnny do well he feels depressed about letting them down, and so does not tell them the truth.

As in most cases it is the last straw that breaks the camel's back; here it could be bullying at school or breaking friends, but there is generally a big build-up behind it. We in The Samaritans should recognise that it is always a serious step to telephone us, so we have no reason to assume that the caller is not feeling desperate. It is not uncommon for young people to experience a very sudden sense of loss and depression, so that for them at the time the situation may seem quite hopeless. The feelings of young people are intense, so they are likely to be very elated at one moment with a dramatic drop to sadness and possible depression. This is one of the reasons why it is most essential for us in The Samaritans to listen to what is said and to note what is not mentioned. The assessment of these situations is by no means easy, and requires good consultation in the Branch. Some doctors and social workers are particularly concerned that much childhood and teenage depression goes unnoticed. Suicides do occur in this age group; whilst this was being written a thirteen-year-old boy killed himself in London.

Clients in this age group will be very sensitive about confidentiality, and whilst they seem mostly to have heard that The Samaritans can be trusted to keep confidences, they will be very cautious at the outset. It is therefore most important not to take any action without the client's consent. This may arouse feelings of anxiety in some about the best not being done in the end for the child; and some may feel just a little frustrated waiting upon the permission of a fourteen-year-old before taking what seems to the volunteer the obviously desirable action.

Some adults have very genuine reactions of anxiety about the need to inform parents or school – in fact the commitment to maintaining confidentiality may be more sorely tested in relation to a fourteen-year-old client than with a middle-aged man on the run for murder or some sex offence. But it is essential for us not to break confidence with the client if we are going to be a means of helping him feel it is good to be alive. The maintaining of this confidence will not only affect him positively, but will encourage others of the same age group to contact us. Once we have built up a good relationship, the boy or girl is usually more than happy for us to contact school or parents or whatever, and if they do not give permission it is for a good reason. As the Samaritans are offering a safety-valve whereby pent-up emotional conflicts can be safely released, it is more than likely that the boy or girl will be capable of taking the next positive steps without the need for Samaritan intervention at home or at school.

If we do have occasion to speak with parents or school teachers we must be careful not to blame them for the situation. They may feel guilty about their little Johnny being so desperate that he had to go to the Suicide people, so they may at first react aggressively. We must listen also to them. With teachers it is generally easier, but it is important to recognise that we are seeking their co-operation and guidance and not telling them how to run their school. Many teachers are pleased with our interest and will often end up by unloading on to us their worries about the particular case and many similar ones.

This increase in our calls from children and teenagers does not indicate that everything is worse than it was in our day – it is simply that young people today know that there are a number of helping agencies available to assist people with problems. They get quite a lot of information about the work of The Samaritans in school and often write up accounts of our work as a special project, so it is not surprising they turn to us. Also present-day society does to some extent encourage people to express their anxieties whatever their age group, and so many more people, instead of suffering in silence as they may have done in the past, now ring The Samaritans. That's what we are for.

Befriending the homosexual – CHAD VARAH

We are all to some extent homosexual, in that we retain from that period in our childhood when we were almost entirely homo-erotic a capability both for deep affection for and sexual attraction to those of our own sex even if soon after puberty we joined the vast majority who find the opposite sex more sexually exciting and desirable.

This may be illustrated by the behaviour of men or women confined in a situation when for a longish period they are cut off from the society of the opposite sex. Homosexual practice in one-sex boarding schools or in prisons or on ships at sea are no proof, by themselves, of predominant homosexual leanings on the part of the participants. Many a public schoolboy has had no difficulty in distinguishing between those of his sexually very active contemporaries who are 'really' homosexual, and who will be observed to continue into adult life; and those who are 'making do', and even on a short exeat will manage to get at some girl. But what of the ones who are apparently equally interested in pretty boys and their visiting sisters? And those who even in term time would rather masturbate while thinking about a girl than engage in sex play with another boy? And those who (whether with a low or high or medium sex drive) strive to avoid sexual arousal and gratification?

A bright schoolboy will come to the conclusion that just as you cannot divide the pupils in your class into 'clever' and 'stupid', because there is an infinite gradation from the sharpest to the thickest academically, so the same lot of boys cannot be divided into heterosexual and homosexual, as if you were bound to be purely one or the other, and as if there were no degrees of interest and lust. Strange, then, that he so often grows up to join the mob of foolish adults who are unaware of this fascinating spectrum, and who, like the old style Western with its goodies and baddies, label everyone 'straight' or 'queer'.

The reason why those of us who regard ourselves as wholly heterosexual are loth to admit that we retain any homosexual potential in our make-up is partly that we have not found ourselves in circumstances when this uncomfortable bit of self-knowledge was forced upon us, and partly that all the weight of conventional attitudes and our natural avoidance of the finger of scorn cause us to flinch away from any such awareness. Indeed, many of those who are, and know they are, markedly homosexual may try to deny this, to others if not to themselves. They want to live quietly without persecution, and who (except those more interested in politics than in love) will blame them if they decide not to 'come out', let alone man the barricades? It is sad to note that many of the most lurid criticisms of post-Wolfenden legislation in this country came from timid homosexuals.

About 4% of the population, both male and female, finds sexual love-making with the same sex more acceptable than with the opposite sex, even though the latter activity may, for some, at a pinch, be feasible. What we do not know is how many of the remaining 96% deserve to be called heterosexual by a similar criterion, namely that they find sexual love-making with the opposite sex more acceptable than with the same sex (which of course includes oneself). When you cut out those who have not yet reached puberty and those who have become asexual through senility, those who cannot use sex in relationship but only in masturbation (which may possibly use another person's body to rub against), those who suffer from a deviation of aim or object (e.g. sadomasochists, exhibitionists, fetishists and transvestites, whose deviant desires may focus on the opposite *or* on the same sex), what percentage of the population is left? An educated guess is that something of the order of 40% deserve to be called heterosexual in the sense that (no doubt with some aid from fantasy) they can enjoy a *person* of the opposite sex. An educated guess about those who deserve to be called homosexual in that they can enjoy a person of the same sex is that they number about 2%; so that leaves a majority of the population in an inferior position from the point of view of truly human, loving sexuality. The distinction, if we feel bound to make one at all, is not between hetero and homo, but between those who can love with their sex and those who unhappily cannot.

Acceptance of these facts so completely that it has become part of our natural and unthinking reaction to the information that a man or woman we encounter is alleged to be homosexual, is the only way the volunteer, whether more hetero or more homo, can befriend a homosexual. Only this attitude, which is scientific and true and humane (and therefore good and Samaritan) can enable us so to befriend the homosexual in crisis, without talking offensive nonsense about perversion or 'cure', that he or she will not only continue to live but probably find life richer for having encountered The Samaritans.

A moment's thought will convince us that a person who is homophile (i.e. capable of love-making with someone of the same sex) is not much more likely to seek the help of The Samaritans about homosexual problems than a 'heterophile' (to coin a word) is to seek our help about heterosexual problems. Both vague categories of human beings suffer from a variety of difficulties which may make their life appear unsupportable at the moment, and a person's sexual orientation will often be largely irrelevant to the sort of befriending he or she needs. Homophiles are a little more likely than heterophiles to want to mention their disposition and to find problems arising out of their belonging to a sometimes persecuted (though not nearly as blackmailable as pre-Wolfenden) minority, and they encounter greater difficulties in meeting a sufficient variety of other homophiles to be likely to find an acceptable partner with whom to set up home. The average homophile has the same need of a secure and mutually rewarding partnership as the average heterophile, and the frequently expressed allegation that 'homosexuals are not capable of lasting relationships' is untrue. What is, sadly, true is that without the support of society and the family which most marriages enjoy, homosexual partnerships may break up when disagreements or infidelities occur as easily as in the less family-integrated heterosexual cohabitations without marriage. Certainly there is often a need for a form of 'marriage counselling' for homosexuals, male or female, in partnerships, and good befriending by Samaritan volunteers may lead to this being found acceptable.

A most important thing for Samaritans to know and tell to others is that when a person has been identified as a male homosexual this does not mean that he is likely to be a pederast, i.e. to be one who gratifies his sexual desires with children. Just as the vast majority of heterosexuals prefer a nubile partner and do not try to seduce little girls, so the vast majority of homosexuals do not try or wish to seduce little boys. Because heterosexuals greatly outnumber homosexuals, far more little girls than little boys are 'interfered with' sexually.

Not all pederasts are violent attackers of strangers. The typical pedophile loves children and relates to them better than to adults and usually does no more than stroking of the genitals of related or known children. But it is understandable that even this arouses anxiety and indignation in their parents and other adults if the child mentions it.

Let a male homosexual, Franklin E. Kameny, have the last word: 'The homosexual, in our pluralist society, has the moral right to be a homosexual . . . (and) to live his homosexuality fully, freely and openly, and to be so and to do so free of arrogant and insolent pressures to convert to the prevailing heterosexuality, and free of penalty, disability or disadvantage of any kind, public or private, official or unofficial, for his nonconformity.'

Bereavement – C. MURRAY PARKES

The effects of bereavement

When we look at the effects of a bereavement, there are four main areas that we have to consider.

There is *grief* itself – that is to say the psychological reaction to the loss.

There are the effects of *deprivation*. For instance, a woman who loses her husband not only suffers from the loss of her husband, but she also has to learn to live without him. She is, from then onwards, a person without a husband. She suffers not only loss but psychological starvation.

Then there is the *role change* that accompanies most losses – the fact that being a married woman, for instance, is not the same thing at all as being a widow. A person in one situation in life has to learn a new set of roles.

Attached to this is the way in which this change in role is perceived by society, particularly in the case of many losses the *stigma* which is associated with the loss. Here again, one can think in terms of loss of a person, or one can think in terms of other types of loss. For instance, an amputee – someone who loses a limb – is undoubtedly stigmatised – he becomes the recipient of sympathy. Sympathy is a very belittling thing. It is very damaging to self-respect. It's a stigma.

This involves more than a negative hostile element which undoubtedly does creep in; it includes the way in which people are frightened and embarrassed by those who are closely associated with loss, particularly where a death is involved. Every widow discovers that there are certain people who find it very difficult to talk to her, who feel somehow threatened by her, and they react in an embarrassed way.

This stigma is less obvious in our society than in many others where the widow may come under quite severe taboos for a period after her bereavement. In one island in the Philippines the widow is not allowed to see or speak to anybody. She walks through the forest with a stick which she taps on trees to warn people that she is coming, and it is believed that even the trees she touches will die, so closely is the widow associated with the death of the person whom she survives. The same fears exist in our civilisation and I think they account for some of the tendency to ignore, avoid and blind ourselves to the needs of bereaved people.

The process of grieving

There are several factors which determine whether a person goes through the process of grieving in a healthy manner or develops one of these abnormal reactions. There are three main considerations: there is the nature of *the relationship with the dead person* and other factors influencing the magnitude of the grief itself. Here I put two things first: dependence and ambivalence. Where the relationship has been a very dependent one with the widow or widower highly involved – to the point that her whole life centred on the other person, she is particularly liable to develop a severe reaction after the loss. There is also the opposite type of relationship. The husband and wife have quarrelled a great deal and perhaps there have been times when one has actually wished the other one dead. When death wishes are gratified the survivor has a tremendous load of guilt to make up. And it sometimes happens that the survivor will do a complete about-turn and say 'I was always quarrelling with my husband, but now I realise he was right'. In order to try to put this right she will spend the rest of her life in mourning for him. There are, of course, other forms which this ambivalent attitude can take.

The second main determinant is the effect of *defence* – the defences of the bereaved person against pain and distress. Now, we all know people who are very good at defending – very good at not facing up to unpleasant fact. We know families, too, where a 'stiff upper lip' is something which is a pride. 'People don't cry in our family.' So this isn't only a personal thing, it's a cultural factor. In fact there are many cultures which place very high value on the ability to control emotions and not to break down or to cry in situations which one would expect would give rise to this. Among the widows about whom I was talking earlier, those who showed the least emotion during the first fortnight of bereavement were uniformly more disturbed three months later than the rest. It appears that one can postpone grief, but one cannot deny the need to grieve. Sooner or later it will break through, and that's why defending oneself in this way doesn't seem to be a satisfactory answer to the problem of grief.

Finally, there are the effects on the rehabilitation of the widow of *the environment* in which she finds herself, and here I would put social isolation as the commonest cause of trouble. If a person has a close warm family who stand by her at the time of bereavement, then she will find during the course of the next few years that there is something left in life, that there are people who can share her grief, and people who can bring her out of it. Socially isolated people tend to get 'stuck' with the chronic type of grief. Rather less common, but also a problem that can arise, is the bereaved person who is over-protected. The tendency for the family to take over is perhaps not a bad thing at first, but in time can tend to be unhealthy, if it goes on after the period when the widow would normally have found herself a job, gone out, and so on. This is particularly the case where there are young unmarried daughters at home who are willing to take over a large part of the role of the widow. We all know the situation that can arise here.

Grief work – Chad Varah

The most important thing Samaritans can do to help someone who has suffered a severe bereavement is to encourage them to do what has come to be called 'grief work'. This involves taking out and looking at the memories of the one who has died, whether these were good or bad, and 'working' through them a sufficient number of times for them to be accepted, assimilated, and gently put away. Nothing prevents a bereaved person from readjusting to life more than the selfish habit of most of their relatives and friends of frustrating this need by changing the subject. They pretend this is for the mourner's good, but it is to protect themselves from embarrassment or boredom. We Samaritans are willing to assist patiently with 'grief work'.

The last act is always tragedy, whatever fine comedy there may have been in the rest of life – we must all die alone.

BLAISE PASCAL

Problems of the middle-aged – CHAD VARAH

When my triplet sons were small, Michael would often point out to visitors that he was the eldest and David, with equal pride, that he was the youngest, if only by five hours, which left Andrew with little claim on any admiring exclamations that might be offered. But one day he announced, 'Well, *I*'m the middlest.'

The special difficulties of the elderly receive almost as much discussion as those of 'youth' and much more than the exciting period Miss Jean Brodie called her 'prime' or that period, practically a synonym for dullness and mediocrity, called middle age. 'I'm getting middle-aged, I suppose' usually means 'it'll be downhill the rest of the way to the grave'. Yet it is from people in this age group that most of the beneficial contributions to our society come. Between forty and retiring age, both men and women tend to know who they are and what they have to give, and to be more conscientious and less likely to be distracted from their duties than when they were young. If they have any skill to offer, it is likely to be at its most practised, and though experience may teach people to keep on making the same mistakes, it is more likely to be a safeguard against bright ideas that won't work.

The middle-aged frequently hold those positions which are with good reason called 'senior', and are in most cases married, with children who are already young adults. If they are owner-occupiers of their houses, this adds to their authority and standing in the community. Women are mostly not yet widowed, and may well be able to choose between paid and voluntary work and at some stage decide how much of their lives to give to the enjoyment of grandmotherhood.

Why, then, safely beyond most of the uncertainties and confusions of youth, and not yet suffering a tremendous weakening of their powers, do so many men and women illustrate the distinction between prime and middle age?

Whilst the middle-aged may suffer any type of problem, just like other age-groups, the commonest ones that bring people to The Samaritans concern occupation and relationships, including sexual relationships.

It is well known that in our society the over-forties, particularly men, find it difficult to change jobs or to get a new one if redundant or dismissed. In those occupations which provide a pension, it is not economic to take on someone who after only a few years of service will become entitled to a pension. Furthermore, a certain seniority in age goes uncomfortably for all concerned with a junior position: those who would be quite willing to take instructions from a younger colleague may find the latter objecting. Junior positions are also likely to have lower rates of remuneration, insufficient for the commitments of many middle-aged persons.

The chief obstacle to one of the over-forties getting a new job may be his/her disinclination to lose status by accepting a position which attracts less social respect than the previous one, even if as well, or better, paid. To reconcile a person imprecisely but impressively described as an 'executive' to becoming (say) a postman may well be a counselling rather than a befriending job, though since it does not require any forbidden 'probing' questions, an experienced befriender may casually introduce into a conversation innocent enquiries about what would relations, neighbours, former colleagues think about the change, and what effect might it be expected to have on the person's health to be humping a bag of mail door-to-door instead of being deskbound when not sitting in a car on the way to sit in front of a television set. Not so long ago, Americans were proud of the number and variety of the occupations they had had experience of before becoming sufficiently prominent for anyone to listen to the catalogue, but increasing specialisation and the need for relevant qualifications and/or union recognition seem to have inhibited this vocational mobility.

Anyone who feels himself/herself to be on the scrap heap clearly needs a sympathetic listener, but may feel that the restoration of some self-respect leaves the problem unsolved. It is true that Samaritans do not pretend to solve problems, but in those cases where nothing less is acceptable they are well advised not to begin befriending without making this clear. Happily, there are cases where the morale-boosting by the volunteer enables the client to see his/her strengths and weaknesses more realistically and therefore to attempt some initiatives on the basis of actual resources, but such a satisfactory outcome cannot be guaranteed. It is good if the client decides not to demand what no one is likely to offer, but not good if he/she is determined not to settle for what is possibly available.

Change of lifestyle can be tricky to adjust to, and if it is not self-chosen it can lead to depression. One of the things to look out for is depression hidden behind an array of seemingly intractable problems.

It is wise for a person to take up new interests as he/she becomes incapacitated for the enjoyment of former ones, but enthusiasts should beware of trying to 'sell' their own interests to clients, and patiently draw out what the person might really wish to explore. There are so many exciting things to do or study, but it has to be remembered what a subjective word 'exciting' is.

Relationships in middle age often cause difficulty: the children no longer listen respectfully, if at all, and a spouse may have so completely triumphed in the long battle to have his/her own way as to leave the other beaten and resentful. Some spouses have become more and more strangers to one another as the things for which familiarity has bred contempt are progressively concealed, and others may have become so used to one another that instead of being as comfortable together as folded arms or crossed knees, they have become so boring that all sexual attraction is lost.

Much has been written about the menopause in women, and in the last decade also about the equivalent some ten years later in the male, but writing about it doesn't make it go away nor are all results of studies about the condition taken in by the general public so as to make them more understanding. The woman suffering tiresome symptoms of the change of life should seek the medical help which is now available, and then settle down to enjoy sex without fear of pregnancy, if she has or can find a partner.

One of the kindest things one can do in discussing their difficulties in life with women in their forties is to make no mention of the word 'menopause', for such women are sick of everything being put down to this, and of being expected to be difficult or unwell. Let any diagnosis come from them or their doctor.

The so-called male menopause isn't the termination of reproductive ability, which may continue in a centenarian, but an almost obsessive attempt to recover lost youth by doing things the young do, particularly in their supposed sexual freedom and prowess. The realisation that one of a man's two feet is in the grave makes him painfully aware of what he missed when the half-way mark was still well in the future. He will sometimes go to extraordinary lengths to feed the illusion that he is as virile as ever he was, and because he is more patient, more determined and more practised, he may in fact be able to enthrall some young thing for a while, to the distress of his self-righteous wife and the embarrassment of his children, possibly older than his mistress. We have to recognise that if he is the client, he is the one with whom we sympathise, not other people who may be inconvenienced by his antics. Ageing and death are not amusing, nor must we find ludicrous the expedients of human beings to take their minds off these horrors, escapable only by dying young, suddenly.

Befriending is often of great help in cases of this kind. The mere fact that the Samaritan does not utter irrelevancies implying disapproval such as 'and you have those three lovely granddaughters' is a relief – one client who was told this by his meenister replied curtly, and most aptly, 'I don't fuck them.' Acceptance of the difficulty as a real one, common to most middle-aged humans, is therapeutic. It's been known for a man to persist in behaviour all his family and friends denounce as ludicrous and unreasonable, and on being befriended by a Samaritan who accepts his behaviour as totally understandable and quite intelligently directed towards getting what he in fact wants, has decided to desist from it on the ground that the price other people are paying for what of course he wants is unacceptably high.

In middle age a man who has lived a heterosexual life with no penchant for homosexuality or the deviations may find that with waning powers or decreasing opportunities, neglected yearnings from his youth catch up with him. If these combine with loneliness and depression, he may engage in some form of sexual behaviour which causes scandal or even gets him in trouble with the police. Or he may simply despise himself for lusts which his conditioning does not allow him to satisfy. In either case he may become suicidal, and it is important for Samaritans to recognise this, to take his romantic longings seriously, and to recognise that those who are 'living, and partly living' may choose death because what they are afraid of is death.

Alcoholism – DAVID DAVIES

Alcoholism is a topic which is riddled with myths and misconceptions. The one that should be disposed of first is the idea that nobody can say what an alcoholic is, but we all know one when we see one. That is quite untrue on both counts. We do know what an alcoholic is, and we don't recognise them when we see them.

All of us – all caring agencies, doctors, nurses, social workers, volunteers of all kinds – must work with alcoholics because of the sheer numbers. It is reckoned there are a million in the population. Whether you know it or not, some among your clients are alcoholics. You may not recognise them as such, but we do know what an alcoholic is and can now give guidance as to how to recognise one. It's not just 'look and see'.

First, what is alcoholism? It is essentially connected with the long-term use of alcohol, and in that respect it differs from just getting drunk, which could happen to anybody – even on the first time that he takes a drink. So that one element in the definition must be continuing use of alcohol over a period of time. Another element must be harm, and that harm could be in any of three spheres. It could be in the physical sphere, e.g. damage to the liver; or in the mental sphere, even to the extent of mental disorders which bring people into mental hospitals; and (what concerns you most) in the social sphere, which covers marital, occupational and economic aspects of life.

Of course, if somebody went into hospital with liver damage due to alcohol and came out a week or two later with his liver restored, which could happen, nobody would dream that he was clear of his alcoholism. His liability to continue drinking in the way that brought on the damage still persists, as does that aspect of him we call dependence. It is no different from dependence on other drugs which, like alcohol, are addictive. So I would suggest that a thumbnail definition which anybody can use is: continual or intermittent ingestion of alcohol leading to dependency or harm. And dependency may be of a physical kind, e.g. where a man has to take a drink first thing in the morning to steady his hand. Or it might mean that he has to take a drink then or at other times not to control any physical symptom, but simply to feel right – to feel able to face the day and do the work he has to do. We shouldn't play down psychological dependence and think that it's any less difficult to cope with than physical dependence, because with some drugs – amphetamine is one of these – there is no physical dependency, and yet dependency of a purely psychological kind on that type of drug can be just as desperate as (say) dependence on heroin.

The other myth that I'm sure everyone has heard, that alcoholics are born, is quite untrue. Alcoholics are made. Nobody is born an alcoholic. And the other thing you read in the textbooks, that the cause is unknown, is also quite untrue. The cause is quite simple: oddly enough, it's alcohol. But one has to say a little more than that; it isn't just alcohol, but the continued use over a period of time of alcohol in quantities and in a frequency which engenders dependency. And this is true of all drugs of dependency, that nobody becomes dependent the first time they have the drug in a particular dose, but if there is repetition, then a sort of Rubicon is crossed when the body is no longer as it was previously, that is to say just the same after the dose as it was before. Now there is left something in the body about which we have learnt a great deal in the last couple of years. There is something left in the nervous system which makes the body keyed up and expectant of the next dose. But that only comes after a certain quantity and frequency. Now all drugs of dependency are harmless in certain dosages and certain frequencies, even if you become dependent. Coffee is a very good example. Most of us are dependent on coffee; we feel the need of it at certain times of the day, and if we don't get it we feel irritable. These are withdrawal symptoms. Very few of us develop damage due to coffee unless we have more than a certain quantity, which in the case of coffee is known to be five or six cups a day. Curiously enough, in the case of alcohol, it's known to be about five or six pints a day, or five or six double whiskies a day. Certainly at that level, physical harm can occur.

So it's possible to be dependent on alcohol and not be harmed by it. This may be a bit academic in a sense. But we must ask: Why then do only about 5% of us become harmed by alcohol? Rephrased, why do 5% drink so much to harm themselves?

The reasons why they drink so much are fairly straightforward and we know a great deal about them. They are sociological reasons. There is pressure to drink for all of us as we grow up, as part of our lifestyle. Some families and some groups of people experience stronger pressures than others. In some occupations, like the drink trade, and waiting, and going abroad in the Army – and including medicine for some curious reason – where there is increased availability, there is an increased likelihood of this developing. And of course, where it's cheap and where there are fewer restrictions, such as lack of licensing controls.

So in the case of any alcoholic, it's possible by taking a careful history to decide which factors have played a part in his case. Then the cause of it is perfectly clear and the treatment is rational. If there's harm, one deals with the harm, and that's no different from dealing with harm in other ways. If it's social harm, then social workers and volunteers like Samaritans are handy to deal with that. If it's physical, then there are doctors, real doctors who look after the body; and if it's mental, there are psychiatrists to look after that aspect. That's not very difficult as a rule, particularly if the trouble is spotted before it has gone too far. But what really is difficult, having got the harm out of the way, is dealing with the dependency. Because dependency is a habit and habits are very, very powerful. If one has practised a habit for twenty, thirty or forty years it's very difficult to get out of the habit. But we know more these days about how to unlearn habits, and treatment of the dependency side of alcoholism has become rational and can be very effective in ways which it wasn't really before.

Well, how do The Samaritans come into all this? I suppose the problem that comes up immediately is the question of suicide. It has been shown that among alcoholics the suicide rate is something like seventy times greater than in the population at large, and attempted suicide also is increased by about that factor. Moreover, the vast majority of alcoholics who either achieve suicide or make a non-fatal suicidal act, at the time they do the act have in fact got alcohol circulating in their blood. Because as I've said you can be an alcoholic with no alcohol circulating in your blood and go for days, weeks or months in that state, and therefore perfectly sober and in touch, but still have the propensity to lapse into your habitual drinking on certain cues or in certain situations. But in the harmful situations which are likely to present to *you*, the alcoholic is very likely also to have alcohol in his blood. So that if you can tide an alcoholic over that particular time, if you like to be with him for a few hours the next day when the alcohol has worked out of his blood, it could well be that though he is still an alcoholic, he is not in fact bent on suicide, and therefore the immediate goal should be fairly clear.

What are you to do then if you do identify the alcoholic? Perhaps one should ask *how* are you to identify him? None of the things you have been told is of any use to you, if I may say so. I should warn you that I am an iconoclast. I would suggest there are no lists of symptoms, or if there are it is because the man has reached such an advanced stage that you can spot him anyway and you don't need him to tell you the symptoms. The great thing is to keep in your mind the question: Is he harming himself by drink? All you have to determine is, in your own mind: Is he drinking enough to account for the harm he's got himself into? There might be other reasons for his harm as well, which might emerge in the course of the conversation and discussions you have with him, so that you have to keep an open mind about it. If his use of drink is not such as to make him vulnerable, simply on quantity and frequency, then that is probably as good a guide as any. Now it isn't easy to find out how much a man drinks, and the worst way is to ask him if he drinks or how much he drinks; but there are ways of finding out, simply by talking to him about his everyday life, how he spends the ordinary day, just listening – and I'm sure you're all very good at listening – and somewhere, while he's telling you about how he spends the day, something will crop up about on my way home from the pub, or to the pub, or in the bar or something, and that's as good a point as any to pick him up conversationally and get him to tell you more about how often he goes there and what he does there and so on. If you could keep a few figures in your mind, anybody who drinks on average something like five pints a day, or five double whiskies, that's roughly half a bottle of spirits (I never can work it out with wine because wine varies so much: it's probably about one and a half bottles of table wine a day) anybody who's been drinking that on an average for some months (and it's more likely years) is vulnerable. Certainly vulnerable to physical damage; and if he's vulnerable to physical damage then he's even more vulnerable to social damage, because the cost of it is enough to bring economic difficulties to many families where economically they live on the margin. Of course, if he's had treatment, and acknowledges this or volunteers it, that's a help.

A very good clue is: the surest way to find an alcoholic is to enquire about the family of a known alcoholic. It does run in families, but not in the sense in which one could indict genetic factors. It runs in families for the simple reason that families share a life style, and if the life style is what the Americans would call positive to drinking, then all the members of the family are likely to drink to a greater extent than a family where, again in the same jargon, attitudes to drinking are negative. So these are the things to look for. Of course, if a man's lost his driving licence on a drink-driving charge that's something to make you prick your ears up and think about it. Certainly if he's done it twice or if he's had a high blood alcohol when doing it, that's almost diagnostic.

But what about the future? The present services are very sketchy. The Health Service has an Alcohol Treatment Unit. There's one in every health region; it's usually located in the old psychiatric hospital, which is usually well away from the urban area where the problems really occur. Of course, a man can be referred there: he can be referred to his doctor, who might refer him there. GPs vary a great deal, they tend to judge an alcoholic on whether he drinks more or less than they do, and some of the stories I hear about unhelpful general practitioners, I'm sure, are true although I'd like to disbelieve them.

There is a network of information centres growing up which actually offer advice as well as information and there are volunteers being trained, and we've been picking the brains of your own organisation and of the marriage guidance people to see how we could best train volunteers to do it. Each year now there will be increasing numbers of volunteers manning information centres, organised by the National Council on Alcoholism. There are of course religious organisations such as the Salvation Army and the AA. They tend in a particular place to cull the kind of man who is best suited for them. But there's no one way to Rome and these agencies, even though they all have a different approach, all have their uses. If a man doesn't do well with one he will quite likely do well with another.

Drug dependence – CHAD VARAH

Compulsive or addictive behaviour is likely to lead to problems for the victim, who will therefore need help. Some of the persons affected will seek this help, at some stage, from The Samaritans.

We are not concerned here with alcoholism, the most common form of gradual, non-admitted suicide in Western countries, nor with compulsive gambling or over-eating or other addiction, but with dependence on drugs.

The term 'drugs' covers a wide range of chemical preparations, solid, liquid or vaporised, which may be ingested, injected, inhaled, sniffed, rubbed on the skin, used as an enema or suppository, or surgically implanted. The vast majority of them are prescribed or self-prescribed for therapeutic purposes, though some are frequently and some occasionally misused – only the hallucinogens have no medically approved use and are therefore procured only illegally for abuse.

In common parlance, 'drugs' is a pejorative word, implying dangerous substances abused by weak-willed and disreputable persons called 'drug addicts'. Even in the sense of a substance of addiction, the victims of the commonest and arguably the most dangerous of these, nicotine, would indignantly reject aspersions on their respectability. Although this article is concerned with drugs of dependence, usually as a result of misuse, it should be mentioned that Samaritans try to preserve the neutral sense of the word, for they often have to reassure callers that they will not become 'drug addicts' by taking medicaments prescribed by a qualified doctor, even over a long period, any more than a diabetic person can be described as an insulin addict. Apart from patients with otherwise uncontrollable pain, such as those with certain forms of terminal illness, doctors rarely prescribe drugs in doses which make the patient dependent on them. Most drugs are not commonly abused and do not lead to dependence.

Among the drugs callers may have had prescribed by their GP, in alphabetical order, are those for alcoholism, for allergies, analgesics, for angina, antacids, antibiotics, anticoagulants, anticonvulsants, antidepressants, antihistamines, antihypertensics, antispasmodics, bronchodilators, corticosteroids, for diabetes, diuretics, for epilepsy, expectorants, hypnotics, inhalants, laxatives, for nausea, opiates, for rheumatism, sedatives, stimulants, tranquillisers, for ulcers, vitamins and for vomiting. Under each heading there may be several or hundreds of preparations, each with a pharmaceutical name and a proprietary one, and it would be beyond the scope of this article (or the competence of this writer) to describe their effects or the effects of an overdose of them. Samaritans who encounter overdoses of unfamiliar substances should not be tempted to act on 'a little knowledge'. The same applies to the effects of failing to take a prescribed drug in the correct dosage at the stated intervals or in the situations laid down.

Many otherwise safe drugs (in the prescribed dosage) become dangerous if combined with alcohol, or in conjunction with certain other drugs.

We are concerned here with drugs that are commonly abused. In alphabetical order, these include amphetamines, barbiturates, cannabis, cocaine, hallucinogens, inhalants, medicines containing sedatives or stimulants, and opiates.

Amphetamines

Amphetamines and similar drugs powerfully stimulate the body and the mind and are therefore nicknamed 'speed'. They may still sometimes be used medically to suppress appetite for slimming. Other nicknames for such 'pep pills' are 'dexies' and 'meth', from Dexedrine (dexamphetamine tablets, yellow), and methedrine (methylamphetamine hydrochloride, white – also in ampoules). There are over a dozen common pep pills, and many less common. They are mostly taken by mouth, and make the user wakeful, alert, not hungry or tired, restless, often confused and/or irritable. After three or four hours tiredness sets in. There can be psychological dependence, with lethargy and depression after withdrawal. Regular use of amphetamines may lead to 'tolerance', i.e. in order to obtain the same effect it is necessary to take more of the drug. If there is psychological dependence, then the user most certainly will increase the dose.

With young clients in big cities showing depression and lethargy, one possible cause is the use of amphetamines.

Barbiturates

Barbiturates have the opposite effect to amphetamines. Where amphetamines tend to make the user excitable, irritable and perhaps violent, the barbiturates are hypnotics, that is to say they induce sleep, and their users are typically confused and drowsy. Like the amphetamines, barbiturates are usually used in pill form, though they may be injected, and at a time when heroin became difficult to obtain, some heroin addicts were 'fixing' with barbiturates partially dissolved – they won't dissolve completely, and some users died of the results of abscesses formed at the point of injection.

The barbiturates most commonly used and misused are Amytal, Gardenal, Luminal, Nembutal, Seconal, Sodium Amytal, Soneryl and Tuinal. They are likely to lead to both physical and psychological dependence, and it is important to remember that tolerance does not develop in the case of barbiturates to the point of preventing the abuser from being poisoned by them.

The abuser of barbiturates may well be confused with a person who is drunk – there is the same stumbling, unco-ordinated movement and the same slurred speech. Barbiturates are in any case often used with alcohol, which intensifies their effect.

It is very difficult for people to give up barbiturates after they have become dependent and the withdrawal symptoms are severe. Naturally, since hypnotics depress the central nervous system and induce sleep, and reduce anxiety, cessation of their use produces insomnia and anxiety, and as phenobarbitone is used to prevent epileptic fits, serious cases of withdrawal can cause the person concerned to suffer convulsions. The physical signs of withdrawal are twitching and trembling, dizziness and nausea.

An overdose of barbiturates slows the movements and slurs the mind and dilates the pupils. If the overdose is great enough, the individual will go into a coma and die.

Because of the danger of barbiturates, doctors are being encouraged to prescribe non-barbiturate hypnotics. The ones in most common use are also the ones most abused, e.g. by being injected or by being used with alcohol: Doriden, Mandrax, Mogadon, Noctec and Welldorm. The most dangerous in overdose is Mandrax, which also (like Doriden) interferes with the action of anticoagulants, if the person has to take these.

Cannabis

Cannabis includes both 'grass', also called pot or marijuana, which is the leaf and flowers of the plant, and hash, which is the resin from the plant compressed into blocks. Either can be smoked – grass by being rolled alone or with tobacco, and hash by being crumbled into tobacco. Both can be put into food or drink. If smoked, it is held in the lungs to increase the effect, which may last for several hours. 'Hash' is short for 'hashish', which strictly ought to be used not for cannabis resin but for cannabis resin mixed with opium and smoked in a pipe. This is the opiate drug of addiction which was used by the Old Man of the Mountain to keep his gang of murderers under his control – they would be made dependent on the hashish, which didn't take long, and then refused it until they had killed the designated person. This is the origin of the name 'assassin' now used for any kind of hit man, though he is more likely to be working for payment than for a supply of drugs.

'Grass' made into a cigarette, with or without tobacco, is called a 'joint', and experienced smokers draw in a good deal of air at the same time as they draw the smoke into their lungs, to increase the effect. This effect is a type of intoxication not unlike that produced by alcohol, but without hangover and with euphoria, laughter and chattiness succeeded usually not by aggression or maudlin burbling, but by quiet introspection.

There seem to be also hallucinogenic effects of cannabis, in addition to sound and colour simply being more vivid: there may be a sort of delirium, depending on the mood of the person and probably the basic character of the person at the time the use began.

It is claimed that as moderate use does not seem to produce any bad effects or physical dependence and it has not been known to cause death, possession and use of cannabis ought not to be illegal. At the time of writing, cannabis and cannabis resin are (like amphetamine) Class B drugs in the 1971 Misuse of Drugs Act. Possession of them can attract up to five years in prison and/or a fine.

The chief objection to regular use of cannabis appears to be that it seems to produce the 'don't care' attitude of the dropout. It may well serve a useful purpose in giving young people something to rebel about and to indulge in a pretty harmless form of law-breaking. Some psychologists consider that if cannabis were legalised, something more dangerous would be taken up as an expression of rebellion against parents and Society by breaking a law.

Cocaine

Cocaine is a strong stimulant made from the coca plant of which none whatever nowadays goes into Coca-cola. It is extracted and refined into a glistening white powder and therefore is commonly known as 'snow', or by the abbreviation 'coke'. Partly because it is very expensive, and partly because it produces exhilaration and a brief pleasure in the sex organs which may even cause orgasm, it has been in recent years an 'in' drug in the United States.

It is usually taken by sniffing into the nostrils, which become damaged and stream with mucus, so that the person appears to have a continuous cold and may use very many tissues per hour. Cocaine can also be injected. Medically, it would be injected as a local anaesthetic: the present writer remembers having it at his school dentist, and round about 1928 having the dentist substitute a synthetic substance called Novocaine, which is nowadays used instead.

Apart from the destruction of the septum of the nose, continued use can produce brain damage. Dependence on it is psychological, not physical, and the usual after-effects are anxiety and some depression. There may also be hallucinations.

Hallucinogens

Lysergic acid diethylamide, or LSD for short, is the most commonly encountered of the hallucinogens, but mention may also be made of dimethyltriptomene (DMT) which is related to the amphetamines but different in its effects; and mescaline.

LSD is only obtainable illegally. It has no medical use, though in the Sixties it was sometimes used as an aid in psychotherapy, and practitioners in clinical psychotherapy were instructed in the use of it.

It should be emphasised that LSD is now a Class A drug under the 1971 Misuse of Drugs Act, along with cocaine, heroin, morphine, pethedine and physeptone. This means the penalty can be up to seven years' imprisonment and/or an unlimited fine.

It should be quite clear to the reader that under the Act, you can be imprisoned or fined if it is proved that you have had a classified drug in your possession, or supplied it to another or offered to supply it to another or been concerned in supplying it to another, or have been in possession of it with intent to supply it, or have exported or imported it.

Among the classified drugs, there are many which may be legally in a person's possession because they have been medically prescribed. In these cases, it is important not to pass them to another person. But in the case of LSD, there is no possibility whatever of obtaining it legally. It is never medically prescribed. LSD is a colourless, odourless and tasteless liquid, and these facts make it all the more dangerous. It will usually be encountered in the form of microdots, though it may be in the form of the powder from which the solution is made or in the form of pills. It is almost always taken by mouth, but it can be injected or sniffed.

Hallucinogens are taken for their psychological effects: the physical effects are not pleasurable. They include loss of appetite, nausea, insomnia, tremors, sweating and respiratory disturbance.

It is the psychological effects which are sought by the users of LSD, and which have given to the English language the word 'trip' in a specialised sense. This word suggests that the user of LSD goes elsewhere mentally for a while, and then comes back. A trip may be good or bad, but even a good one may make the person aware of material from the unconscious which may be very upsetting – this was the reason for its use in psychotherapy until this was stopped.

Enthusiasts for LSD, who have an almost religious fervour about it, speak of the aesthetic and emotional value of what they call a 'psychedelic' experience (surely 'psychodelotic' would be the correct word?). Sensory impressions are intensified and may be confused, and 'peak' experiences give to some devotees a religious sense of oneness with the universe and ineffable feelings of joy and peace. On the other hand, we should set against this the deaths which occur to users by the delusion that they can walk on water or fly out of a skyscraper window.

Persistent users may become psychotic, and those who have used LSD only once may have 'flashbacks' for years afterwards. These have particularly been encountered in victims to whom the drug has been administered without their knowledge and consent. A horrifying example was the schoolgirl to whom it was administered by the vicious boy-friend of her nasty sister in a café. The girl ran wildly along a busy street weaving back and forth amongst the traffic and narrowly escaping death, and when picked up by the police all they kept saying to her was that they wouldn't tell her parents if she said where she had procured the stuff. The only thing she wanted was to be taken *to* her parents, and she suffered terrifying experiences before being able to persuade the police to take her home. She came to the notice of The Samaritans because of brief recurrences of this bad unsought trip. Fortunately one of our consultant psychiatrists knew the appropriate treatment and was able to instruct her family doctor.

Inhalants

School children in search of kicks are likely to find substances such as glues and industrial solvents which can be sniffed or inhaled and which are easily procurable and not costly. Some commercial solvents are similar to volatile substances used medically as anaesthetics. Glues used in model aircraft construction, and carbon tetrachloride and toluene used in dry-cleaning, have a sedative effect but are also toxic and they can damage the liver. Lighter fuel, nail polish remover, and some kinds of paint can be sniffed in order to produce dizziness and a feeling of intoxication. Hallucinations can result from continued abuse.

Chloroform and ether are of course anaesthetics and if inhaled are likely to produce unconsciousness.

Medicines containing sedatives

Medicines containing *sedatives* come mostly under the heading of cough mixtures. Many cough mixtures contain such drugs as derivatives of morphine, and because they don't only suppress coughs but sedate and give a sense of well-being, they are quite often abused: Collis Brownes, Gees Linctus, Pholcomed and Romilar for example.

Antihistamines also have a sedative effect and may be abused for this purpose.

Opiates

Finally we come to the *opiates*, the derivatives of opium, all of which are listed as Class A drugs under the 1971 Act. The most important opiate of dependence in Britain is heroin, which is diamorphine. Pethidine addicts may sometimes be encountered.

In addition to analgesic-sedative-euphoric derivatives of opium such as heroin, morphine and Pethidine, there are now synthetic opiates of which the most commonly abused is methadone, commonly called Physeptone in Britain: and Fortral and Romilar.

The opiates do, of course, have a medical use in controlling severe pain, e.g., in terminal illnesses. The present writer once had a small injection of Pethidine after having had a frozen shoulder manipulated to tear loose all the adhesions. The anaesthetic given for the operation was of short duration. The agony of this one-sided crucifixion receded like the tide going out, leaving a sense of peaceful drowsiness, after one administration of Pethidine which was never repeated.

Pure heroin is in the form of small white tablets called 'jacks', similar to saccharine tablets. It is dissolved in water for injection, and pure distilled water should be, but usually isn't, used. Heroin bought on the black market may be tablet or powder and the very impure type known as Chinese heroin looks like very fine brown sugar. Heroin from Iran is even darker, which is why it is known as 'brown belt' heroin, typically sold in cling film from chewing-gum wrappers. The large Iranian community in London makes it the chief market in Europe, and the situation has become much worse since the fall of the Shah, in the confused situation under the new regime. Not all heroin addicts know that Iranian 'smack' is immensely stronger than other kinds available on the black market and may therefore overdose.

Heroin abusers use a tourniquet to make the vein stand out and then inject the solution with a syringe. Many get infections by using blunt and dirty needles.

Though the unaccustomed user, or the regular user taking a much larger dose than he or she is accustomed to, may suffer nausea and vomiting, and there have been many deaths by inhalation of vomit, the normal experience of the regular user of heroin is a drowsy feeling of well-being and a quasi-sexual feeling of bliss, which is greatly desired and forms the psychological dependence. Physical dependence is, however, even more important: users of heroin dread the pains of withdrawal, and find it almost impossible to reduce the dose when their inclination is to increase it to obtain the same effect as when they first began. A few hours after each 'fix', pains of withdrawal begin and increase for several hours. It may take as much as a week for them to die down if there is no further injection. Muscle cramps, perspiration, gooseflesh, sniffles, yawning, twitching and diarrhoea combined with restlessness and anxiety make the withdrawal symptoms very disagreeable indeed. It is too much to expect that a person dependent on heroin will give it up and suffer all these difficulties together with the deprivation of an extreme pleasure, without any encouragement, emotional support and medication. The addicts who have been helped to wean themselves from heroin have mostly had the withdrawal symptoms reduced to bearable proportions by the substitution of physeptone or some other sedation. Physeptone, which normally comes already dissolved in ampoule form, is itself an opiate but, as stated above, it is synthetic. It is itself addictive, but the basis of treatment in the Treatment Centres is that the withdrawal symptoms are less intolerable than those of heroin, so if physeptone is gradually substituted for heroin, the physeptone by injection can then be replaced by a physeptone linctus taken orally. Many dependents find difficulty at this stage, because the act of 'fixing' is itself part of the addiction, which will seem strange to those of us who dislike having injections at all.

Heroin dependents, who are known as 'junkies', have a low expectation of life, partly because of the danger of overdoses, hepatitis and infections, and partly because of their generally unhealthy way of life. They are often homeless and inadequately clothed and fed: everything revolves around securing their next fix, and few can afford to maintain a heroin habit on the black market without resorting to crime or prostitution. The junky is extremely unlikely to be able to hold down a job sufficiently well paid to buy heroin on the black market. Nobody who has been closely associated with a junky will envy him the allegedly better-than-orgasmic pleasure which is bought at such a terrible cost.

The media do not continue indefinitely to highlight the same problem, because novelty is lost and people get bored, but what is not reported does not invariably lose its following. Heroin and other addictions caused such a scare in the Sixties that government Treatment Centres were set up, but in spite of these the number of addicts has risen steadily and in the summer of 1979 there were warnings from, for example, the Standing Conference on Drug Abuse that there were signs of an approaching heroin 'epidemic'. Though the word was ill-chosen, the statistics were alarming: the number dependent on 'hard' drugs who were under treatment had risen by 19% to 2,408 and the number of new dependents notified for the first time was up by 22% to 1,332. As the Home Office pointed out, these figures do not include the many times larger number of persons obtaining their drugs illicitly. In the 1960s, when there was alarm over only about 750 addicts, the chief source of illicit drugs was a small number of doctors who over-prescribed, in some cases allegedly on demand. The Treatment Centres stopped this by having the prescription of heroin by doctors outside such centres banned, but black market sources have multiplied and boomed.

It may be that only 12,000 to 15,000 people in Britain are dependent on heroin/physeptone, as against tens of thousands using amphetamines, hundreds of thousands using barbiturates, and millions abusing alcohol. Comparatively few though they are, even in London and other big cities, the junkies present a very serious problem which tempts Samaritans to seek a quick and easy solution.

This temptation must be resisted. Not only is it totally against the principles of The Samaritans to try to change the habits of another person without his or her consent, but it is also bound to be a source of frustration and eventually disillusionment to have the motivation for so difficult a task as giving up a drug of dependence inside a different person, from the one who is dependent on the drug and has little or no motivation.

How Samaritans can help

We Samaritans have learnt to be realistic and to recognise that the majority of those who are dependent on drugs are either psychopathic or inadequate personalities bordering on the psychopathic, and in any case weak and self-indulgent characters who are incapable, even with encouragement and support, of the effort and sacrifice needed in order to be freed from dependence on a drug which they do find it possible to obtain. Only a minority who have got hooked have within themselves a strong desire to be liberated from their dependence. This minority is as worthy of the enormous amount of time and energy and patience involved as the majority is totally unworthy because their nature and character would make it certain that the effort would be totally wasted. Furthermore, the fact of attempting the impossible with the psychopathic drug abuser creates a relationship which the latter will not be slow to exploit, so that the foolishly sentimental volunteer is likely to end an unproductive involvement with the knowledge that he/she was merely facilitating the continuation of the drug dependence.

There are few things which 'sort out the men from the boys and the women from the girls' in Samaritan circles better than contact with the emotionally immature and egocentric or demanding and manipulative, of whom it must be asked if they are allegedly *not* dependent on drugs, why aren't they? Those who, in Oscar Wilde's words, 'can resist anything except temptation', are sure to be offered drugs on the streets of our big cities, and may be expected to use them if they can afford them.

A drug-dependent client of The Samaritans is a person who provides an excellent test of our principles. His or her situation will present a great temptation to the volunteer to do the forbidden thing, namely to 'solve the problem', with or without the client's consent. The desire to *do* something is understandable, but it must be restrained. The inclination to change the way of life of the client to one which would be more acceptable to the volunteer betrays the presence of a non-Samaritan in the organisation. The drug-dependent client is pre-eminently a case for befriending, which will only lead on to counselling and/or treatment if the client very much wishes this.

The listening, acceptance and concern which are included in the befriending relationship will not only establish the facts and create good rapport in those cases where a request for definite help may in due course be made, but will also assist those who do not really wish to be helped to face the reality of their situation in a way that may bear fruit at some later stage in their lives. At worst, the volunteer will avoid wasting time and energy and ending with the frustrating feeling of having been conned.

Endless patience and tolerance will be required of the volunteer in those cases where there is a genuine desire on the part of the drug dependent person to end his or her dependence. A volunteer should not be left alone with such a situation, but should work under the guidance and with the support and encouragement of a colleague. The 'enemy' may be not only the drug of abuse, but also the subculture in which it is found and which may form the environment of the drug abuser, particularly if a youngster who has come to a big town from the country. Junkies, in particular, have their own fraternity and thus minister to the drug dependent's desire to 'belong'. The junky freemasonry is so strong that any junky who appears to be escaping from it is the object of sustained attempts to win him or her back, even to the point of *giving*, freely, expensive drugs to those who have just completed a 'cure'. The Samaritans have to be seen as a group of friends who have no axe to grind and nothing to 'sell', who are befriending the drug-dependent person out of pure beneficence, and compare very favourably with the subculture in which the drug-dependent person became dependent.

Counselling and psychotherapy are beyond the scope of this essay, and as for treatment, the safest thing is to get in touch with the person's family doctor in any country where family doctors are usual. Not all countries have Treatment Centres like those in Britain, where classified drugs may be prescribed free of charge in a course of gradually diminishing dosage. The aim of the Treatment Centre is to make it unnecessary for the drug-dependent person to purchase illegal supplies, but to stick to their prescribed and gradually diminishing dose. There are areas in Britain where there are no Treatment Centres at all, in which case it is to be hoped that the Branch can obtain help from a local psychiatrist or from the casualty department of the local hospital. In extreme cases, in-patient treatment may be obtainable.

Once off the drug, the person will have to face whatever it was that caused him or her to take up the drug in the first place. Rehabilitation may be very difficult if the client cannot get a place in one of the hostels specially for this and cannot get out-patient treatment at a hospital regularly.

It has not been possible to mention more than a small proportion of the medicaments Samaritans may encounter, but every Branch should have a copy of *The British National Formulary*, which lists drugs under their chemical and proprietary names and tells what they are for and other useful information. In addition there is 'MIMS', the monthly index of medical specialities, which the Branch could obtain through a friendly GP.

Although the proportion of drug-dependent clients whom The Samaritans are able to help effectively is very small, it has added up over the years to quite a crowd of people, all of whom must be included as having been saved from a form of slow and unadmitted suicide.

He felt the enormous relief of speaking without prudence to someone who, he believed, understood him. The eyes seemed to offer complete friendship, the smile encouraged him to lay down for a short time the burden of secrecy.

from *The Human Factor*, GRAHAM GREENE

How can Samaritans be protected from useless manipulation by the psychopath?

— DOMINIQUE ALESSANDRI

The statement of a young volunteer after a year's experience in The Samaritans seems to be a good introduction to this question.

'I came here thinking that we ought to do everything possible to help those who ask for it – now I see clearly that there are some people for whom we can do nothing more.'

This was by no means the remark of a discouraged person – her faith and enthusiasm for the actions of The Samaritans remain undiminished. At first glance this seems to present a contradiction; yet it does not. For the Samaritan of the Gospel performed two very distinct acts:

First, he brought immediate assistance to a man in need.

Secondly, and much more importantly, he gave him the possibility of setting out again in life, freely and with dignity.

This is the story of an action which is completely exemplary: an anonymous act (the choice of a Samaritan is free of any religious or moral conviction), disinterested, efficient, and limited in time. This action in no way left the recipient dependent on the Samaritan but, on the contrary, free to return to live among other men. In addition, the action did not inconvenience the Samaritan in any way. He possessed the material means (time and money) to bring this help without neglecting his own occupations – this, too, is not without importance. And it is this special meaning of the Samaritan's help that the parable emphasises.

Two essential questions now arise that define the limits of this help.

Will the Samaritan's help have this liberating power for the person to whom it is granted, or will it be only temporarily effective, leaving the recipient in a state of dependence on his helpers and society?

Can the Samaritan's help be effective without carrying a prejudice (either moral or material) towards the organisation, which would endanger its capacity to help other clients?

In the case of people given the rough, general label of 'psychopaths', these questions have a very special relevance. Psychopaths, or 'immature personalities', comprise all categories of individuals whose emotions have remained blocked at an infantile stage. The extent of this blockage, as well as the stage at which it occurs, varies, as do their disorders and degrees of psychopathy.

If we limit ourselves to plain psychopathy, the business of enumerating, describing and classifying psychopathic disorders is of only very limited interest for Samaritans. There would even be a certain degree of danger for Samaritans in believing that one can, by reading descriptive and theoretical work, learn to 'label a client' and anticipate the surprises and dangers that he has in reserve. By so doing, The Samaritans' spontaneity – one of the most important qualities in their response – risks being weakened.

It seems infinitely more appropriate during the volunteers' training to prepare them to face these dangers when they present themselves in practice. Two distinct aspects of this topic should therefore be considered. The first would summarise the most obvious and frequent traps laid by these psychopaths, according to the characteristics of their personality. The second, and the most essential, would be to get The Samaritans to ask themselves why they fall into certain traps, and to consider both the need for and the means of avoiding them.

Certain characteristics often found in psychopaths

An enormous emotional greed: their demands for help constitute 'the proof that they are loved', but no sooner is this proof of love obtained, than it is rejected – deemed insufficient. And so their demands will be renewed. They can be materialistic (money, social aid), or emotional (a desire to monopolise attention, a desire for pity, a desire to challenge through aggressive behaviour, then see just how much they can be loved despite this). These demands and challenges can only become more and more incessant and abusive. With this 'emotional greed' is associated an incapacity to love of surprising magnitude. What they are looking for is to seduce, to attract pity, to manipulate. Other people are for them only the instruments of their desires. Aggressiveness always lies behind their demands. The more one has, in acceding to their demands, given them the hope that they can always be satisfied, the less able they are to tolerate frustration. Here we must point out a danger for Samaritans. If they allow this kind of hope to develop in a psychopath, a perilous 'return to reality' is to be feared the day they refuse to go further in befriending him. Faced with frustration, the psychopath's aggressive nature will be released, often in an impulsive and destructive manner, be it against himself (in impulsive suicide or some sort of auto-destructive act), or against a Samaritan or the entire organisation.

It seems that in most cases the psychopath is incapable of overcoming his drive or controlling his behaviour. In extreme cases, criminal acts are committed without the psychopath feeling in any way responsible. He does not know 'what came over him'!

The psychopath, in an attempt to obtain something, or in an act of revenge, will also take more elaborate measures such as various forms of blackmail, of which the most delicate – threat to commit suicide – should be noted by Samaritans. In dangling the threat of suicide, the psychopath tries simultaneously to obtain what he wants and specifically attack The Samaritans. While trying to burden them with the responsibility for his death, he will try to spread uneasiness, remorse and scandal within The Samaritans. This blackmail is sometimes followed by impulsive suicide. However, usually it concludes with a simple attempt or fake attempt. But what would one get involved in if one gave in to this blackmail? The manipulator is going to obtain what he wants, and that will defuse the conflict for the moment. But it will begin all over again, and each time for motives which become more and more frivolous. Thus one becomes involved in a particularly dangerous relationship, destined to failure. If such a case presents itself to Samaritans, it seems important, from the moment a response is to be made, to think of future consequences, after having, of course, weighed the suicidal risk.

Besides the true delinquents and criminals whom one will be dealing with among these psychopaths, there will be all sorts of 'social cases' among The Samaritans' clientele: people incapable of holding down jobs, unable to take care of a family, accumulating debts, continuously having problems with neighbours, involved in minor delinquency, alcoholics, drug addicts, sexual deviants, and so on.

The stories told by these people of their sad lot can be very upsetting for those who listen. It seems that throughout their lives disaster has followed them, they are rejected by everyone, catastrophe accumulates along their path. The Samaritans must learn to control their own feelings in response to such touching stories. They must realise that it would be unwise, out of excessive emotion, to take any decision without expert advice.

Sometimes there is a really urgent need for social aid, and this cannot, in these cases, be systematically refused.

But if one is clear-headed enough to control these emotions, impose firm limits to their demands, and not, under any circumstances, allow the assistance given to be detrimental to the needs of other clients, the risks that one takes can be greatly reduced. Furthermore, when having any dealings with a psychopath, it is of the utmost importance that The Samaritans stick together, and that all the members concerned are aware of what is acceptable and what is not, in each case. The psychopath has a particular flair for discovering even the smallest weakness in the cohesion of a group. He will *always* try to get from those in the group who seem more hesitant (in general the most inexperienced) what he has been unable to obtain from the others. If he succeeds in this, he will not only achieve his ends but, in so doing, will cause one or more Samaritans to infringe the discipline of the organisation and have to be penalised. His hope is thus to stir up trouble within the group.

It seems worth while to underline the cunning (and sometimes downright perverted) aspect of certain cleverer psychopaths. These cunning psychopaths find a great pleasure in hurting, scandalising, and spreading discord. This pleasure will be even more intense if the object of attack is a source of respect to others. This is what makes The Samaritans a perfect target. If the psychopath cannot spread dissension among The Samaritans, he can try to discredit the organisation by slandering the work of the group, by the use of violence against one branch of the organisation, or by trying to push Samaritans to the use of force themselves. Having achieved this, he will claim that The Samaritans are not at all what they claim to be . . . He can try to make the group spend large sums of money (for example by making frequent reversed-charge calls), or to monopolise their time endlessly (by repeated telephone calls) – in short, to sabotage the organisation by every means at his disposal. These cases are extreme and fortunately rare, but can be a cause of real damage to the organisation. The best attitude to adopt to counter this behaviour and render it harmless seems to be one of strict neutrality. The least show of irritability on the part of Samaritans can feed the destructive force within these psychopaths. But equally dangerous would be lack of firmness or useless tolerance of their attacks. From this it is clear what a delicate matter it is to choose the right attitude. Those volunteers who are less experienced must learn to refuse to deal with these problems and to refer them to those with more experience (Director, Samaritan-in-Charge).

The means at the disposal of The Samaritans

During their training, the new volunteers have an assortment of methods at their disposal. They can listen to potted case histories which expose problems already encountered with psychopaths. In this way they can get an idea of what it is all about, how these critical situations arise, and the consequences of the errors already committed. They can also learn how necessary it is to prepare oneself to avoid these situations. Above all, the various types of 'role-play' have an immense advantage by giving them an opportunity to play an active part. If during one of these role-plays the volunteer falls effectively into one of these traps, the question of why the trap worked should immediately be raised. Rarely (except in the case of a very skilful liar) is it the client's fault. Usually the volunteer will at this time have certain questions to ask himself:

What is his idea about his role as a Samaritan? Does he perhaps think that he must be able to do everything to help all the clients, and that the greater the effort the Samaritan's course of action demands, the better it must be?

Is it his sensitivity which led him to perceive too keenly the need of the client for more pity or interest, and caused him to lose his own capacity to evaluate the situation calmly?

Does he have a certain naïveté which renders him incapable of even conceiving of the existence of the means used by psychopaths arising out of their total lack of scruple and regard for others?

Does he panic in the face of blackmail?

Does he lack the training to reflect on the long-term consequences of the help given, and have too short-sighted a view of the interest of the client?

Is it a fact that he likes to feel needed? This is a very natural feeling for a person beginning Samaritan work, since something was required to give him the impulse to offer himself. If he can recognise the existence of this tendency in himself, without guilt, that can contribute one of the most essential stages in his development.

Does he suffer from an inability to say 'no' firmly but without aggressiveness? This can certainly be acquired only with experience and through total conviction.

Many other questions can be asked as the role-playing exercise becomes more and more developed and detailed. For the volunteer to learn to question himself in a positive manner – that is to say with the aim of understanding the problem better, without systematically accusing or torturing himself – can be a difficult task. A totally new and different way of thinking is sometimes necessary. To a new volunteer this exercise might seem unnecessarily painful, even frightening. Nevertheless, if he directs himself in this manner and if he is also helped by those who are experienced and of goodwill, he will quickly see the benefits that result from such instruction. He will soon see that his case is far from unique, and that many others – perhaps all – will have the same problems and that, by discussing them, they can often be effectively overcome.

For certain volunteers, their reluctance to question themselves in the preparation classes may come from an exaggerated fear of seeming inadequate in the eyes of others. But to refuse to face this questioning can only aggravate the fear, isolate the person from the group, and exaggerate the difficulties of the task. Thus the instruction of these anxious applicants requires that those who help them use great tact, take sufficient time before setting them to work, and encourage them more actively to develop a sense of self-confidence. If, on the other hand, others do not see the necessity to question themselves in this manner, this could be the result of a sense of false confidence. These applicants consider that they have already done enough self-questioning to meet successfully all the circumstances which might arise. Sometimes it is especially difficult and delicate to integrate these applicants into the team, and in this case it is more a question of slowing down their initiative without shaking their convictions too much. It is, perhaps, reasonable to allow them to face a real situation and make mistakes. After this, those who have made mistakes, and who are honest enough to admit it, can have a fruitful discussion with those Samaritans assigned to help them. These should not judge severely but, on the contrary, by being friendly and positive, should integrate them into the team without risk of further error. In certain cases, unfortunately, it seems from experience impossible to integrate new applicants successfully into the team, and their exclusion from The Samaritans should be considered.

Practice has shown (and we have also just seen) how important group discipline is within The Samaritans, particularly where psychopaths are concerned. Learning to work as a team instils a natural reflex of delegating responsibilities to the most competent, whenever this is judged necessary, or at least asking for advice without hesitation. Perhaps it is a training-ground for a certain modesty? It also teaches a respect for discipline: volunteers should under no circumstances undertake, without warning, any hasty action which contravenes the common mind of the group, even if they think themselves more capable of judging the problem than others. This is not to say, of course, that each member must obey blindly without having his personal opinion. When there is disagreement, discussion and debate should be encouraged. But this must precede any action, so that, when action is taken, it will be in a coherent manner, making it impossible for the psychopath to find occasion to sow discord amongst The Samaritans.

Of course, all volunteers may make mistakes with psychopaths, letting themselves be manipulated and abused. In such cases the Directors and the Samaritans-in-Charge have an essential function.

It would be highly regrettable for a volunteer who has realised his mistake, especially when dealing with a particularly tricky psychopath who has disillusioned him, if he became discouraged and lost confidence in the efficacy of Samaritan work. It would be equally regrettable if he became exaggeratedly suspicious in the hope of defending himself from a repetition of this experience. He should seek an interview with someone more experienced than himself, as this can sort things out and restore his confidence. But after many experiences, sometimes unhappy, isn't the development of a good sense of humour the best protection of the volunteer? Once he has gone beyond this stage of disillusionment, he realises that he cannot do everything, or succeed with every client, but that what he does is 'not so bad'.

Dangerous sentimentality – Chad Varah

How do so many psychopaths get accepted as clients in the first place, in spite of our precautions?

They have allies within the branch. Not usually fellow-psychopaths – few of these wangle their way in, and none remains long undetected – but muddleheaded sentimentalists who can be manipulated into breaking the rules. These are as dangerous as the psychopaths, and should be eliminated promptly.

Brenda's first five years – ROSEMARY HANSON*

Five years ago Suzan Cameron from the London Branch told the delegates at the Annual Conference held that year at Lancaster University about a way of befriending telephone masturbators which had developed in her Branch and was called 'The Brenda System'. Since then Brenda has caused quite a stir – she's certainly been talked about a lot. She's quite bruised from the number of brickbats that have come her way but has blushingly received a few compliments too. Other branches have followed suit, although we're not sure how many – it would be nice to know – and others again have devised their own methods of dealing with a problem which isn't just national but international. I hope Brendas will share their experiences with the rest of us. For those not yet initiated into the ways of Brenda, I cannot recommend too highly Chad Varah's book 'Telephone Masturbators and the Brenda system for Befriending them', but I thought you might like to hear, straight from the horse's mouth, how we've been getting on during the last five years.

First I'd like us to take a step back into the past . . . before Brenda befriending was introduced, every female volunteer coped as best she could with the 'What colour are your knickers?' calls. We had a situation something like this:

Role play 1

Volunteer answers phone.

Client: Have you got big tits?

Vol.: Well . . . er . . . about average I suppose . . . Why do you want to know?

* Introduction to Workshops at The Samaritans' Annual Conference 1978 and 1979.

Client: What colour bra have you got on?
Vol.: Well, what colour do you like?
Client: Aren't you going to help me? (pause) I like nice big tits in a black lacy bra. Do you wear see-through blouses?
Vol.: My name's Susan – What's yours? (pause) I think we've spoken before, haven't we?

Client hangs up abruptly ...

Volunteer (to audience): I didn't get anywhere with him ... We all know him – he rings four or five times a week, sometimes more. He just keeps trying till someone helps him wank. Even that doesn't satisfy him – he's back on the line in no time ... we're just going round in circles ... frustrating in every sense.

Perhaps some people recognise that conversation? Answering 'Why do you want to know?' is counter-productive, we find, though tempting. Counter-productive because it starts us on a childish conversational ball-game, with each side refusing to give way ... and tempting because it gives the volunteer time to collect herself and puts her on the offensive instead of the defensive. But it results in stalemate. After all, both sides know why, and neither is being honest. Much better is something like 'What colour/size do you like?' or a sympathetic 'Are you feeling frustrated?'

Brenda, who is somewhat precocious for a five-year-old, has taken nearly 5,000 calls. She has coded 107. Of those coded, thirty-six are not ringing currently, five are disabled, four have been put on Standing Orders 'X' (i.e. are black listed). I expect they are ringing other branches and telling them how useless we are. They are our *dis*satisfied customers.

Now for the satisfied ones ... five have thanked us and said positively that they don't need us any more. Many more have expressed their thanks and ring only occasionally. We are touched that some of these ring us from time to time to find out how *we* are, to report progress with a girlfriend perhaps, or just to wish us a Happy Christmas, or Easter, or whatever. We have even been sent flowers once! Seven have been referred to a psychiatrist or a psycho-sexual clinic by us and are undergoing treatment of various kinds. One of the things we have learnt is that very few of our callers have *only* a sexual problem. Many are severely depressed or suffering from a variety of personality disorders – the sex call is the presenting problem, a kind of cry for help, if you like.

After Brenda started, at least we knew *who* was calling – in fact we often found that Brian, John, Peter and Bill were the same person, so the number of callers dropped quite dramatically. I know other branches have found the same. We frequently found that clients who seemed *un*helpable (rather like the client in the role play just now) after ringing for some time, because they got a uniform response suddenly became helpable, revealing all sorts of serious problems. Secondly, volunteers who had felt they couldn't cope with these sorts of callers felt relieved, and in general the Branch seemed to feel that we were trying in an organised way to help callers who had been blocking the lines. Of course, we had to put up with a great many jokes and, more hurtful, some people thought we must be pretty odd (or no better than we should be) to want to shut ourselves away for two hours at a time and talk about our knickers . . . The novelty seems to have worn off and we seem to be accepted now. There were dark mutterings about the danger of Brenda volunteers being turned-on by clients, though anyone who's ever taken Brenda calls would say that they are more likely to be moved to tears than ecstasy by the plight of so many men leading such impoverished, isolated lives. The only other emotion commonly provoked is boredom. Once you've heard one man wanking, quite honestly you've heard them all.

The right volunteers are neither over-keen nor disapproving. The 'knack' (which we think should *not* entail giving personal statistics or details of your own sex life) of helping someone wank on the phone comes easily to some and means nothing to them – it is just part of the compassion they feel for the client. These are the ones who should be Brendas, otherwise the volunteers *and* the clients will put too much emphasis on a small part of the befriending relationship. We soon found that the most taxing part of being a Brenda is not the *subject* of most of the calls, but the more directive, assessing role that we find ourselves in.

All this was a step forward, but soon we found a situation like this arising – here is a volunteer referring a call to Brenda:

Role play 2

Vol.: The Samaritans, can I help you?
Client: Will you help me?
Vol.: I'd like to . . . how can I help you?
Client: It's very big . . . I've got a terrific hard-on . . . would you like to see it?
Vol.: Oh dear, I'm afraid you're on to the wrong person . . .
Client: You said you wanted to help me . . .
Vol.: Yes, I *do*, but not in that way . . . the thing is, I can't really help you to wank, you see . . .
Client: What was that word you used?
Vol.: I think you should really talk to Brenda . . . Oh dear, I *am* sorry, I see she's not here today, but she will be here tomorrow – could you ring back tomorrow?
Client: But I need help now! I can't wait till tomorrow . . . Why can't *you* help? It'll only take a minute . . . please . . . you don't have to do anything, just stay on the line.
Vol.: No, no, I can't. But Brenda will help you tomorrow – she's much more experienced than I am – she really knows about these things.
Client: Just this once!
Vol.: No.
Client: Oh *please* . . . no one would know, would they? What am I going to do otherwise?
Vol.: Oh dear, I don't know. I am sorry you're feeling so frustrated . . . but if you could just hang on till tomorrow . . . I promise Brenda will help you.
Client: You don't understand, do you? (hangs up).

The volunteer clearly got more anxious as the client insisted that he wanted help *now*, not tomorrow. In her anxiety she was ready to promise the world. By the time the client did get to Brenda he would have a very clear expectation that she would help him to wank immediately. The Samaritan was probably left with the feeling that she hadn't really helped – indeed, that she'd just upset the client – that it was unfair to ask him to ring back, and that anyway it was somehow un-Samaritan to reject a caller by referring him to someone 'special'. The worst of all worlds. A sort of delayed dial-a-wank.

We find it extremely important to train volunteers to use the Brenda service properly (the clients seem to have no difficulty, it's the volunteers who have problems). This means very carefully and gently referring clients and *only* those who want the volunteer's help in masturbating – not, as often happens, the poor man who's worried because his wife doesn't have an orgasm, or the boy who thinks he's got a girl pregnant, is panic stricken and frantic for information about sex. In fact, we have found that most clients, however desperate, when they find that there is someone there who really wants to hear about their problem as well as their prick (which may *seem* to be the same thing) are prepared to wait.

Remember that for most of our callers, sex is not a pleasure – in the same way that for an alcoholic a drink is not usually a pleasure. He craves it and needs it, which is quite different. Many of our callers are quite literally addicted to sex – they will disparagingly describe themselves as sex-maniacs. Like alcoholics, while the thirst is on nothing can deter them. As alcoholics have A.A. it seems only right that sex-callers should have B.B. These rather appropriate initials stand not only for Brigitte Bardot but also for Brenda Befriending. Far from creating the addiction, as so many people fear, Brenda tries to help the caller free himself from it. As with drinkers, the first stage is very difficult and may take months of patience. But you are half-way there when the client acknowledges that it *is* a problem and he does want help – not just another drink or wank. Many coded callers are very demanding at first, and very *un*demanding – they ask for pitifully little from us – once they have the security of knowing they can ring.

At a recent workshop in London on sexually demanding callers a volunteer from another branch expressed the opinion that we seem to do things the wrong way round – you refuse to help them masturbate if they won't talk about the whole problem, then just when you're getting somewhere and building up a rapport, you *do* let them wank. He clearly saw this as a retrograde step. But what we have found is this: that wanking 'on demand' amounts to a dial-a-wank service with the client *invariably* putting the receiver down just as soon as he's 'come'. This is not surprising. Most of these clients, especially if they are obsessive telephone wankers with a long history of making random obscene calls, are full of guilt and shame at what they're doing. If the volunteer has been kind, the moment the tension has been relieved, they are even more ashamed because they feel they've treated someone badly who was trying to help them. They hate themselves for 'conning' her into it. They want to forget about it as quickly as possible – until the next crisis of frustration. And so the pattern continues, with us inadvertently reinforcing the client's own low opinion of himself. Of course, our refusing to help in the first instance is bad luck on those very rare clients for whom 'just this once' would have been right. But we are trying to break a pattern. I think it's possible to turn something negative into something positive. As Chad Varah explains in his book, helping a client wank can be beneficial, leading him to revise his opinion both of himself and of women. But should we allow wanking to go on indefinitely? What if the client becomes hooked on Brenda? We have found that wanking becomes less and less important for most clients. If it doesn't, we are able to talk to them about the possibility that they are swapping one addiction for another. Several times we've rather nervously broached the subject, only to find the client relieved to discuss it and, often, he has suggested himself that he should limit his wanking calls, while feeling free to ring us to discuss how things are going in between them. As usual, *we* get steamed up about things which clients solve for themselves! However, we have noticed with certain types of callers – usually married and with good jobs, perhaps their own business (*not* people who are socially isolated), that a domestic crisis or extra pressure at work can trigger off renewed frenetic wanking activity. When this does happen, if we are clever, it can be used to give the client a new insight into the cause of his problem.

When we first started, we were all exceedingly anxious about our lack of 'expertise' in the field, and when we consulted experts and they told us we probably knew more about telephone masturbators than they did, this was scarcely reassuring. I'm sure we did, and still do, make a lot of mistakes. We spent hours unloading our worries on to each other and we still find it necessary to have very regular meetings as a group.

Just occasionally, our failures turn out to be successes. I remember a time when I persuaded a flasher to do up his trousers and talk instead of wank. I thought I'd been very cool and composed. During a conversation some weeks later he told me that I'd looked *so* frightened – terrified, he said – that he'd taken pity on me. Although *I* was mortified, he said that it had made him think much more seriously about his exposing and he eventually decided to ask for psychiatric help.

Incidentally, quite a number of men come in and expose. It usually happens so quickly – is this where the expression 'quick as a flash' originates? – that we have no warning. It is very definitely something we don't encourage and we usually say that we will leave the room for a few minutes and come back when they've 'come'. Wanking in the centre can precipitate distressing scenes with the client in tears, overcome with guilt, and the volunteer very upset because she has made him worse, not better. Interestingly, a number of volunteers to whom this has happened have noticed an expression on the client's face just before flashing that can only be described as childish. One volunteer put it: 'He looked just like my little girl when I've told her she can't have something she wants.' So now we look out for this warning sign. The sad thing is that few exposers find they can ring us instead of flashing. The point about their particular obsession is that they need to be seen and not heard. And if they do come in they will probably find it impossible to 'control themselves' – they know we will not report them. In many cases this fear of being caught and the public humiliation of prosecution is no deterrent: simply the cause of appalling anguish *after* exposing. Many of them say that something 'takes over', something which however hard they try to resist, they can't, although they know on a rational level it is self-destructive. The most we can say about the very many exposers who have been to us, is that we have kept some out of prison and have been instrumental in getting a few to accept professional help. It's rare, in our experience, that they will accept befriending by a male volunteer, due to their embarrassment at what they are doing.

I must now say something about the vexed question of Getting Them In. Many people believe that if a sex caller is serious about wanting help he must be prepared to come into the Centre. I think we shouldn't under-estimate the fear that clients may feel at this prospect. After all, many have never made any kind of relationship with a woman before. On the other hand, as we've seen, exposers will come in at the drop of a hat. In between these two extremes, are clients who benefit greatly from face-to-face befriending, though they will usually be too embarrassed to ask the same volunteer to help them wank on the phone in future. It comes down to our treating *each* as individuals with different needs.

In trying to assess what progress Brenda is making, I have read literally hundreds of reports recently. Some are boringly repetitious with those few clients who, as Chad puts it, want to make Brenda feel bad, rather than wanting Brenda to make them feel better, cropping up again and again – but it's encouraging how quickly they are spotted and how little time is now wasted on them. In fact, difficult as some clients are to befriend, time and again reports start 'This is a really nice man . . .' Amongst those clients whom volunteers consider not helpable by us are a number of unemployed young men; they are *generally* depressed and bored. For them it is almost a hobby – very rarely do they have difficulty in 'pulling birds', although they complain that they can't afford to go out much. We think it's important to discourage them from getting addicted. A similar pattern has emerged among shift workers – single men whose social lives are non-existent because they work nights, and married men who get home several hours before their wives and children.

Some reports are heart-rending. There was the married man who finally screwed up his courage and went to his doctor about his impotence. 'I'm having trouble in bed,' he said. The doctor instantly wrote out a prescription – for sleeping pills. It was only surprising that he didn't take them *all*, that night. In fact, later he did overdose, but was found. This client started as a typical 'Have you got big tits?' caller. After years of phoning us, he suddenly came in, and it turned out that he was an epileptic; we were able to refer him to a more understanding doctor, and it seems likely that the epilepsy pills were causing the impotence which had been causing deep distress for seven years.

Then there was the seventeen-year-old who kept ringing aggressively, wanting endless sex information. We wondered if he really could be so naïve and why he didn't make the effort to go out more. The break-through came when we discovered that he is disabled and one of us visited him to assess the situation. The poor boy had the normal adolescent sexual feelings in spite of being paralysed and obese. He lived alone with his elderly father who also worked at home. He had no privacy and no experience to base fantasies on. We were able to get his attendance at a day centre organised, to supply him with some mild porn magazines, an educational book or two and a male befriender to visit him and take him out.

I'd like to end on a lighter note, so I'll tell about the time when at the end of a long busy session a Brenda was asked yet again 'What size tits have you got?' and, for once, told him. She was flabbergasted when he replied in a concerned voice: 'That's not very big . . . do you find you can get a man with such small tits?' The boot was on the other foot that time!

You will see that we have learned a lot in the last five years – certainly our vocabularies have been enlarged . . . Perhaps the most important thing we have learnt is that it is not expertise that most of our clients want, but befriending.

Why do people make sexually demanding calls to The Samaritans? Many of them are depressed, and some are suicidal.

It is easy to understand that sexual problems can *cause* depression. Fetishists or sado-masochists obviously can't make loving sexual relationships and so become isolated. For a man to become impotent is depressing. It is less often recognised that both sexual problems and sexually-demanding calls can be *caused by* depression. The client who wants to discuss his problem intelligently in the hope of finding some solution can be befriended by any volunteer. Only Brenda deals with those who want the volunteer's participation in his sexual fantasies to enable him to ejaculate. It is foolish to say of the latter that if they really wanted help they'd come in and wouldn't mind speaking to a male volunteer.

The listlessness and lack of energy associated with depression may make it impossible for a man to do much about his frustration, and depression often robs the sufferer of the imagination needed to fantasise. It also reduces his ability to communicate, so he can't make relationships and rarely asks for medical help. When a caller says he can't wank on his own, it is unsafe to assume that this must be a 'con': it will be true of some depressed callers, who may say that to masturbate whilst telephoning a strange woman requires the least energy and commitment, or may speak in a low, flat tone, answer in monosyllables, and seem curiously apathetic or unexcited even when obviously masturbating.

The contemptuous dismissal of these callers as 'just doing it for kicks' (sometimes said of Brenda too) doesn't fit in with Brenda's experience of 'obscene' callers in tears, seeing their sexual desires as causing only unhappiness. 'I wish I could cut it off.' If such a client has seldom or never had a girlfriend and has few or no friends, no hobbies or interests, no job or no interest in his job, Samaritans would do well to manage the conversation in the way they're taught to do with someone who is suicidal.

N.B. Reports from Brendas all over the world will gladly be received (*not* anonymously) by Brenda, The Samaritans, 39 Walbrook, London EC4N 8BP.

The book *Telephone Masturbators and the Brenda system for Befriending them* by Chad Varah will only be supplied to Branches undertaking not to let it be seen by non-Samaritans. It costs £1.50 plus postage. The shorter version *Telephone Masturbators and how to befriend them* costs £1 post free. Both from Befrienders International, St. Stephen Walbrook, London EC4N 8BN.

How to start a Branch of The Samaritans

— JEAN BURT

The first question to be asked by anyone who feels moved to suggest a new Branch is: Does this town or rural area need a Branch of the Samaritans? Is it not sufficiently served by a nearby Branch?

It is wasteful to set up several Branches in small catchment areas where one Branch could provide an effective listening and befriending service for the whole area. A large town needs a Branch and most in the British Isles now have one.

The Regional Representative is involved at an early stage – and indeed throughout the life of the Branch – and brings the proposals for a new Branch to the Executive Committee of the Council of Management. If they think a new Branch is needed and could be self-supporting, a steering committee with a Convenor is formed. That Convenor should be someone locally respected. He or she need not be a potential Director. A public meeting is held to obtain potential volunteers, local support and publicity, and to inform the invited representatives of the various social services of what The Samaritans will and will not be doing and how they fit in without trespassing on existing services.

The most important part of starting a Branch is the choice of people who are going to care for the clients, namely the Director and the volunteers. It is best if a neighbouring, experienced Branch helps with the selection and preparation of the volunteers for the new Branch. The greatest care is taken in looking for the Director. If the Regional Representative and the Executive Committee are satisfied with the nominee, the nomination is recommended to the Council of Management, which alone has the power to open (or close) a Branch and to appoint an Acting Director and later a Director.

A sufficient number of volunteers should be prepared to provide a double-manned twenty-four-hours-a-day service to clients. About 120 volunteers are needed for this, but some Branches have started with fewer and have survived. At least two telephones, one emergency and another auxiliary are required.

Premises have to be found by the steering committee. These should be central, near public transport, light, warm, quiet, and reasonably comfortable. Ease of access and privacy are of paramount importance. If suitable premises are available, the money should be found to pay for them, rather than that premises be found to suit the available funds. The formation of a body of 'Friends' of the Branch to help with fund-raising and other practical matters is desirable.

Due attention should be paid to publicity since the Branch cannot help clients unless people are aware of the services offered. Guidance is given in The Samaritans Publicity Manual. The local media should know that a Branch is in preparation for the area and should be informed of the opening date. A regular advertisement in the local newspaper is one effective form of publicity, and creates good will which may lead to better editorial coverage of the Branch's service and activities.

The Director will recruit consultants, the most important being a psychiatric consultant. Among others may be a doctor in general practice, and a lawyer.

When the Branch is opened the members should elect a Branch committee. The most important provision of the model Branch constitution is the separation that it makes between the work of the Branch which is the responsibility of the Director, and the administration and financial support for the work, which is the responsibility of the Branch committee. The Chairman of the Committee must be a Samaritan, and most, if not all, of the members should be Samaritans, if possible.

The Director should ensure that the leadership is firm and supportive. He or she cannot be in the Branch twenty-four hours of the day and will need to delegate, but remains solely responsible for 'hiring and firing' volunteers and for decisions about clients.

For at least the first year of its work, the Branch is on probation. The probationary Branch is entitled to send an observer to meetings of the Council of Management but may not vote. At the end of this first year it may apply to be considered as a full Branch, with a voting representative on the Council, elected at the Annual General Meeting of the Branch, which also nominates a person to be considered by the Council for appointment as Director.

One of the most important things to bear in mind when starting a Branch in the 'Eighties is that there is now a wealth of experience within the movement. So why learn the hard way?

On being a volunteer – NUALA KELLY

There are many unusual aspects to Samaritan life: aspects which can only be seen when one stands back after a couple of years and tries to look objectively at an organisation that has become a part of one's life. The most unusual aspect is the extraordinary ability of The Samaritans to enrol people who are active by nature, verbally and physically concerned for their fellow men, and to turn them into passive, compassionate listeners; to put in the background the very 'self' that first attracted the volunteers to this particular type of work.

Samaritans soon learn that the simple requirement of a listening ear carries with it many demands. The natural compassionate response to someone in distress has to be guided by a degree of detachment that leaves the volunteer free of emotive judgements and at the same time allows him to be emotionally concerned for the client.

The Samaritan does not need to be versed in psychiatry, psychology or the social services but he needs discipline . . . he must be prepared to feel inadequate and accept this blow to his ego. He has to trust his fellow volunteers to take over clients from him, fully confident that each one of them will be just as efficient as he is himself, sometimes even more so. He has to avoid pre-judgement, free advice, snap summing-up of problems; he has to accept that he is required to do some office-work so that the best service can be given to the client at all times. He has unfortunately to change the initial picture of himself sitting with phone in hand, his heart full of concern, his ear attuned to every nuance in his caller's voice and divine inspiration endowing him with just the right word at the right moment all the time.

Divine inspiration and an ear well tuned-in we all need, but usually it is in retrospect that we realise the deficiencies of our contribution to conversations and we remember all too late some of the cardinal rules we learned in training.

Volunteers have to resist their natural impulse to solve some desperate cases by giving material comfort . . . they have to accept that a client's sworn promise to phone next day is often not kept . . . they have to accept that gratitude doesn't necessarily follow weeks and months of time spent on cases . . . that often the person helped doesn't even remember his name. The volunteer discovers that he is what he actually chose to be – faceless, nameless, just a voice or an ear and nothing more.

It is hard to be so anonymous, and often the volunteer's own personality refuses to accept such a low profile. The desire to build up problems, to over-emphasise situations or to decide without consultation that certain people seeking help are merely a nuisance, is very tempting. The volunteer has to accept that what appeared easy and natural to his personality demands greater effort and discipline, discernment, concern and self-effacement than at first realised.

The attraction of working as an individual under the umbrella of a recognised organisation still remains but the responsibilities this brings to the volunteer usually become apparent only after practical application of training. Volunteers meet other volunteers so they can't keep their concern only for the telephone or the consulting room, it has to encompass their fellow workers, the upkeep of the premises, the running of the organisation, the flag-days and the ongoing training programme that are all part and parcel of The Samaritans. Those who come seeking an outlet for their compassionate natures suddenly find themselves asked to do the very work that they had run from in other organisations. The Samaritans demands the essence – that great dichotomy between the active and the passive . . . it requires ordinary people to be extraordinary even if only for a few hours a fortnight.

It requires that people of diverse interests and backgrounds work together conscious that personalities often don't blend, and that the volunteers who take on far more than the normal work load need the co-operation of the others, or at least the understanding that what they are doing is an answer to one of the needs of the organisation and not just glory-seeking. The critical faculty which our training endeavours to eradicate for the benefit of our clients should not rear its head in the confines of the Centre and be directed to those who volunteer or who are asked to take on more onerous duties. Each one, no matter how elevated his position in the organisation, is still a Samaritan giving the full measure of the time and ability which he can afford to this voluntary work.

The clients create us; for them we exist. We have to refrain from the danger of creating ourselves into something superlative, in manipulating our clients just to boost our own ego – even if our clients very often manipulate us to their own advantage.

Care of the volunteers – JOHN ELDRID*

Who cares for the Volunteers?

For every Director of a Samaritan Branch this is a vital question as care of the volunteers is his responsibility. I emphasise *responsibility*, because it does not imply that the Director cares for all the volunteers personally, which is generally impossible and in many situations not beneficial; but the Director is responsible for seeing that the volunteers are cared for, by himself/herself, Deputy Directors, Leaders and any one else appointed for the job.

But before the Director can effectively be *responsible* for the care of volunteers, he/she must have appropriate care for himself or herself – and indeed have accepted his own personal need for care. The Lord says, '*Love your neighbour as yourself*'. This implies, first, that you know how to love yourself. How you do this is your personal business. You will need to recognise that the emotional, spiritual, sexual and social aspects all need attention and satisfaction. You may effectively be cared for by your wife, husband, friends, homosexual partner, or as part of a religious order, but I do not think the Director should expect to rely for total care on the members of the Branch.

I do not mean that volunteers should not and do not care for their Director. I am very much aware of the great care I have received from Portsmouth and London Branches. But there is a need for the Director to have loving, caring relationships outside the Branch. I recognise that working in The Samaritans may change one and enrich one's personal life and relationships, but this is not the same thing as a total dependence on The Samaritans for a meaning to life. This also applies to volunteers though there

* Talk given at a School for Leaders, Swanwick, March 1976.

are some differences, since the task of the Director is more demanding than that of a volunteer, so it is possible for volunteers to have a wider area of dependence for personal and social needs on The Samaritans than a Director can have. We come back to the Director's responsibility for care of volunteers. Let us first draw out the areas of concern and need, and secondly, suggest ways to meet our responsibility.

Areas of concern and need

Anxiety is one of the major problems for all of us. I would be so bold as to suggest that the only real problem in The Samaritans is the anxiety of the volunteers, and not necessarily the problems of the clients. If we can cope with our own anxiety, then we are likely to befriend our caller well. This means that volunteers, new and old, will want to have opportunities for talking about their anxieties regarding calls, outside befriending and so on. As we know, neurotic anxiety is the result of a situation of conflict. So if a volunteer feels anxious, it may be because the caller has triggered off some unresolved emotional conflict. No matter how carefully selected volunteers are, it is likely that at some time a caller will awaken some unresolved emotional problems in them. It is always rather a shock when the caller outlines his problems and difficulties and you find you have more or less the same difficulties!

From my experience in The Samaritans it would seem that on the whole volunteers cope quite well with bearing and sharing the distress of our callers, but the trouble comes when the caller touches or triggers off a neurotic fear, sexual problem, or pet hate. So when a volunteer seems unduly anxious about a caller, we may need to ask, 'What has the caller started off in the volunteer?' The volunteer's anxiety about the caller may be only the 'presenting problem'!

I am well aware that volunteers are remarkable and special people, but I am realistic enough to recognise we all come with mixed motives. From the evidence of a recent questionnaire, some of us are rather nervous about recognising that we have mixed motives for joining. Even after careful selection, the motives for seeking to reduce personal inner loneliness, or to gain power or the satisfaction of sexual curiosity, are still likely to be present. I know that most Directors, at some time or other, have experience of those who have not resolved their neurotic need for power. So we can in spite of careful selection expect to be troubled by some of these common feelings.

This means that often volunteers will need help to find ways of coping with and redirecting such motivations. We must be realistic about them and not be afraid to look at the so-called darker side of our personalities. We can thus help our volunteers to become more mature persons. Carl Rogers' little book called 'Encounter Groups' is well worth reading. Many Samaritans have experience of Encounter Group activities. I am not suggesting that Encounter Groups will give us all the answers, but his book and such group experience are worthy of our attention.

Some volunteers will find it hard to accept direction and guidance. They want to 'go it alone'. A lot of potentially good volunteers seem to have problems about Branch discipline, so we need to handle them with understanding.

We have to recognise that volunteers may become tired and lose – for a time, anyway – their ability to fulfil the emotional demands of our work. In many Branches, especially in the large cities, the pressure of work is very demanding. I am keenly aware of this in London. On the other hand, in less busy Branches volunteers may lose heart through not having enough to do.

The volunteer who is in contact, whether long term or short term, with a client who kills himself/herself, will feel very vulnerable for a time. I personally have been closely involved with a number of suicides and some of the emotional scars still remain. So we should expect such volunteers to have a bereavement period, often with a lot of guilt feelings which are not justified. Many of our volunteers have suffered from quite serious depression and I am not suggesting this affects their quality as volunteers, for any of us may be depressed, but we may attract people who are more likely to become more depressed and suicidal than the average person. I think it is worth bearing this in mind in the choice of volunteers.

How we carry out the responsibility for care of volunteers

I suggest there are five ways in which this responsibility may be carried out, by the Director, Deputy Directors and Leaders, Tutors to new volunteers, Groups and the Branch as a whole.

First, the Director is responsible for doing all he or she can to develop these five avenues of care. This kind of set-up presupposes the concept of a shared responsibility and leadership. So the Director, who knows that if he or she should die or move suddenly, Joe or Mary will take over, is already realistically caring for the volunteers.

I have already said it is impossible in a large Branch for the Director to care personally for all the volunteers, and it is probably unhealthy for this to happen in a small Branch where it *is* possible. I do, however, consider the Director should see all volunteers who are involved with a client who kills himself/herself. Special attention should also be given to volunteers who are involved with police or a court case. Quite apart from expert guidance, the volunteer may need a lot of befriending support.

Where volunteers have to be sacked it is the Director's business to do it. We would hope all volunteers know the Director is available to talk with them about personal matters or serious Samaritan problems. At the same time, the fact that you are the Director may stop some volunteers from coming to you with personal problems, because the Director's first responsibility is to serve the clients, and also the Director is concerned with Branch discipline.

Secondly, most of us will have found that at least one Deputy Director or Leader will emerge as the confidant(e) of many volunteers. This can be most helpful, but it is better if this can be a shared responsibility. Deputy Directors and Leaders should be the kind of people who are able to care for volunteers as well as for clients. They can do much valuable work by being sensitive to the needs of volunteers who are emotionally upset by a client's problems. The attitude of the Deputy Directors and Leaders in general will of course very much reflect that of the Director. If the Director is able to share responsibility and care of the volunteers and indeed the whole Branch, then the Deputy Directors and Leaders are more likely to express their own special gifts of leadership and care. In this way the care of volunteers is able to develop naturally. How you organise and care for volunteers who are befriending callers outside the Centre depends on local Branch needs, but it is essential for volunteers to feel able to talk to Leaders about their anxieties regarding ongoing befriending. We have to recognise that some volunteers feel guilty about bothering the Director, Deputy Directors and Leaders, so they need encouragement. Expecting them to send in regular 'follow-up' reports is useful, and of course to report any worsening or improvement of the client's situation.

The third point concerns the 'Tutor System', especially for helpers. I suggest that when you become a helper you should automatically join a helpers' group and have your own tutor. This helps to reduce anxiety and gives the helpers opportunities to talk freely among themselves and with their tutor. It is very good if the helpers can meet at their tutor's home, but this is not always possible. In a large Branch it takes a while to get a tutor system going well, so a lot of patience and faith is needed. But it is extremely valuable in many ways, e.g. often it is through the care and counsel of a good tutor that a rather shy volunteer may blossom into a very confident Samaritan. The tutors also enable the Director to make a fairer assessment of a volunteer's suitability to become a Member. And of course helpers do seem to be very willing to bring their personal worries to their tutor.

The fourth way of caring is through groups. I am thinking especially of the building up of area groups of volunteers who live within a reasonable distance of each other. Such a group, with a Leader or other experienced Samaritan, has regular meetings during the year, usually once a month or every six weeks. The Director, Consultants, or others can be invited from time to time. The main business of the group of about twelve volunteers is to share their anxieties, befriend each other, and further their Samaritan education. Again you need a lot of patience in getting such groups going.

Lastly, there is the care given by the Branch as a whole. This is very important to develop and is much easier in a small Branch than in a large one. Some Branches have regular Branch meetings and I am sure this is beneficial, but we should always recognise that a lot of inter-communication between more than fifteen or so people is not really likely.

It is possible for a large Branch meeting to split into groups for a while, but the value of a Branch meeting is surely to experience the togetherness of the Branch and this can be expressed in social functions with some limited business. When possible I think it is good to be able to invite non-Samaritans, especially husbands, wives and so on, to socials, as there is a danger of volunteers becoming a kind of club.

As part of the care of volunteers the Branch should offer opportunities for on-going education and encourage the Branch to realise they are part of a great association of Branches.

The key points in the care of volunteers are lots of consultation, shared leadership, and firm direction.

Varieties of fund-raising – DAVID M. JACKSON

There was a wonderful response to a questionnaire we sent out on fund-raising. Two memos were dispatched to the Treasurer of every Branch: one for the Branch and one for the Friends or whatever outside organisation the Branch might have. In each case, the answers from a 'Friends' group have been amalgamated with the answers from a Branch so that 124 *Branches* is a true figure. This represents replies by nearly 75% of the Branches in the British Isles.

Because of the many different interpretations of the questions asked, figures cannot be exact, but they provide information and food for thought. It will be obvious that some replies did not tell me everything done or intended to be done. For instance, it seems unlikely that only fifty-five of the 124 Branches indulge in 'Chance' activities (raffles, draws, etc.) and only twenty-four stated that they get money from talks.

Various headings grew as the analysis developed. Some of the items don't quite fit, but let them speak for themselves. In the following pages you will note that there is no Table III. It was deleted because so often Tables VA and VB mixed with it. It was called Annual Appeal. Only a few Branches mentioned an actual Annual Appeal, but those that did used the circulation of the Annual Report widely with or without begging letters and vice-versa. Involvement of the media whenever possible for new items and special advertising (e.g. sponsored pages) is particularly geared to annual meetings and annual appeals.

'Don't know' appears in the Tables simply because the Branch didn't answer that particular question, not because they *said* they didn't know.

With regard to the use of Friends, it was felt that the greater 'busyness' of the Branch much affected the need for recruitment of non-Samaritan fund raisers, although this was by no means always the case. Sometimes 'busyness' went with a poor financial position and sometimes there was no outside help because there were so many volunteers in the Branch. Out of the 124 Branches, forty-one used Branch members only, eight used Friends only, seventy-four used all sorts (both inside and out) and one 'didn't know', the percentages of 124 being 33%, 6.5%, 59.7% and 0.8% respectively. Four Branches were in the process of starting Friends.

It is interesting that only half of the 124 Branches mentioned a principal source. It seems to show that some Branches (with or without Friends) go for one big 'do' a year while others use a tremendous number of small events. This is not strictly so. Quite a number of the Branches with a principal source use many others as well, and in some cases, Branches mentioned two principal efforts.

Activities vary very much in size. A raffle, for instance, might be in a Centre, at a fete, or by itself, i.e. anything from a box of chocolates to a motorcar. A coffee evening – as the Tables show – might be a large or small event.

While some Branches were specific about the success or failure of a particular fund-raising activity, there was not sufficient information given for me to condemn or praise any of them as being all bad or all good. One problem that has to be resolved is whether an activity which raises a large sum of money is worth the amount of work involved, but remember, even if efforts fail, the publicity is always of great value.

I *Principal sources*

(N.B. 13 Branches mentioned two, the others one or none).
Branches involved 62 (50 % of 124)

Flag Days	35
House to house and street collections	11
Shops	4
Fairs (fayres, fêtes, etc.)	3

Stalls (markets, joint charities etc.)	2
Bazaars	2
Dances	2
Income from capital investments	2
200 Clubs, etc.	1
Draws, lotteries	1
Teddy Bears' Picnic	1
Donations from business houses	1
Sponsored walks, runs and climbs	1
Regatta	1
It's a Knock Out (shared)	1
Nearly New	1
Sales (all sorts)	1
Concerts, musical evenings	1
	72

II *Measure of needs*

Above your needs	(+)	15
Adequate	(=)	71
Below your needs	(—)	33
Don't know		5
		124

IV *'Chance' sources*

Branches involved: 55 (44.35 % of 124)

Auctions	3
Bingo	2
Clock competitions	2
Clubs (200, etc.)	10
Draws (wholly sponsored)	12
Draws (shared)	1
'Fruit machine' tickets	1
Raffles	35
Teddy Bears' Picnic	1
Tombola	2
Watch competition	2
	69

VA	*Donations and Income (Regular)*	
	Branches involved 112 (90.32% of 124)	
	Business houses	23
	Capital investments	23
	Charities	45
	Churches	51
	Covenants	54
	Local Authority	92
	Schools	6
	Social services	5
		299
VB	*Donations (Casual)*	
	Branches involved 40 (32.25% of 124)	
	Business houses	7
	Callers (clients)	2
	Charities	15
	Churches	12
	Hospitals	1
	Legacies	10
	Local Authority	3
	Subscriptions	14
		64
VIA	*Events, wholly sponsored*	
	Branches involved 40 (32.25% of 124)	
	Boxing	1
	Cycling	3
	Darts	1
	Football	2
	Golf	1
	Hockey	1
	Horse ride	2
	Knit-in	4
	Quiz	2
	Regatta	2
	Slim-in	2
	Stallion parade	1
	Swim	10
	Three legged race	2
	Walk	20
		54

VIB *Events shared*

Branches involved 14 (11.29% of 124)

Bonfire night	1
Donkey Derby	4
It's a Knock Out	1
Medieval day	1
Rag week	5
Run	2
Swim	1
	15

VIIA *Collections (outdoor mobile)*

Branches involved 89 (71.77% of 124)

Bingo halls	3
Carnivals	8
Cinemas	2
Clubs	4
Carols	17
Flag days	70
House to house	45
Precincts	3
Sporting fixtures	6
Stores	2
	160

VIIB *Collections (outdoor static)*

Branches involved 97 (78.22% of 124)

Antiques	2
Art exhibition	2
Bazaar	10
Boxes (on counters, etc.)	11
Discount goods	5
Fairs (fayres, fêtes)	30
Flower festival (show)	9
Jumble	50
Mile of coins	1
Nearly new	9
Pitch on 'Prom' (shared)	1
Sales (all sorts)	13

Schools	1
Shops	36
Stalls (market, fair, etc.)	27
Supermarket (competition)	1
Vintage car fair	1
	209

VIIIA *Social events (large)*

Branches involved 80 (64.5% of 124)

Barbecues	9
Coffee mornings and evenings	8
Concerts (all sorts)	33
Dances	49
Dinners	1
Fashion shows	21
Film nights	3
Garden parties	7
Hair styling spectacular	1
Music hall	4
Revue	1
Social evenings	6
	143

VIIIB *Social events (small)*

Branches involved 71 (57.25% of 124)

Beetle drives	2
Bring and buy	14
Bottle stalls	5
Bridge drives	4
Coffee mornings and evenings	50
Open days (local factories)	2
Pies pickles and plonk	3
Ploughman's lunch	1
Skittles	1
Strawberry teas	1
Tombola	1
Tupperware	2
Wine and cheese	33
	119

IX *Talks and sundry sales*

Branches involved 11 (8.87% of 124)

Buy a brick	1	
Bees (honey)	2	
Christmas cards	3	
Paper (waste)	6	
Pens	2	
Stamps (used)	5	
	19	
Talks	24	(19.35% of 124)

X *Gifts in kind*

A Peppercorn rent	2
B Unspecified (light, heat, etc.)	7

GENERAL FIGURES

Total of listed sources	106
Total number of all the activities	1,184
Average per Branch	9.5

SOURCES MOST MENTIONED		% *of* 124
Local authority grants (regular)	92	74.19
Flag days	70	56.45
Covenants and other individual subs	54	43.54
Churches, regular donations	51	41.12
Jumble sales	50	40.32
Coffee mornings (small)	50	40.32
Dances	49	39.51
House to house and street collections	45	36.29
Charities and trusts	45	36.29

Local Authority funding in the UK

— LAURENCE BIGGS

In December 1978 a short form of enquiry went to all Branches on this subject. 129 Branches kindly replied (76%) and these notes summarise the information forthcoming.

1. Cash benefits from Local (and County) Authorities

The 129 Branches between them collected £70,088 (average £543)
but 13 Branches got nothing
and 9 Branches between them got £24,730 (mainly in unusual circumstances)
Hence 107 between them received £45,358 (average £426).

So an 'average' Branch with an intake under £400 could find it worth while having another look at the Branch's approach to the Local Authority.

The successful approach seems to be the following:

A well-typed letter of request, signed personally by the Chairman of the Branch, supported by a clean smart copy of the last Accounts and Report, with explanatory notes; and a letter setting out the prospects for increased service to the community in the coming year. References to the hard slog of the past year will not be so productive as the prospect of increased benefits in the next, and so on.

2. Trends in Local Authority assistance

Branches replied as follows:

Did the 1974 reorganisation affect you?

For the better	30	23.25%
No	64	50.00%
For the worse	11	8.50%

Since 1974 have grants increased (in real terms)?

Yes	24	18.60%
They have kept pace with inflation	30	23.25%
They have fallen behind	54	42.00%

Local Authority grants as a percentage of expenditure were:

0% – 10%	52	(41.0%)
11% – 20%	31	(24.2%)
21% – 30%	18	(14.0%)
Over 30%	7	(5.5%)

Support in kind: 52 Branches (40.62%) reported that Rates Rebates were received and/or that Rents were reduced, sometimes to nil.

So any Branch adversely affected by the 1974 reorganisation has some handy facts to use on the successors of the old Authorities. If more than 9 out of 10 have done as well (5 out of 10 doing better) then representations could make a strong point.

Similarly, if the contributions have fallen behind in real terms (and 42% think they have) then this point can be brought out in a letter. Applications should do more than mention the fact: they should work out the sum needed to keep pace with inflation from 1974 and bring the matter to notice again next year if ignored this year.

But, generally, special circumstances are needed if the contributions are to cover much more than about 15% of total expenses, and the average noted above (£426) hover around 10–12% depending on Branch circumstances.

3. County Council assistance

At least two counties, Essex and West Midlands, have taken the intelligent course of viewing The Samaritans' Service on a County basis. They call for information, and then make a grant to the movement in the County, leaving Branches to divide the spoils.

This approach could well be developed, and the Regional

Representative, with the Treasurer and Chairman of the Regional Committee, might help in setting forward and co-ordinating the approach. The letter should be clearly written from a Regional standpoint, and the funding handled at that level. The Accounts submitted could be The Samaritans Incorporated Accounts, reinforcing the point that this is not a local affair, but worthy of County attention. Mention could be made of the fact that ours is an entirely voluntary service, that nobody is paid, and nobody is ever charged a penny. The various things The Samaritans do that have the indirect *financial* effect on local and county funds, should be set out, for example:

We keep people out of hospitals who might otherwise require treatment.

We keep people in employment (and off Social Security Benefit) when they might fall by the wayside.

We keep families together – children out of care – mothers and children safe from physical danger, and some old people less unhappy through contact with our centres. Not to mention the inevitable drunk who haunts us, and might otherwise become a candidate for the mental hospital . . . and much more, which can be described graphically.

In short, County Council help is worth looking at, but at Regional level.

4. Rate reliefs (and other benefits)

Over 40% of Branches mentioned Rating benefits, and most Branches now make some attempt to get 'something off' the Rates.

An expert (i.e. a Samaritan Treasurer who is a Borough Treasurer) has kindly looked at the subject, and advises as follows:

'The Rating (Disabled Persons) Act 1978, which applies from 1st April 1979 contains a clause on rebates for Institutions (such as The Samaritans) that the rebate should, under this Act, be equal to the Rates chargeable (i.e. 100% relief).

'But, in practice, sewerage and water rates (which are paid

separately) will remain chargeable on the full rateable value of the property.

'The overall result will be a very substantial reduction in Rates paid.'

But . . . Branches will have to lodge an appeal under this Act to obtain the benefit of the relief. 'This is the time for all good Treasurers . . .'

5. Tailcorn

It would be a dull day if all Samaritan Branches were to receive identical treatment.

They do not – a few examples follow:

(a) From a seaside town: 'No help to purchase our new premises, but Local Council granted us a site on the Seafront for 2 weeks in summer without charge. We raised £2,000.'

The moral seems clear: if one way does not work, try another! No sea, no seafront? What about a street market? But bear in mind that, whenever The Samaritans appear in public we get clients, even if we are looking for cash – so we should be prepared.

(b) A small but growing Branch received assistance under the 'Local Government Grant (Social Need) Act 1969, Urban Programme for Capital and non-capital projects' – and a Branch making a good case might get a grant for capital use, or help with telephone bills, or with rent.

(c) A busy Branch reported that the Local Authority agreed to help, provided they had a representative on the Committee! This could not of course be permitted but eventually they paid up without *any* strings.

(d) A Branch (overseas) – 'We used to be Rate free, but Rates were abolished so we lost that benefit. The Electricity Board treats us very kindly – their man forgets to read the meter.' Ah well!

(e) Some Branches have suggested that The Samaritans Incorporated should take a hand, by writing to all Local Authorities pointing out the service that the movement renders, and drawing attention to the Branch in the immediate area.

This would be an innovation, and would only be adopted if a substantial majority of Branches thought that it would help. It could be done, and at no great expense.

Branch visits – JOHN WILLIAMS

Visits by members of the Executive Committee of the Council of Management, or by members of the Panel of Visitors (chosen by the Executive Committee after visitors' Conferences) are carried out every two and a half years. They serve a dual purpose. The first is to help the Branch to evaluate the work it is doing. The second is to give the Executive Committee an up-to-date report on the state of the Branch so that proper and effective continuing support can be given.

The intimate relationship between caller and volunteer, created either on the telephone or face to face and being normally entirely private, can only be properly evaluated by those who shared in it. The caller knows whether what took place was helpful or not but, even so, his feelings may not be an accurate guide. The volunteer will also have some feeling as to whether or not the caller was being helped. By consulting with colleagues afterwards a more thoughtful appreciation can be arrived at. Whether or not the caller returns for a second contact or more is not necessarily an indication of the value of the first. Yet, if the caller does contact the Branch again, it can be concluded that the first contact was valued.

Day Leaders have to assess the value of what took place and, in discussing with the volunteer the course of future action, are bound to come to some conclusions as to the volunteer's performance. At meetings of Day Leaders not only is client care a major topic but also the effectiveness or otherwise of particular volunteers. In other words, some evaluation of what took place between caller and volunteer always occurs. It will be a blend of fact and feeling.

A Branch is the means by which client care is made continuously available in a particular area. Visitors have to try to help Branches evaluate the service they are offering. The number of clients who call is the first indication. The number of those who call again, and the number of those to whom continuing care is properly given, is the next. The number of para-suicides admitted to local hospitals could be a contra-indicator; whilst a continuing fall in the local suicide rate might be accepted as a pro-indicator. The entries in the log book and other Branch statistics can all yield their evidence. The attitude of the volunteers revealed in conversation and the ethos of the Branch generally show whether or not it is dedicated to caring for the suicidal and despairing.

Before the visit the Branch is asked to send to the visitors, one copy to each, a completed questionnaire, a copy of the Annual Report and Accounts, and any other material likely to be of interest.

It is important that the members of the Branch should be told about the visit well in advance and encouraged to take every opportunity to talk to the visitors when they come. They should be able to do so without any of the Directors or Leaders being present.

The programme of the visit should be worked out as soon as possible and agreed with the visitors so as to give them every opportunity to discuss or look at as many aspects of the work as possible. In the course of the visit they will need to meet the Director, the Deputies, the Chairman of the Branch Committee and members of that Committee, including the Treasurer and the Publicity Officer, and also the Day Leaders. One of the visitors will need to have a leisured quiet conversation with the person responsible for the selection and preparation of volunteers. It is essential that there should be a Branch meeting and that this should be carefully planned to involve those present either in actual case discussion, or in some carefully prepared group discussion about client care. One of the visitors will be prepared to start off the meeting with ten minutes or so explaining about Branch visits, and they both can be expected to answer questions, but the bulk of the programme is provided by the Branch itself.

There is no need for the Director to be in attendance throughout the visit. The visitors will not be able to look at everything and will have to concentrate on particular matters to which their attention may be drawn. They should be given time during the visit to be alone together and encouraged towards the end of their visit to share some of their immediate reactions and to bring out into the open things that have worried them. At the same time, the fact that they may feel it necessary to reserve certain matters for further reflection should be respected, together with their responsibility to report to the Executive through the Regional Representative. It should always be appreciated that however skilful the visitors are, they only have a very limited amount of time to spend with the Branch and that, therefore, they can really only apply a 'dipstick method'.

The purpose of the questionnaire is to bring into focus all aspects of the work of a Branch and to highlight matters which merit particular attention during the visit.

The first section about *clients*, attempts to measure the 'busyness' and effectiveness of the Branch. Some very busy Branches may not have time to offer continuing care to the clients. Some less than averagely busy may well be effectively offering a high standard of continuing care. Some very unbusy Branches may be so simply because clients feel it is not worth while calling a second time.

Section II is about the *volunteers*, and seeks to explore selection, preparation and continuing instruction as well as turnover. Section III covers *leadership*, and the various ways of solving the same basic problems. Section IV relates to *administration* other than care of clients and volunteers. Section V is about *publicity* and the relationship between this and the 'busyness' of the Branch. Finally the last section deals with *facilities* and allows the Branch to take a look at these again through the eyes of the visitors.

Busyness is measured by total calls – all old, new, 'sex' and unidentified approaches – over the telephone, in person and by letter per 100,000 catchment population (for purposes of comparison).

New clients are those who are 'identified'. This specifically excludes 'silent calls' and also other calls when no identification is achieved and nothing much communicated. But many anonymous callers do communicate a lot else and should be counted.

Ongoing befriending is a term used for befriending specifically arranged for the continuing care of particular clients by particular volunteers. It does not include the continuing care of clients who ring or call whenever they feel the need and to whom no one has specifically been allocated as a 'befriender' because this seems not to be necessary.

The 'R' factor is arrived at by dividing the *total* number of calls minus the *new client calls* by the number of *new client calls.* The average of 196 Branch returns in 1975 and 1977 was 3.6. The standard deviation was 1.4. This means that for Branches outside the limits 5.0 and 2.2 the question 'why' needs to be asked.

Visitors should study carefully the material received from the Branch, together with the Regional Representative's comments. The last visit report will also be available. Thus some evaluation of the work being done can be arrived at beforehand. During the visit this evaluation can be tested in terms of the people met and the relationships discovered. It should be agreed beforehand who will do what and it is worth while spending half-an-hour alone together about two-thirds of the way through the visit so as to share impressions so far gained.

Branches will want to know how the visitors feel about them and if they have any suggestions or criticisms to make. Visitors are in the difficult position of being too closely involved at the time to ensure a reflected judgement and there may well be matters on which they would wish to reserve comment. Nevertheless, it is important to be as frank with one another as possible.

Branches can make a new assessment of their work for themselves immediately after the visit, bringing into focus what came out during the preparations they made beforehand, what came to light during the visit, and their own reactions to any comments the visitors may have made. Thus new and helpful ideas can be made effective without delay.

Both visitors should write concise reports which should include:

(a) a brief statement of his/her own critical evaluation of the service offered by the Branch.

(b) any comments needed by way of explanation of the recommendations including the reasoning behind them.

(c) any additional comments likely to prove helpful to the Executive Committee in assessing the Branch.

(d) any thoughts as to what should happen next in the Branch.

All reports, together with both copies of the completed questionnaire, should reach the Regional Representative without delay. He then adds his own comments to the summary report form. This is put before the Executive Committee at its next meeting together with any additional reports or comments he may consider necessary. After the meeting he returns to the Branch drawing attention to the special commendations of the visitors and discussing ways of carrying out the recommendations which the Executive Committee has endorsed.

Suggested form for inter-branch visits

(Volunteers are asked to obtain this form from their
Director and get it signed by him/her after filling it up.)
FINAL DATE OF VALIDITY OF THIS FORM ______________________
day month year

____ of
Title First name Surname

______________________________ ______________________
address town

is a member of the Branch of The Samaritans entitled
______________________ in ________________ ________________
name of service town country

(*OR* is a member of an organisation called
in ________________ ________________ not affiliated)
town country

He/she is working in the service as ______________________
and is hereby certified to be in good standing at this time.
We shall be grateful if he/she may be received as a
colleague in the Centres in ____________ ____________ ____________
____________ ____________ ____________ ____________
(and be permitted to take part in the work) DELETE IF NOT APPLICABLE.
Our office telephone number is ______________________
and our address for enquiries is ______________________
(FOR INTERNATIONAL VISITS: his/her Passport Number is ____________)

(Signed)
______________________ Director.
______________________ (Date:)

Our future leadership – MICHAEL YORKE

We all know how The Samaritans has grown in every way since becoming nationally organised in 1963. This is due to the validity of the original inspiration, the wisdom of the early leaders in organising us in the way they did, and the obvious need for our service in the community.

At every point growth has been the keynote since that date: e.g. in the number of Branches, and volunteers and clients, the amount of owned property, and public awareness of our service. We like to think that we have learnt from such mistakes as we have made.

One thing has not changed, and this is to be applauded: we are still almost totally a voluntary, grassroots, locally organised charity. It is the desire and the role of the Chairman and other elected officers and of the General Secretaries to be available to assist those who do the frontline work in the Branches. It is not their role to be dictatorial or detached. With three exceptions all Executive members are practising, duty-doing Samaritans in their local branches.

But the situation in the way that it has changed provokes serious questions. We cannot avoid the results of size and prestige. These are particularly relevant when we consider how we run, and who runs, our branches. Let us look at three roles within the movement.

Branch Director

How far does the Branch take for granted what the Director does for it? Many Directors work full time but without pay for us. Many receive no expenses and are reckoned to cover the cost themselves. One Branch Director who travels to the Centre four times a week has to pay 60p a day for parking alone.

Many branches are now considering secretarial assistance. If a branch does not do this, is it because it is taking advantage of the goodwill of volunteers? The issue, of course, raised by both the above, is that we have been requiring not only people with time *ad lib.* but also reasonable financial resources. Is it fair and right that our future development should rest critically upon such people's goodwill?

Maybe we ought to consider at least office holders in the branch on a different expense basis. As far as time is concerned, we all know the problems of recruiting volunteers because, for instance, more women now go out to work; how will such factors affect our future recruitment of directors and other leaders? Are we in fact permitting a situation which will be destructive for us in the long term?

These questions are relevant not only to large city Branches where the workload is great, but also to rural ones where the workload may not be so pressing but the travel distances are far greater.

The role and the situation of each Director should be seriously examined.

Regional officers

The expectation of the Movement about its regional officers is now quite different from what it was even in 1967. Regions are now mostly well organised, with full and invaluable education and support facilities. This regionalisation has enabled the Movement to keep the essential common touch and enabled everyone to get to training programmes if they wish to and their circumstances allow this.

But has it been considered what it means to be a Regional Representative? He or she is both a messenger of the Council (through the Executive) and a friend and counsellor to the Directors and Branches in the region. Representatives are expected to be at two all-day Council Meetings and six overnight Executive Meetings a year; the Swanwick Schools (ideally all of them);

Branch meetings, regional schools, and Committee meetings. In addition, they must punctually write letters, be ready to give talks, and be available at home on the telephone. The question of expense for these officers is not a major problem because they all receive their fares or 10p a mile when they drive their cars, the proportion of the telephone bill used for Samaritan work and their postage costs. Such payments are surely not excessive. One Regional Representative did 6,500 miles driving last year for The Samaritans. The main problem for regional officers is the enormous time commitment. It should be remembered that they are still expected to be active volunteers in their local Branch. Are we expecting too much from such volunteers?

Officers of The Samaritans Inc.

The situation regarding the Chairman and Vice-Chairmen is also one which needs careful thought. The demands on the former as the leader of a charity of our size are obviously considerable both in time and effort. The Vice-Chairmen are now given areas of responsibility to assist the Chairman and they have a great deal of work under this category. They, too, are practising volunteers and are sometimes Regional Representatives as well.

It is obvious how much the Movement owes to its General Secretaries and office staff at Slough. Without them it would be difficult to remain a coherent movement. But we still need to look at the question of whether we are creating an impossible task for the volunteer leadership of the Movement. The style has really not changed since 1963 whereas the framework of the role has changed almost beyond recognition. I am concerned that we are moving towards a situation which requires the Chairman and other officers who are volunteers to be people who have the power in their working lives to order their own time, like the clergy, retired persons, or non-employed women. Any person with a 'normal' job simply could not lead us. If this analysis is true then it is a serious matter. If we wish to continue with volunteer leadership, as is our tradition, then we must be realistic in our expectations and the role which we want our leaders to fulfil.

I am myself one of the fortunate people who can order their time, and the Church has allowed me to treat my work for The Samaritans as part of my professional duties – even if it is unpaid. But what is to happen in the future is of far greater importance. We seem to be at present in a settled period of leadership so now is the time to look at these big issues in a thoughtful and leisurely manner. I conclude with a series of questions which I hope Branches will give adequate time to examining. We cannot go on doing things as we have always done them if they appear unrealistic in contemporary situations.

The questions for each Branch are:

1. What does the Branch expect as a work load from its Director; and how does it assist him or her in fulfilling it?

2. What expenses are paid to the Director and other Branch officers, as of right, and what should they be?

3. What priority to such expenses does the Branch give? Are manpower expenses paid when other things have been settled?

4. What is the Branch's attitude to employing:

(a) a paid Director, if necessary,
(b) a secretary
(c) a Samaritan Consultant?

The concept of a Samaritan Consultant was suggested at a recent meeting of the Directors of very large branches. Such a Consultant would be a Samaritan of long and wide experience who would assist a Branch or group of Branches in selection and instruction of volunteers, and in their personal support. He or she would also help in the assessment of client needs at Leaders' meetings and would thus be an assistant to the Director and Day Leaders.

5. What are the issues raised by the possibility of a great increase in Samaritans?

6. What does the Branch think is the role of the Regional Representative? Are there any people in the Branch who could do it if they were asked? If not, why not?

7. Should we begin to consider the employment of professional regional field officers even though this runs against our Samaritan tradition? What are the important implications of this?

8. What is, and what should be the role of a volunteer Chairman?

9. Are the regions as presently constituted the right pattern for the next ten years? What adjustments should be made, taking into account that each region needs a representative on a committee that is not too large?

These are fundamental and far-reaching questions of great importance for the future well-being of our Movement. They need to be faced courageously and honestly. None of us is clear yet about the answers and the decisions must be made by the Movement at large.

The Samaritans: 25 years on—plan for a school

In November 1978 the work of The Samaritans reached its twenty-fifth anniversary. We thought it a good time to add to the more usual fare at the Schools for Directors and Leaders some opportunity to look at developments over the past years and at likely changes in the years ahead. The 1979 Schools were therefore organised in three 'modules', each consisting of a plenary or demi-plenary, a workshop and the chance to talk out issues raised (or anything else) in small groups. The modules were as follows (numbered A, B and C):

(Module A – The Opening Plenary)

Befriending and the community

Evidence suggests that we permeate the community indirectly and directly – *indirectly* in that it is known that The Samaritans are always there and available, even if not used – a sort of talisman. We are known through publicity, professional links and the grapevine, also through recruitment and fund-raising which is also publicity. This awareness leads to a sense of dependence and security that something precious is being preserved.

But *directly*, how far have we managed to put suicide on the agenda of public and professional concern? How far does the public really understand the nature and limitations of our work? What is the proper response to their expectations and trust?

> 'Talisman: Anything that acts as a charm or by which extraordinary results are achieved. 1784.' (*Shorter O.E.D.*, 1972.)

The Samaritans in the '80s

(Extra Demi-plenary)

Society, suicide and The Samaritans over the last and the next twenty-five years

Having passed our twenty-fifth anniversary, it is appropriate to look back at the changes in society since we began – probably greater than in any other quarter century – especially in relation to suicide, confidentiality, the law, the family, corporatism, attitudes to authority, attitudes between the generations, expectations of relationships.

Also there is a need to try to anticipate the next few years, for change will continue. Are we able to meet emerging needs? Are we a movement or an institution?

> 'The Samaritans simply lacked the way of adjusting to novel situations'. (*The Scientific American*, January, 1977.)

Befriending and the community (Workshops)

(Workshop A 1)
Liaison with local professional and voluntary agencies

'Your branch is lucky, we have no Consultants.'

'Surely we've outgrown Consultants – don't need to depend on professionals.'

'What do Samaritans do anyway? Shouldn't we discourage them from meddling with this patient of ours?'

'There is a need for a new sort of service halfway between a Citizen's Advice Bureau and a crisis centre, staffed by volunteers where people can go when . . .' (Evidence of the Conference of Chief Probation Officers *Marriage Matters*, Home Office 1978).

'The Samaritans represent an extreme in isolationism . . .' (*The Scientific American*, January 1977).

In this workshop, participants will meet with a consultant psychiatrist, a social worker and a general practitioner and will explore how healthy are our relationships with our friends with whom we share the care of our callers.

(Workshop A 2)
Getting the message across

This workshop stresses the commitment of leaders (and all members) to the general policy of the Branch. Publicity affects the potential clients and volunteers who do or do not approach us. The way in which we treat clients and others who have occasion to ring us is the principal means of publicity and cannot but do good or harm. So does even the style of fund-raising and the content and manner of talks.

But to most of us the media represent not a means of publicity but a threatening intrusion on the cosy life of the Branch. So let's have a look at it.

> 'The media is a whore. Screw it – or you'll get screwed by it.' (Anon. journalist, 1979).

(Workshop A 3)
Getting the right people, or making a match

In this workshop we consider the nature of the attachment between the volunteer and Samaritan (Branch) work. The framework chosen as illustration is that of a marriage or close friendship and the purpose is to raise the kind of questions which members can readily apply to their own Branches. The essential relationship is *mutual compatibility* rather than one partner 'selecting' the other. The sub-headings we shall use are – Early Initiatives, A Developing Relationship, Living Together, The Parting of the Ways.

> 'Getting to know you,
> Getting to know all about you;
> Getting to like you,
> Getting to hope *you* like *me*!' (O. Hammerstein II)

(Workshop A 4)
Public relations and fund-raising

This workshop examines the ethics and the publicity involved in attracting funds. While many members do not *have* to fund-raise, they should, as part of their commitment to the Branch, be aware of the Samaritan implications of fund-raising and all that goes with it. What means should we not use? Are some Friends failed Samaritans? They still represent and speak for the Branch. Does the Branch budget get published to the Branch? Does it provide for all it should? What about the Annual Report?

> 'The naughtiness of the silver.' (Bishop Latimer on a previous bout of inflation.)

(Workshop A 5)
Anonymity

If a caller exercises his or her right to remain unnamed, does it hinder befriending? Do we press too hard for the name sometimes? Are we more anxious to fit the 'case' into the Branch's experience (index system) than to establish a relationship at the caller's desired level?

Anonymity is our defence from too close an attachment by the caller. It is also a safeguard against the seeker after public acclaim who is attracted to voluntary work. But does it hinder real befriending? And is the effort of the volunteer in avoiding discovery of their Samaritan involvement really necessary?

> 'But still keep something to yoursel'
> Ye scarcely tell to ony.'
>
> (*Epistle to a Young Friend*, Robert Burns)

(Module B: Demi-plenary)
Befriending the individual (Workshops)

This session concentrates on our work with individual callers. 'Befriending' is the word we use to describe the relationship with all callers from the beginning and also the one-to-one relationship set up in cases of ongoing need. It needs to be distinguished from ordinary friendship: what are the distinctions? Can a Branch be said to 'befriend' in any recognisable sense of the word? Doesn't this deny the need for real one-to-one relationships for lack of which the callers come to us? Or are we talking about counselling anyway? What about advice-giving and problem-solving? We deny them and yet answer the phone

'The Samaritans. Can I help you?' when we mean 'The Samaritans. Can you help yourself?'

> 'He had probably never set himself up to understand . . . he had been content to play the holy humble role of service . . . to provide the sound of his voice to distract me from the crying of the silence.' (*The Waterfall*, Margaret Drabble)

(Workshop B 1)
Monitoring one-to-one befriending

This workshop concentrates on the leaders' (or befriending secretary's) role in helping the process of ongoing befriending away from the Centre. Are befrienders properly prepared for the task, briefed as to what is expected of them and warned of possible dangers? Sample role-plays may show the setting up of a befriending relationship, a befriender becoming possessive of his/her client, and the switching or termination of a befriending. What are the criteria for this latter? Do we appreciate the client's reaction to a switch or switching off? Are we prepared for the befriender's sense of loss, or resentment of the Leader's need to probe what's going on?

> 'Oh, do not ask, "What is it?"
> Let us go and make our visit!'
> (*The Love Song of Alfred J. Prufrock*, T. S. Eliot)

(Workshop B 2)
Befriending the elderly

This workshop will ask, What is the attitude of society to the elderly? Are there new problems that the elderly did not face in past generations? It will point to the intensification of loneliness through deafness and immobility, the sense of running downhill and being useless. Is current propaganda for euthanasia adding to this? Ought the Samaritans to become an adoptive family? Or one's Samaritan an adopted daughter? The problems posed by some old people's irrational pride. The extent to which we can and should liaise with other agencies. The valuable contribution of the old in befriending (inside and outside Samaritan work).

Sample role-plays could include the lady who is very neglected but won't accept help for fear of having to be put away in the asylum, and the exhausting repetition of an old person's conversation.

(Workshop B 3)
Befriending the young

Our publicity is doing much to attract the young – do we know how to cope with them when they phone or visit? The workshop examines the difficulties, such as the tendency to exhibit parental reflexes – anxiety, problem-solving, 'talk to your parents/teacher,' 'you ought to be home by now, they'll be worried about you'. The question of matching young callers with young volunteers – is it always right? Can we listen directly to a mid-teens client without all sorts of luggage getting in the way? What about 'hoax' or testing calls?

We have more young volunteers in some branches than in others. Can our attitudes to young volunteers be the touchstone for our attitudes to young callers? Does the Branch welcome and use a student who is a Samaritan at college elsewhere?

> 'So many ways to be unsure or bold.'
>
> (*The Young Ones*, Elizabeth Jennings)

(Workshop B 4)
Befriending the addicted, or Barbs, booze and us

This workshop examines and endeavours to make clear to members the main addictions and how we may be affected by them; and what help it is possible for us to give. It considers especially the problems that may lie behind the addiction; our relations with other agencies; and our care as Leaders for those befriending the addicted.

Why do addicts not contact us more? Are we perhaps frightened of addiction?

> 'Every form of addiction is bad, no matter whether to Narcotics, Alcohol, Morphine or Idealism.' (C. G. Jung.)

(Workshop B 5)
Befriending the befriender

This workshop tries to work out the best ways of supporting the befrienders of our callers and to look at their various sources of support when their ongoing befriending or 'one-off' contacts leave them with a sense of strain and failure (or indeed ought to and don't).

> 'I politely answered, but after a while I could detect in his voice the same note that I could hear in my own – a note of diffident, hopeless, anxious concern, striving with immense effort to sound detached and unconcerned. I felt so sorry for him, poor useless man, I knew that he was like me, equally afflicted and that that was why he was there on the end of that line at one o'clock in the morning, and I did not want him to know how irrelevant his questions were and how inexpressible my true complaints, so I tried hard to sound more cheerful to cheer him up so that he could ring off thinking that he had done a good job with me.'
>
> (*The Waterfall*, Margaret Drabble)

(Module C: Demi-plenary)

The boundaries of befriending

How far have the frontiers of Samaritan work been extended in recent years, and what have been the pros and cons? How far can they be extended in the future without breaching basic Samaritan principles? With the use of duos, trios, small groups and open discussion, this Demi-plenary session will begin to examine some vital areas, including training, support, accessibility and 'specialisation'. Have we tended to diversify because of the seeming success of our work shown in a reduced suicide rate, and are we now in need of rediscovering our original calling?

> 'Old men ought to be explorers.' (T. S. Eliot.)

(Workshop C 1)
Where and how do we draw the line?

The Boundaries of Befriending – which clients are unhelpable?

Which might be harmed by befriending? What are the criteria? What are the priorities? How does this assessment affect the caller? . . . the volunteer? ' . . . the leader?

> 'If you want a client very well befriended, just put up a notice forbidding it.' (Anon. Director to another, *c.* 1973.)

(Workshop C 2)
Samaritan Branches befriending in the open: The Festival Branch shares its experience

Since 1973 the Festival Branch has been befriending clients at pop and folk festivals, and other events. We have found that the way in which we work varies in some important aspects from that of static Branches. In this workshop we share what we have experienced and look at ways in which other Branches might learn from this and get involved in similar work.

> 'I couldn't help thinking of cosy Branches, and warm clean Centres, with the phone between you and the client. Here they came and you were face to face, and they could see your eyes and feel your hands, and you couldn't lounge back in the swivel chair and sip your coffee. I was sitting in the open with a distraught girl in floods of tears, and I held her hand, and she talked and talked. Will she visit her local Branch and accept befriending? I don't know – but here at Blackbush we were a crisis organisation, and isn't that what "Sams" is all about?'
> (Volunteer attending her first Festival.)

(Workshop C 3)
The third party call

In June 1976 the Council resolved that we could respond much more to Third Party calls than before. This workshop explores the difficulties in deciding how to respond to differing types of call and then in either making an approach to the named person or in refusing to do so.

The workshop also considers who are the 'gatekeepers' who should know about our befriending and availability, e.g.

policemen, night porters, chemists, caretakers, porters, bus conductors . . .

> 'Could you come and do something about our Alice? She was out until 9.30 *again* last night and she's only twenty-seven.'
>
> (Anon. caller)

(Workshop C 4)
Bigger is better or small is beautiful? What sort of Branches do we want?

There have been changes in the pattern of coverage, e.g. fewer new Branches are being formed and more sub-groups (but not many). Some sub-groups have stopped manning for lack of business. This workshop is not so much to advocate policy as to explore the advantages and disadvantages of working as volunteer and leader in the very busy Branch or in the very quiet sub-group – the problems of giving supervision, guidance and support, and the problems of morale. What are the likely changes in e.g. telecommunications and advertising?

> 'Not too little, not too much, but just right.'
>
> (The classic advertisement for Erasmic.)

(Workshop C 5)
What are the lessons and limits of Brenda?

The workshop explores the question of the Sexually Demanding Caller as a problem for Branches with a Brenda system and without one, especially as experienced by a male or female Leader responsible for female volunteers taking such calls. The problems that occur in referring such callers from a Branch without Brenda to a Branch with Brenda.

> 'But are they all horrid, are you sure they are all horrid?'
>
> (Catharine Morland in Jane Austen's *Northanger Abbey*.)

Fanaticism—CHAD VARAH

The Samaritans are listeners. Whatever their human failings in the world outside, when they come on duty they leave behind their self-regard and self-concern in order to be as far as possible what the clients wish them to be, need them to be. They have to accept the caller as he is, and befriend him whilst he seeks his own way forward at his own pace. That is why Samaritans are not permitted to try to 'sell' their own views or beliefs, which would not fit the caller and in his vulnerable, suggestible state could approximate to brainwashing or at the least deter him from frankness in confiding his doubts, fears and hopes.

The implacable opposition of The Samaritans to crisis intervention services dominated by religious bodies whose members may exhort instead of respecting the caller's own philosophy does not mean that devout believers (or supporters of a political party) are barred as volunteers. A person may hold firm religious or political convictions without being a fanatic. There are some religious sects or political parties which no one but a fanatic would join, but others whose rigid beliefs are imposed only on their own members, even though they may have some fanatical adherents who wish to impose them on everybody. The Samaritans themselves have principles which are binding on members.

How does one recognise a fanatic? He feels threatened if anyone disagrees with his pronouncements, and becomes anxious if any part of his beliefs is challenged, lest the whole structure be undermined. His satisfaction in imposing his ideology on others is short-lived and needs regular renewal. He would like to be a dictator whose decrees are obeyed without question. Some fanatics have been.

The fanatic tries to embody his beliefs in legislation, so that people who do not share them may be forced to act in accordance with them, or be punished. Nothing could be more contrary to the spirit of The Samaritans.

Three subjects on which fanatics try to impede the work of The Samaritans are abortion, homosexuality and pornography, all related to human sexuality and therefore emotive. It should be clear to all Samaritans that their private attitudes to these matters and the practice of themselves and their families are their own business. But fanatical attempts to impose these attitudes on the public at large, or to mention them to callers, absolutely disqualify the person from being a Samaritan.

The caller has been offered befriending, not indoctrination or condemnation. A caller with an unwanted pregnancy must be befriended and thus calmed sufficiently to consider what she wants to do about the situation. All possibilities should be frankly discussed. When she has made her choice, whether termination or continuing to term, she must be told where she can get expert advice and help. A Samaritan whose private religious convictions are totally against abortion has no problem about keeping these private and giving the information required. Naturally, because Samaritans believe in the caller's freedom of choice, as an organisation we have to be against removal of that freedom by making one of the options unavailable.

The homosexual caller must be befriended, and thus helped to find his or her way to a fuller sexual life such as a heterosexual is free to have, without any mention being made of any religious objections the volunteer may have been taught. As an organisation we cannot but be glad that the Wolfenden Committee recommendations were passed, decriminalising homosexual acts between consenting adults in private. Similar freedom for the autoerotic client dependent on pornography for his sexual gratification, recommended by the Williams Committee, must obviously be similarly welcomed by Samaritans as an organisation.

Our tenderness towards the clients, and our respect for their right (and indeed, duty) to make their own moral decisions, makes us many enemies. Let them all be outside, in the cruel world that drives the clients to seek refuge in Samaritan befriending.

O eloquent, just and mighty Death! Whom none could advise, thou hast persuaded; what none hath dared, thou hast done; and whom all the world hath flattered, thou onelie hast cast out of the world and despised. Thou hast drawne together all the farre stretched greatnesse, all the pride, crueltie, and ambition of man, and covered it all over with these two narrow words, *Hic jacet* . . .

Unfinished History of the World, SIR WALTER RALEIGH

List of Branches of The Samaritans in the United Kingdom and the Republic of Ireland

All the branches whose name is in bold type offer befriending 24 hours a day by one means or another. Those offering less than a 24-hour-a-day service have the name in small capitals.

Each branch has a serial number, which indicates its seniority. At international gatherings this number is followed by /1, signifying that the branch is part of The Samaritans Inc., i.e. is in the United Kingdom or the Republic of Ireland.

To the right of the serial number is a letter showing the category of service provided according to the following code:

A = at least two Samaritans on duty at the centre for telephone calls and for personal visits by clients 24 hours a day.

B = at least two Samaritans on duty at the centre for telephone calls 24 hours a day and for personal visits not less than 12 hours a day, with arrangements whereby one or more Samaritans may be sent to meet clients away from the centre during the hours when the centre is not open for face-to-face befriending.

C = same as B, but only one Samaritan on duty at the centre for not more than 3 difficult hours out of the 24.

D = same as C, but single-manning for not more than 9 hours out of the 24.

E = two Samaritans on duty at the centre for telephone calls and personal visits for not less than 12 hours a day, telephone calls being transferred (automatically or by an operator) for the remainder of the 24 hours either to another branch or to Samaritans on duty in their own homes.

F = a lesser service than the above, but providing attention 24 hours a day even if at times there is only one Samaritan on duty at the centre or if callers at certain times are transferred to the home of a Samaritan or are requested by a recorded message to ring another number.

G = double- or single-manning for 12 or more hours a day; no service at other times, but the nearest branch offering a 24-hour-a-day service advertised.

H = same as G, but manned for less than 12 hours a day.

Branches have been placed in the category nearest to that described in their replies to a questionnaire, so it is up to them to see that their service continues to match the classification.

The categories give an approximate indication of the *quantity* of service provided, and make no judgment of the *quality*. Category B is the norm to which branches should aspire, except that if there are more than two lines, double-manning is not enough – there should be a Samaritan to answer every telephone. Category A is perhaps not possible in big cities, where people wishing to sleep on the floor would be likely to prevent the branch functioning. One of the A branches admitted to taking one of the phones off the hook when a volunteer was busy interviewing, thus giving a poorer service than if it were B.

The number of branches in the various categories is: A, 12; B, 70; C, 39; D, 25; E, 6; F, 7; G, 6; H, 5.

The serial number not only indicates the branch's seniority (except in the case of associate branches, which use the number of the parent branch with a p = probationary or part-time), but also follows the individual Samaritan's own number in his or her branch at inter-branch meetings. At international gatherings a further number (given in the list headed Befrienders International) indicates the country in which the branch operates. Thus every

Samaritan in the world has a number in the form abc/def/gh which if unique to him or her, since the numbers are not re-used when people leave. E.g. Monica Dickens, author of *The Listeners*, began as 1222/1/1 (no. 1222 in the first branch in the British Isles), then became 12/1/12 (no. 12 in the first branch in the 12th country, New England, USA), and then 1/2/12, no. 1 in the second branch in that country).

The initials after the name of the town refer to the region to which the branch belongs. Until these regions are revised to give their representatives a reasonable number of branches to look after, the regions and their 1979–80 representatives are:

E = Eastern, Ted Davies; EM = East Midlands, Patrick Revell; I = Irish, Catherine Boyle; L = London, Susan Flint; NE = North East, Eric Miller; NW = North West, Roy Punton; S = Southern, Sylvia Montgomery; SC = Scotland, Kay McMillan; SE = South East, Brenda Bridge; SW = South West, Walter Fielding; WM = West Midlands, Frank Byrne; Y = Yorkshire, Albert Jewell.

The names in brackets after the regional designation are that of the person appointed by the Council of Management to be responsible for the branch, followed by that of the person elected by the branch to represent it on the Council of Management. Where there is only one name, the same person holds both offices. The names given are those for 1979–80.

Just as each full branch elects a member to the Council of Management of The Samaritans Inc., so each region elects one representative to the Executive Committee. These are listed above. Also on the Committee are the Officers and the Consultants.

In the list of branches, the telephone numbers given after the Director's name are either for all calls, or different for those seeking help and for other callers. Except in the cases of Tunbridge Wells and Wakefield, emergency numbers should not be cluttered up with business calls. Callers other than clients should use the office numbers, remembering that these will not be answered at times when the centre is not manned. Clients are requested not to use office numbers, which may be answered by someone who is not a Samaritan on duty to befriend them.

Where postcodes are given, the county (if mentioned) is in brackets, being no part of the postal address. Postcodes should form the last line of an address and be in capitals, not joined up, with a space between the two parts. Do *not* underline or punctuate postcodes.

The dialling codes given may in some cases not apply when ringing from the provinces. The codes given for places in the Republic of Ireland are not for use from outside that country. From the UK, substitute 0001 for 01 to dial Dublin, 0002 for 021 for Cork, 0005 for 051 for Waterford, 0006 for 061 for Limerick, and 0009 for 091 for Galway; otherwise dial 100 and ask the operator.

The Chairman of The Samaritans is Nancy Kerr and the Vice-Chairmen are John Eldrid, Nat Smith and Bob Withers.

The General Secretaries are Jean Burt and David Evans, 17 Uxbridge Road, Slough (Berks) SL1 1SN – telephone 75 32713.

6 B **Aberdeen** (Sc) (Helen Barron) 0224 574488/9 & 53990
The Samaritans, 60 Dee Street, Aberdeen AB1 2DS

163 C **Aberystwyth** (WM) (Norman Lloyd) 0970 4535 & 4567
The Samaritans, 5 Trinity Road, Aberystwyth, Dyfed SY23 1LU

ADDLESTONE – see Weybridge

AMERSHAM – see Chilterns

133 C **Ashford** (SE) (Ms Pat White) 0233 24606/7 & 29561
The Samaritans, 22 Beaver Road, Ashford (Kent) TN23 1RP

169 D **Ashington** (NE) (Brian Hays) 0670 814222 & 818717
The Samaritans, Central Hall, Woodhorn Road, Ashington (Northumberland) NE63 9TT

70p H AYR (Sc) (Jane Fison) 0292 84000 & 84548
The Samaritans, 23 St Leonard's Road, Ayr
Manned 19.00–22.00, other times answering machine refers callers to Kilmarnock

155 C **Ballymena** (I) (Harry Neill) 0266 43555 & 43556
The Samaritans, 45 Mount Street, Ballymena (Co. Antrim) BT43 6BP

32p G BANBURY (S) (Betty Garland) 0295 57575 & 57576
The Samaritans, Albert Street, Banbury (Oxon) OX16 8DG
Manned 11.30–08.00. Answering machine gives number of Oxford branch 08.00–11.30

143 A **Bangor and North Down** (I) (Joan Doherty) 0247 63036/7
The Samaritans, 92 Dufferin Avenue, Bangor (Co. Down) BT20 3AD

115 B **Barnsley** (Y) (Pam Gibson – Douglas Drye) 0226 83339, 83330 & 87888
The Samaritans, 11 Victoria Road, Barnsley S70 2BB

BARNSTAPLE – see North Devon

121 D **Barrow** (NW) (Roy Punton) 0229 25656 & 25799
The Samaritans of Furness, 16 Hartington Street, Barrow-in-Furness (Cumbria) LA14 5SL
Manned 10.00–08.00

87 D **Basildon and Thurrock** (E). (Prue Baker – Stephen Wright) 0268 412000 & 412044
The Samaritans, 16 Little Lullaway, Basildon (Essex) SS15 5JJ
Manned 11.00–23.00

139 D **Basingstoke** (S) (Kate Child) 0256 62333/4 & 21039
The Samaritans, 5 Essex Road, Basingstoke (Hants) RG21 1TA

52 B **Bath** (SW) (David West) 0225 29222 & 25353
The Samaritans, 2 New King Street, Bath (Avon) BA1 2BL

37 B **Bedford** (EM) (Robert Labe) 0234 52200 & 52317
The Samaritans, 69 Gwyn Street, Bedford MK40 1HH
(Associate Branch at MILTON KEYNES)

13 B **Belfast** (I) (Sydney Callaghan) 0232 24635/6 & 669944
The Samaritans, Thomson House, 46/48 Stranmillis Road, Belfast BT9 5AD

BEXHILL – see Hastings & Rother

25 B **Birmingham** (WM) (Doreen Fisher – Peter Calvert) 021 643 8001 & 2000
The Samaritans, 3 Brasshouse Passage, Broad Street, Birmingham B1 2HR

105 B **Blackburn** (NW) (Sheila Shaw) 0254 662424 & 667450
The Samaritans of Blackburn, Hyndborn and Ribble Valley, 105 New Park Street, Blackburn (Lancs) BB2 1DF

171 A **Blackpool** (NW) (Geoffrey Sherman) 0253 22218/9 & 22210
The Samaritans, 16 Edward Street, Blackpool, Lancs

118 A **Bognor Regis** (S) (Jill Dent) 024 33 26333/4 & 20544
The Samaritans, 13 Argyle Road, Bognor Regis (Sussex) PO21 1DY

68 D **Bolton** (NW) (Roland Arthur) 0204 21200 & 26666

The Samaritans, 16 Bark Street, Bolton (Lancs) BL1 2BQ
Manned 09.30–07.30

BOSTON – Associate group of Lincoln

9 B **Bournemouth** (S) (Roslyn Aish – Reg Maidment) 0202 21999 & 28090
The Samaritans of Mid-Wessex, Blue Pillars, Upper Terrace Road, Bournemouth (Hants) BH2 5NW

168 B **Bracknell** (S) (Avis Ellis) 0344 55555/6 & 21728
The Samaritans, Griffin House, High Street, Bracknell (Berks) RG12 1LB

15 B **Bradford** (Y) (Judith Avis) 0274 494949/0 & 498412
The Samaritans, 21 Marlborough Road, Manningham, Bradford BD8 7LD

82 B **Brent** (L) (Donald MacArthur) 01 459 8585 & 7382
The Samaritans of Brent, 7 Meyrick Road, London NW10 2EL

BRENTWOOD – see Chelmsford

173 C **Bridgend** (SW) (Stanley Stevens) 0656 62333 & 63867
The Samaritans, 14 Wyndham Street, Bridgend (Glam) CF31 1EF

BRIDGWATER – Associate group of Taunton

BRIDLINGTON – Associate group of Hull

137 C **Brierley Hill** (WM) (David Brown) 0384 78111 & 78780
The Samaritans, Hill Street, Brierley Hill (Staffs) DY5 2UE

99 D **Brighton** (SE) (Roy Waters) 0273 772277 & 726273
The Samaritans of Brighton, Hove & District, 102 Clarendon Road, Hove (Sussex) BN3 3WQ

48 A **Bristol** (SW) (Roy Pearson – Jack Colley) 0272 298787 & 298780
The Samaritans, 37 St Nicholas Street, Bristol BS1 1TP

BURNLEY – see Pendle

BURTON upon TRENT – Befriending group of Derby

131 B **Bury St Edmunds** (E) (Mike Howell – Ms Pat Lewis) 0284 2345 & 62161
The Samaritans, 46 Well Street, Bury St Edmunds (Suffolk) IP33 1EQ

BUXTON – Associate group of Macclesfield

23 B **Cambridge** (E) (Peggy Hadrill) 0223 64455/6 & 356420
The Samaritans, 1 Parker Street, Cambridge CB1 1JL

103 D **Canterbury** (SE) (Flavia Taylor) 0227 60000 & 62035
The Samaritans, 14 Ivy Lane, Canterbury (Kent) CT1 ITU

72 B **Cardiff** (SW) (Nan Nixon) 0222 44022/3 & 41459
The Samaritans, 18 Park Grove, Cardiff (Glam) CF1 3BN

112 E **Carlisle** (NW) (Tony Reffell) 0228 34567 & 28053
The Samaritans, 12 Corporation Road, Carlisle CA3 8XB
Manned 11.00–23.00

CENTRAL SCOTLAND – see Falkirk

CHATHAM – see Medway

69 D **Chelmsford** (E) (Sandra Watson) 0245 237357 & 355111
The Samaritans, 12 Critchett Terrace, Primrose Hill, Chelmsford (Essex) CM1 2QN

39 D **Cheltenham** (SW) (Gil Abel) 0242 515777 & 514488
The Samaritans, 3 Clarence Road, Pittville, Cheltenham (Glos) GL52 2AY

86 B **Chester** (NW) (David Coppack – Ken Skelton) 0244 22999 & 25885
The Samaritans, 36 Upper Northgate Street, Chester CH1 4EF

154 C **Chesterfield** (Y) (Clare Marston) 0246 70000 & 32407
The Samaritans, 2 Rose Hill, Chesterfield (Derbys) S30 1LW

93 C **Chilterns** (S) (Aubrey Morley) 02403 5000 & 21222
The Samaritans, 149 Station Road, Amersham (Bucks) HP6 6LZ

47 B **Colchester** (E) (Rosemary Powell-Davies) 0206 61234 & 61236
The Samaritans, Markham's Buildings, Vineyard Street, Colchester (Essex) CO2 7DG

116 H COLERAINE (I) (Donald McDonagh – Marjorie McKay) 0265 4545
The Samaritans, 33 Abbey Street, Coleraine (Co. Derry) BT51 3LA
Manned 10.00–13.00 & 19.00–22.00

125 B **Cork** (I) (Donal Dorney) (021 Cork) 21323 & 21325
The Samaritans, 11 Liberty Street, Cork, Ireland

57 B **Coventry** (WM) (Peter Wilson) 0203 22550 & 24900 & 21540
The Samaritans, 5a Priory Row, Coventry CV1 5EX

160 B **Craigavon** (I) (Betty Lawder – George Miskimmins) 0762 34136 & 34137
The Samaritans, 162 Thomas Street, Portadown (Co. Armagh) BT62 3BE

CRAWLEY – see Horsham

54 C **Crewe** (WM) (Glenys Jones) 0270 55500 & 213445
The Samaritans of South Cheshire, 99 Edlestone Road, Crewe CW2 7HP
Manned 09.30–07.00

28 B **Croydon** (L) (Cyril Franks – Kay Coulter) 01 681 6666/7
The Samaritans, 2b Kidderminster Road, West Croydon CR0 2UE

CUMBERNAULD – Associate group of Falkirk

92 B **Darlington** (NE) (Ted Cox) 0325 55353/4 & 50454
The Samaritans, 13 Woodland Road, Darlington DL3 7BJ

DARTFORD – in preparation

8 A **Derby** (WM) (Ms Pat Tinniswood) 0332 364444/5 & 48993
The Samaritans, 110 Burton Road, Derby DE1 1TG

152 C **Derry** (I) (John Evans) 0504 64061 & 64062
The Samaritans, 16 Clarendon Street, Derry BT48 7ET

33 C **Doncaster** (Y) (Peter Johnson) 0302 27474 & 65557
The Samaritans, 36 Thorne Road, Doncaster (Yorks) DN1 2JA

DORSET – see Weymouth

110 B **Dublin** (I) (Kevin O'Higgins – Joan Dillon) Dublin 778833/4 (U.K. code 0001)
The Samaritans, 66 South William Street, Dublin 2, Ireland

19 B **Dundee** (Sc) (Lawrence Williams – George Brown) 0382 26666/7 & 25678
The Samaritans, 28 South Tay Street, Dundee DD1 1PD

62 D **Dunfermline** (Sc) (Connie Muir – Alex Allan) 0383 22222 & 22271
The Samaritans, 30 Maygate, Dunfermline (Fife) KY12 7NS
Manned 11.00–07.00

122 B **Durham** (NE) (Sheila Roberts) 0385 63737 & 63777
The Samaritans of Central Durham, 26 Sutton Street, Durham DH1 4DW

128 D **Ealing** (L) (Betty Lowe) 01 579 6666
The Samaritans, 4 Windsor Road, Ealing, London W5 5PD

63 D **Eastbourne** (SE) (Vi Endacott – Douglas Warner) 0323 29933 & 24884
The Samaritans, 27 Susans Road, Eastbourne (Sussex) BN21 3LP

EAST SURREY and NORTH SUSSEX – see Reigate

2 E **Edinburgh** (Sc) (Mary Macdonald) 031 225 3333/5
The Samaritans, 54 Frederick Street, Edinburgh EH2 1LN
Manned 09.00–07.30

141 F **Elgin** (Sc) (Helen Barr-Cochrane) 0343 3000 & 2609
The Samaritans, 13 Commerce Street, Elgin, Morayshire
Manned 09.00–23.00

147 B **Enfield-Haringey** (L) (Brenda le Voi) 01 889 6888 & 3044
The Samaritans, 40 Queens Road, Bounds Green, London N11

42 B **Exeter** (SW) (Lady Angela Horsley – Jack Rycroft) 0392 77755 & 57572/3
The Samaritans, 2 Wynards, Magdalen Street, Exeter EX2 4HX

73 B **Falkirk** (Sc) (John Crocks) 0324 22066/7 & 20940
The Samaritans of Central Scotland, 2/4 Leslie Place, Kerse Lane, Falkirk (Stirlingshire) FK11 1RH

168p C **Farnborough** (Roy Dyer) 0252 513222/3 & 514405
The Samaritans, 41 Lynchford Road, Farnborough (Hants) GU14 6AN

149 FESTIVAL BRANCH (L) (Peter Woodley) 01 626 2277
c/o Lynn Taylor, c/o The Samaritans, 39 Walbrook, London EC4N 8BP

43 B **Folkestone** (SE) (Winifred Marshall – Cyril Griggs) 0303 55000 & 57262
The Samaritans, 65 Guildhall Street, Folkestone (Kent) CT20 1EJ

167 B **Galway** (I) (Luke Dillon-Mahon – Michael Higgins) 091 (Galway) 61222 & 61224
The Samaritans, 2 St Brendan's Avenue, Wood Quay, Galway, Ireland

4 B **Glasgow** (Sc) (Douglas Ferguson) 041 248 4488 & 7922
The Samaritans, 218 West Regent Street, Glasgow G2 4DQ

121X C **Gloucester** (SW) (Nan Willson) 0452 36333/4 & 32100
The Samaritans, Basement, 1 Belgrave Road, Gloucester GL1 1LT

GRANTHAM – Associate group of Lincoln

158 E **Great Yarmouth** (E) (Helen Smith – Nicholas Lawrence-Smith) 0493 2800 & 56658
The Samaritans, 62 North Quay, Great Yarmouth (Norfolk) NR30 1JB
Manned 09.00–23.00

56 C **Grimsby** (EM) (Christine Peterson) 0472 53111/2 & 55835
The Samaritans of Grimsby, Cleethorpes & District, 55 Alexandra Road, Grimsby (S. Humberside) DN31 1RD

30 F **Guernsey** (S) (Roy Harding) 0481 23731/2 & 23033 (Director 63061 any time)
The Samaritans, 2 Forest Lane, St Peter Port, Guernsey, CI
Manned 19.00–21.00, Weds. also 13.30–15.00

34 B **Guildford** (SE) (Grace Keirnan – James Wreford) 0483 72345/6 & 68333
The Samaritans, 69 Woodbridge Road, Guildford (Surrey) GU1 4RD

22 C **Halifax** (Y) (Michael Blackburn – Bill Dobby) 0422 58585/6 & 62020
The Samaritans, Warwick Chambers, 37 Southgate, Halifax (Yorks) HX1 1DL

136 C **Hamilton** (Sc) (Sandra Morrison – Robert Clark) 069 84 429411/2 & 420604
The Samaritans, 4 Selkirk Street, Hamilton (Lanarkshire) ML3 6RQ
Manned 09.00–07.30

HARLOW – see Herts/Essex

162 B **Harrogate** (Y) (Denys de la Hoyde) 0423 55655/6 & 57450
The Samaritans, 3 Mount Parade, Harrogate (Yorks) HG1 1BX

66 B **Harrow** (L) (Sue Erickson) 01 427 7777 & 863 7769
The Samaritans, 2 St John's Road, Harrow (Middx) HA1 2HA

111 C **Hartlepool** (NE) (Barbara Gainey) 0429 72929 & 66719
The Samaritans, 58 Avenue Road, Hartlepool (Cleveland) TS24 8AT

38 D **Hastings & Rother** (SE) (Delia Fox) 0424 436666 & 426622
The Samaritans, 26 St Andrews Square, Hastings TN34 1SR

16p G HAVERFORDWEST (SW) (Peggy Lawson) 0437 5536 & 5627
The Samaritans, 6 Tower Hill, Haverfordwest, Dyfed SA61 2LJ
Manned 14.00–07.00

64 B **Havering** (L) (Maggie Hawes) 0708 751111 & 40000 & 66600
The Samaritans of Havering, 107 North Street, Romford (Essex) RM1 4MT

HEMEL HEMPSTEAD – see Watford

135 B **Hereford** (WM) (Nan Raper) 0432 69000 & 55570
The Samaritans, 21 King Street, Hereford HR4 9BX

10 C **Herts/Essex** (E) (Faith Coles – Gavin Cooke) 0920 4099 & 61030
The Samaritans, 14 Cross Street, Ware (Herts) SG12 7AH

138 D **Hillingdon** (L) (Maureen Cornish – Doris Gibbons) 0895 (Uxbridge) 53355 & 34216
The Samaritans, Communicare, Redford Way, Uxbridge (Middx) UB8 1SZ

HITCHIN – see North Herts

140 C **Horsham** (SE) (Ernie Mouls) 0403 2271 & 2272 & 0293 (Crawley) 34549
The Samaritans of Horsham and Crawley, 21 Denne Road, Horsham (Sussex) RH12 1JE

98 C **Huddersfield** (Y) (Ken Chilvers) 0484 33388/9 & 28672
The Samaritans, 28 St Peter's Street, Huddersfield HD1 1RA

14 B **Hull** (Y) (Helen Buttle) 0482 23456 & 29477
The Samaritans, 75 Spring Bank, Hull (N. Humbers) HU3 1AG

ILFORD – see Redbridge

142 D **Inverness** (Sc) (Michael Haines) 0463 34000 & 31779
The Samaritans, 66 Tomnahurich Street, Inverness IV1 1JJ

29 B **Ipswich** (E) (Peter Hill – Ron Kenwright) 0473 51000 & 58488
The Samaritans, 19 Tower Street, Ipswich (Suffolk) IP1 3BE

172 G ISLE OF MAN (NW) (Peggy Pilsworth) 0624 (Douglas) 28211
The Samaritans, 9 Victoria Place, Douglas, IOM
Manned 17.00–08.00

ISLE OF WIGHT – see Portsmouth

11 F **Jersey** (S) (Daphne Minihane) 0534 25555/6 & 36880
The Samaritans, Waterloo Lane, St Helier, Jersey, CI
Manned 10.00–22.00

KETTERING – Associate group of Northampton

70 E **Kilmarnock** (Sc) (Jane Fison) 0563 31313/4 & 25353
The Samaritans of Ayrshire, 43 Titchfield Street, Kilmarnock KA1 1QS
Manned 09.00–07.00, Sat & Sun 24 hours

153 B **King's Lynn** (E) (Clare Cook) 0553 61616 & 3018
The Samaritans, 26 Queen Street, King's Lynn (Norfolk) PE30 1HT

97 A **Kingston on Thames** (L) (Frank Giles – Ms Ben Finney) 01 399 6676/7 & 390 0610
The Samaritans, 12 St Andrew's Road, Surbiton (Surrey) KT6 4TD

164 F **Kirkcaldy** (Sc) (Walter Todd – Cecil Ritchie) 0592 65444 & 69501
The Samaritans, 46 St Clair Street, Kirkcaldy KY1 2QE
Manned 11.00–07.30, automatic transfer 07.30–11.00

132 C **Lancaster** (NW) (Ann Catchpole – Bernice Boardley) 0524 61666 & 69229
The Samaritans, 21 Sun Street, Lancaster LA1 1EW

58 B **Leatherhead** (SE) (Derek Swaine) 03723 75555/6
The Samaritans, 7 Church Road, Leatherhead (Surrey) KT22 8AT

79 B **Leeds** (Y) (Malcolm Robinson) 0532 34567 & 39081
The Samaritans, 93 Clarendon Road, Leeds LS2 9LY

65 F **Leek** (WM) (Harold Scott) 0538 384100 & 384527
The Samaritans, 34 Fountain Street, Leek (Staffs) ST13 6JR
Manned 16.00–23.00, Wed & Sat also 09.00–16.00

44 A **Leicester** (EM) (Mike McIntyre) 0533 700007/8/9, 700000 & 705500
The Samaritans, 1a Elmfield Avenue, Leicester LE2 1RB

100 B **Lewisham** (L) (Yvonne Earle – Joy Drewett-Bourne) 01 692 2266 & 5228 & 3330
The Samaritans, 134/6 Lewisham Way, London SE14 6PD

159 D **Limerick** (I) (Terence O'Brien) 061 (Limerick) 42111 & 42000
The Samaritans, 25 Upper Cecil Street, Limerick, Ireland

74 C **Lincoln** (EM) (Triss Bell) 0522 28282 & 23400
The Samaritans, 17 Hungate, Lincoln LN1 1ES

3 B **Liverpool** (NW) (Duncan Perry) 051 708 8888 & 709 2212
The Samaritans of Liverpool & Merseyside, 21 Clarence Street, Liverpool L3 5TN

1 B **London** (L) (John Eldrid) 01 626 2277 (4 lines) for all calls (01 626 9000 also retained)
The Samaritans, 39 Walbrook, London EC4N 8BP

In addition to the London Central branch, the London Region includes the branches at Brent, Croydon, Ealing, Enfield-Haringey, Harrow, Havering, Hillingdon, Kingston, Lewisham, Orpington, Putney and Redbridge (q.v.)

LONDONDERRY – see Derry

LOUTH – Befriending group of Grimsby

120 A **Lowestoft** (E) (Gordon Mitchell) 0502 2800 & 63010
The Samaritans of Lowestoft and Waveney, 14 Beach Road, Lowestoft (Suffolk) NR32 1EA

77 C **Luton** (E) (Margaret Rees – Stanley Smith) 0582 20666 & 36110
The Samaritans, 32 Napier Road, Luton (Beds) LU1 1RF

80 C **Macclesfield** (NW) (Angela Tingey) 0625 26000 & 27000 & 610112
The Samaritans, 1 Exchange Street East, Macclesfield, Cheshire

MAIDENHEAD – see Slough

157 D **Maidstone** (SE) (Bob Jesshope) 0622 674444/5 & 64027
The Samaritans, 48 Grecian Street, Maidstone (Kent) ME14 2TS

MALDON – Associate group of Chelmsford

7 B **Manchester** (NW) (Hilary Forrest) 061 834 9000 & (until the move) 832 4688
The Samaritans, Livesey Street, M4 5HF; moving to 87 Oldham Street, Manchester M4 1LW

126 C **Mansfield** (EM) (Arthur Annabel – Ms Rob Scholey) 0623 31515/6 & 641904
The Samaritans, la Grove Street, Mansfield (Notts) NG18 1EL

76 B **Medway** (SE) (Bill Bridges) 0634 44846 & 42222
The Samaritans, 42 Ross Street, Rochester (Kent) ME1 2DF

MERSEYSIDE – see Liverpool

MIDDLESBROUGH – see Teesside

37p G MILTON KEYNES (E) (Mary Fitch) 0908 313131
The Samaritans, 6 Church Street, Wolverton, Milton Keynes, Bucks
Manned 09.00–23.00, other times machine refers callers to Bedford

NELSON – see Pendle

NEWBURY – see Reading

67 C **Newcastle** (NE) (Judith Hunt – Bill Short) 0632 27272 & 21523
The Samaritans of Tyneside, 144 Westgate Road, Newcastle-on-Tyne NE1 4AQ

90 C **Newport** (SW) (Alwyne Fuller) 0633 59000 & 62439/4
The Samaritans of Newport and Gwent, 43 Stow Hill, Newport (Gwent) NPT 1JH

144 G NEWRY (I) (Maeve O'Reilly) 0693 2633 & 5013
The Samaritans, 11 Lower Catherine Street, Newry, Co. Down
Manned 10.00–13.00 & 16.00–08.30, other times calls transferred to Belfast

59 E **Northallerton** (NE) (Ann Rider) 0609 6161/2
The Samaritans of Northallerton & The Dales, 7 Crosby Road, Northallerton (Yorks) DL6 1AA
Manned 09.00–21.00

95 C **Northampton** (EM) (Maurice Walton) 0604 715555 & 711000
The Samaritans, 15 Birchfield Road, Northampton NN1 4RF

88 C **North Devon** (SW) (Trevor Harris – Ms Marsh Taylor) 0271 4343 & 4290
The Samaritans of North Devon, 2 Summerland Street, Barnstaple (Devon) EX32 8JJ

146 C **North Herts** (E) (Olive Whenn) 0462 55333 & 53100
The Samaritans of N. Herts & Stevenage, 5 Nunns Close, Hitchin (Herts) SG5 1EP

NORTH SUSSEX and EAST SURREY – see Reigate

78 H NORTHWICH (NW) (Christopher Sampson – George Agar) 0606 3211/2 & 3513
The Samaritans of Mid-Cheshire, 1 St Paul's Place, Witton Street, Northwich (Cheshire) CW9 5DZ
Manned 09.30–15.30 and 19.00–22.30 (Sun not 09.30–15.30), other times calls transferred automatically to Manchester

46 A **Norwich** (E) (Brian Garrood) 0603 611311 & 613055
The Samaritans, 19 St Stephen's Square, Norwich NR1 3SS

18 B **Nottingham** (EM) (John Carter) 0602 40506 & 46464
The Samaritans, 2a Standard Hill, Nottingham NG1 5HQ

161 E **Omagh** (I) (Una Hunt – Edith Hadden) 0662 44944/5
The Samaritans, 20 Campsie Road, Omagh (Co. Tyrone) BT79 0AG
Manned 10.00–12.00 & 14.00–08.00

71 D **Orpington** (L) (Barbara Swinyard – Margaret Colson) 0689 33999 & 33000 & 29262
The Samaritans, 9b Station Road, Orpington (Kent) BR6 0RZ

32 B **Oxford** (S) (Andrew Meynell – Ms Bronac Holderness) 0865 722122/3 & 44044
The Oxford Samaritans, 123 Iffley Road, Oxford OX4 1EJ
(Associate branch at BANBURY)

151 C **Pendle** (NW) (Enid Lord – Joan Silver) 0282 694929 & 693025
The Samaritans of Pendle and Burnley, 15 Market Square, Nelson, Lancs

113 C **Perth** (Sc) (Elizabeth Irvine) 0738 26666 & 27826
The Samaritans, 59 King Street, Perth PH1 5TF

119 F **Peterborough** (EM) (Marielyn Hollowell) 0733 64848 & 65936
The Samaritans, 41 Eastfield Road, Peterborough PE1 4AP
Manned 09.00–07.300, Sat & Sun 24 hours

134 B **Plymouth** (DW) (Liz Carter) 0752 21666 & 21759
The Samaritans, 20 Oxford Place, off Western Approach, Plymouth PL1 5AJ

17 B **Portsmouth** (S) (Shiela Langford) 0705 691313/4/5 & 65241
The Samaritans of Portsmouth & District & Isle of Wight, 296 London Road, North End, Portsmouth (Hants) PO2 9JN

109 A **Preston** (NW) (Ada Forshaw – Elizabeth Shepherd) 0772 22022 & 59000
The Samaritans, 11 St Wilfred Street, Preston (Lancs) PR1 2US

123 C **Putney** (L) (Maureen Burgess) 01 789 535 & 0544
The Samaritans, 106 Felsham Road, Putney, London SW15

24 C **Reading** (S) (Tony Giles) 0734 54845/6 & 57318
The Samaritans, Trinity Church Hall, Sidmouth Street, Reading (Berks) RG1 4QX

81 D **Redbridge** (L) (David Wilkins) 01 478 7273
The Samaritans, 2a Woodlands Road, Ilford (Essex) IG1 1JJ

53 B **Reigate** (SE) (Tim Spinney) 073 72 48444/5
The Samaritans of East Surrey, 42 Holmesdale Road, Reigate (Surrey) RH2 0BQ

RETFORD – Associate group of Lincoln

145 B **Rhyl** (NW) (Mabel Owen – Marie Nuttall) 0745 54544 & 54917
The Samaritans of Clwyd & Gwynedd, 23 Bedford Street, Rhyl LL18 1SY

83 H ROCHDALE (NW) (Derek Parsons) 0706 59999 & 31181
The Samaritans, 4 Oldham Road, Rochdale, Lancs
Manned 18.00–24.00. Manchester also advertised

ROCHESTER – see Medway

ROMFORD – see Havering

ROTHERHAM – Associate group of Sheffield

RUGBY – Associate group of Coventry

26 C **Salisbury** (S) (Adelaide Oates) 0722 23355 & 3708
The Samaritans, The Samaritan Centre, St Martin's, Church Street, Salisbury (Wilts) SP1 2BP

148 B **Scarborough** (Y) (Stanley Chapman) 0723 68888 & 68368
The Samaritans, 35a St Nicholas Cliff, Scarborough, YO11 2ES (All correspondence: PO Box 999, Scarborough, Yorks)

130 SCOTTISH CORRESPONDENCE BRANCH (Sc) (William Aitken – David Arthur) 0786 (Dunblane) 823650
PO Box 9, Stirling FK8 2BT

49 B **Scunthorpe** (EM) (Geoffrey Ward) 0724 60000 & 62757
The Samaritans, 31 Dunstall Street, Scunthorpe (S. Humberside) DN15 6JZ

61 B **Sheffield** (Y) (Margaret Platts) 0742 77277/8 & 77279
The Samaritans, 30 Rockingham Lane, Sheffield S1 4FW
(Associate groups at Rotherham & Worksop)

SHEPPEY – Befriending group of Medway

SHERBORNE – see Yeovil

51 D **Shrewsbury** (WM) (Ms Pat Ross) 0743 69696/7 & 52401
The Samaritans, 4a St Alkmunds Place, Shrewsbury (Salop) SY1 1UH

SITTINGBOURNE – Befriending group of Medway

102 D **Slough** (S) (Nan Macara – Di Bowen) 0753 31011/2
The Samaritans of Slough, Windsor & Maidenhead, 13 Bath Road, Slough (Berks) SL1 3UF

150 B **Solihull** (WM) (Cynthia Leonard) 021 704 2255 & 705 8848
The Samaritans, 9 Herbert Road, Solihull B91 32E

35 C **Southampton** (S) (Mary Millier – Barbara Killick) 0703 32888/9 & 34659
The Samaritans, 64 St Andrew's Road, Southampton SO2 0BA

75 D **Southend on Sea** (E) (Bernard Crix) 0702 42200 & 43739
The Samaritans, 54 Hamlet Road, Southend on Sea (Essex) SS1 1HH

170 B **Southport** (NW) (Don Rawlings) 0704 38038 & 38488
The Samaritans, 152a Lord Street, Southport (Lancs) PR9 0QA

40 G STAFFORD (WM) (Lynn Winmill) 0785 55333 & 55337
The Samaritans, Chell Road, Stafford ST16 2QA
Manned 10.00–08.00, Sat and Sun 24 hours

STEVENAGE – see North Herts

STOCKTON – see Teesside

21 F **Stoke on Trent** (WM) (Carole Holder) 0782 23555 & 23202
The Samaritans of North Staffordshire, 3 Shelton New Road, Shelton, Stoke on Trent (Staffs) ST1 4PF
Manned 10.30–08.00, Sat & Sun 24 hours

108 C **Sunderland** (NE) (Sheila Coggrave – Allen Bird) 0783 77177 & 77427
The Samaritans, 4 Vine Place, Sunderland SR1 3NE

16 A **Swansea** (SW) (Prudence Edwards) 0792 55999 & 52589
The Samaritans, 5 Willows Place, Swansea (Glam) SA1 6AA

91 B **Swindon** (S) (Dinah Moon) 0793 37373/4
The Samaritans, 37a Regent Street, Swindon (Wilts) SN1 1JL

94 B **Taunton & Somerset** (SW) (Carol Wren) 0823 5242 & 89456
The Samaritans, 16 Wood Street, Taunton (Somerset) TA1 1UN

96 B **Teesside** (NE) (Norman Keir – Ewen Hatchwell) 0642 21777 & 247614
The Samaritans, 147 Borough Road, Middlesbrough (Cleveland) TS1 3AT

156 B **Telford** (WM) (Antoinette Wright) 0952 48888/9 & 47627
The Samaritans, 115 King Street, Wellington, Telford TF1 1NU

THANET – Associate group of Canterbury

55 B **Torbay** (SW) (Bob French) 0803 (Torquay) 25355 & 25850

The Samaritans, 21 Warren Road, Torquay (Devon) PQ2 5TQ

114 D **Truro** (SW) (Keith Duffelin – Ted Barton) 0872 77277
The Samaritans, 19 Treyew Road, Truro (Cornwall) TR1 2BY

85 B **Tunbridge Wells** (SE) (Elizabeth Samson – Jean Ross) 0892 32323
The Samaritans, 7 Lime Hill Road, Tunbridge Wells, Kent

TYNESIDE – see Newcastle

124 B **Wakefield** (NE) (Joan Nettleton) 0924 77011
The Samaritans, 1/3 Jacob's Well Lane, Wakefield WF1 3NN

106 C **Walsall** (WM) (Keith Greenaway) 0922 24000 & 20000 & 611805
The Samaritans, Bott Lane, Walsall WS1 2JQ

WALTHAM FOREST – Associate group of Redbridge

WARE – see Herts/Essex

104 D **Warrington** (NW) (Tom Ireland) 0925 38808/9
The Samaritans, 107 Sankey Street, Warrington WA1 1NN

166 A **Waterford** (I) (Mona Halligan) 051 (Waterford) 72114 & 76099
The Samaritans, 1 Waterside, Waterford, Ireland

107 B **Watford** (E) (Graham White) 0923 33333 & 32344
The Samaritans, 2 Local Board Road, Watford (Herts) WD1 1LJ

WESTON-SUPER-MARE – Associate group of Bristol

50 B **Weybridge** (SE) (Margaret Whitaker) 0932 44444 & 47622 & 81 (Staines) 62200
The Samaritans of North West Surrey, Samaritan Centre, Woburn Hill, Addlestone, Surrey KT15 2QB

117 C **Weymouth** (S) (Ron Price – Elizabeth Blades) 030 57 71777/8 & 70910
The Samaritans of Dorset, 13 King Street, Weymouth, Dorset, DT4 7BJ

84 H WHITEHAVEN (NW) (Bernard Sweeney) 0946 4266 & 3370
The Samaritans of West Cumbria, 9 Church Street, Whitehaven (Cumbria) CA28 0AY
Manned 19.00–23.00 (Mon to Fri) 19.00–21.00 (Sat)

127 D **Wigan** (NW) (Derek Wade – Dilys Hall) 0942 491222/3 & 47303
The Samaritans, 73 Dicconson Street, Wigan, Lancs

165 B **Winchester** (S) (Alan Jones – Elaine Constable) 0962 60633 & 2555
The Samaritans, 10 Parchment Street, Winchester (Hants) SO22 6RN

WINDSOR – see Slough

WITHAM – Associate group of Chelmsford

60 B **Wolverhampton** (WM) (John Parker) 0902 26422/3 & 26424
The Samaritans, 181 Newhampton Road East, Wolverhampton WV1 4PQ

36 B **Worcester** (WM) (Mike Taylor – Michael Stewart) 0905 21121 & 28961
The Samaritans, 9 Sansome Place, Worcester

WORKSOP – Associate group of Sheffield

101 B **Worthing** (SE) (Gwen Evans) 0903 205555/6 & 35757
The Samaritans, 2 Lennox Road, Worthing (Sussex) BN11 1DA

129 C **Yeovil** (SW) (Joyce Best) 0935 6455 & 23466
The Samaritans of Yeovil & Sherborne, 10 Everton Road, Yeovil (Somerset) BA20 14F

89 B **York** (Y) (Sylvia Maynard) 0904 55888 & 26952
The Samaritans, 89 Nunnery Lane, York YO2 1AH

List of Branches of Befrienders International (The Samaritans Worldwide outside the British Isles)

Branches of Befrienders International are printed in bold type, with the name of each branch preceded by a number, indicating its seniority and of the country to which it belongs. The number to the right of the oblique is that of the country, according to the following code:

2 = Hong Kong and Macau
3 = India
4 = Zimbabwe-Rhodesia
5 = Pakistan
6 = New Zealand
7 = Australia
8 = Poland
9 = Brazil
10 = Singapore
11 = Malaysia
12 = New England, USA
13 = Republic of South Africa
14 = Zambia
15 = Sri Lanka
16 = France
17 = Spain
18 = Sweden
19 = Austria
20 = Mauritius
21 = Argentina
22 = Trinidad and Tobago

23 = Minnesota, USA
24 = Uruguay
25 = Japan
26 = Thailand
27 = Surinam
28 = Egypt
29 = Barbados
30 = Chile
31 = Venezuela
32 = Italy
33 = Colombia

It so happens that at the time of going to press there is a great number of places where active preparations are being made to start a branch but it is not yet possible to give an address and telephone number for suicidal and other despairing people to use. In these cases, the name of the town is given in small capitals, and the name of our correspondent or convenor is given if he or she would welcome offers of help or recommendations of potential Samaritans in the vicinity.

There are many suicide prevention and crisis intervention centres throughout the world now using the method of Befriending (discovered and pioneered by Chad Varah in London in 1953) which has enabled Great Britain and Western Australia to reduce their suicide rates dramatically. Most of these centres with which we are not formally affiliated are not known to us, but some are known and are included in the following list with the qualification 'Independent of us'. San Mateo, for example, has had a 'Befriending Program' since 1974; in Japan, branches of Inochi no Denwa seem to any Samaritan visitor to be 'just like us'; Orlando, Ottawa and Scarborough have made Chad Varah an honorary member, and Vancouver was founded after his visit in 1967. We shall be glad to include in the next edition any centres which give primacy to Befriending, i.e. the *first* person encountered by the client is not a professional or expert but a befriender, a fellow human being who will listen with acceptance and personal concern so as to strengthen the client's ability to find his or her way out of the crisis. If they wish to join and be recognised by Befrienders International (as some on the list already do), they must satisfy us that they are truly befrienders working in accordance with the Twenty Principles of The Samaritans.

We hope that our next edition may see active branches in the places which are at present 'in preparation', and in other towns as yet not listed. Our expansion depends to some extent on luck, such as our training someone to start a branch in Iceland who is then transferred to the Philippines, but mostly it depends on the effort and initiative of our Continental Representatives and of the members of the extension committees in those countries which are nationally organised.

In Africa, our Representative Graham Piearce of Kitwe (q.v.) has had to concentrate on trying to set up a national organisation in Zambia like the one in Zimbabwe-Rhodesia (which has doubled the number of branches), and will need to be assisted by people in the East, South and West and possibly the North. The Republic of South Africa needs only one more branch to qualify for its own national organisation.

In America Central and South, our Representative Jacques Conchon of São Paulo has not only (with a little help from the Chairman) quadrupled the number of branches in Brazil, which he has made our fastest-growing country, but has also got all the Spanish-speaking countries of South America to prepare branches, those in the Argentine and Uruguay being already in operation. Clearly, all he needs is a Spanish assistant and the transfer of the Guianas and Central America (along with Mexico, from America North) to a new Caribbean area.

Jacques Conchon's outstanding work received an ovation at The Samaritan's annual Conference at the University of York in September 1979, when 1,000 Samaritans were assembled for the first time, and it has been recognised by his being appointed Vice-Chairman of Befrienders International.

In America North, our Representative Sally Casper, who during her term of office had the advantage of five months' work in England, has seen the beginning of the longed-for spread of our work in the USA, with hopeful signs outside New England. In the spring of 1980 The Samaritans of New England will be formed from the present three branches. If we take the futurologists' three conurbations as our most urgent targets, Boswash is on the move and will be greatly strengthened by the transfer of our psychiatric consultant Dr Richard Fox to New York; Chipit is making a start with our budding branch in Chicago; and we have allies in Sansan.

In Asia East, our Representative Andrew Tu of Hong Kong is a public figure in the fields of education and refugee problems, as well as in suicide prevention, and has concerned himself very much with the 'boat people' as well as with students who have failed their examinations. He has rightly concentrated on making the colony's two branches effective. The rest of East Asia is unpromising, except for Thailand. Japan is independent of us and Taiwan belongs at the time of writing to an exclusively Christian organisation called Life Line. Singapore has its own national organisation of The Samaritans.

In Asia West, our Representative Vijayan Pavamani has understandably had his hands full with the endless problems of Calcutta, where he is launching out into other enterprises. He has not been able to spread the work even in the rest of India, except for some preparation in Madras. India, Malaysia and Sri Lanka are expected shortly to have their own national organisations, and the Arab world may best be linked with North Africa. Israel has joined the European organisation IFOTES.

In Australasia, David Woodroffe of Perth took over from John McKechnie as our Representative for Australia, New Zealand having achieved a national organisation, as indeed has Western Australia. Both are making great endeavours to extend to all the major centres of population. Les Freeman is our New Zealand Representative.

In Europe, Befrienders International has a committee formed of representatives of all the countries where Samaritans are at work, with Tadeusz Kielanowski of Poland as Representative in addition to the Chairman.

The Samaritans Inc. also promotes Befriending through its

membership of IFOTES, of which Ellen Balaszeskul of West Berlin is the President and John Eldrid of London, who represents The Samaritans Inc. on the committee of Befrienders International, is a Vice-President. Expansion in most of Europe is inhibited by the existence of other crisis-intervention organisations, whose use of Befriending varies from place to place.

Most of the expansion of our work during our first five years of independence has arisen from the extensive journeys made by the President of Befrienders International, Chad Varah, who is also the elected Chairman of the Intercontinental Committee. Whilst some others have visited existing branches, he has made a point of including in his itineraries places where there is a chance of initiating new work, often visiting the same place more than once.

All the places in the list have been visited by Chad Varah, except Albany, Belém, Évora, Gwelo, Kelowna, Lobatse, Martha's Vineyard, Memphis, Oporto, Port-au-Prince, Port Hedland, St Nom La Breteche, St Thomas, Tarawa and Trivandrum.

ACCRA, Ghana – in preparation. Correspondent: Mrs Julia Sowu, Royal Military Hospital

5/7 **Albany**, Western Australia (Carl Bylund) 098-41 4777
The Samaritans, POB 991, Albany, WA 6330

ALICE SPRINGS, Northern Territory, Australia – in preparation.
Correspondent: Ted Marron, POB 3, Alice Springs, NT 5750; tel. 21024

18/9 **Aracatuba**, Brazil (Mirson Duarte)
CVV-Samaritanos, POB 380, CEP 16100

ASUNCION, Paraguay – in preparation. Correspondent: Dr Mario Aguayo Zayas, Av. Carlos Antonio López 1802

ATHENS, Greece – in preparation. Correspondent: George Assimakis, 58 Odos Anagnostopoulou, Athens 135
(There is also Telefoniké Symparástase, POB 3358; tel. 644 2211)

BAHRAIN, Arabia – in preparation. Correspondent: Dr Ramzy Fayez, c/o The Red Crescent

5/3 **Bangalore**, India (R. Somarsekhar & G. Gajendra)
The Samaritans, c/o Somarsekhar, 33 DBI Colony, Sarakki Layout, Kanakapura Road, Bangalore 560011
(There is also Suicide Prevention, c/o Dr Joyce Siromani, St Mark's Hospital, Bangalore)

1/26 **Bangkok**, Thailand (John Taylor & Don Willis) 235 4000
The Samaritans, 14 Pramuan Road

BARBADOS – see Bridgetown

3/9 **Barra Funda**, Brazil (Joel Beraldo) 826 1025
CVV-Samaritanos, Rua Vitorino Carmilo 717, Anexo ao Pronto Socorro, Barra Funda, CEP 02253, São Paulo, SP

2/20 **Beau Bassin**, Mauritius (Iboo Mansoor & Charlie Yip Tong)
The Samaritans, 16 Leishman Street

BEER-SHEVA, Israel
(Independent of us, branch of ERAN; tel. 057 32111)

23/9 **Belém**, Brazil – in preparation (José Fernándes da Silva)
CVV-Samaritanos, Travessa 1° de Março 241, Sala 106, CEP 66000 Belém, Pará.

8/9 **Belo Horizonte**, Brazil (Anastaçio Valdyr Chaer) 442 0505

CVV-Samaritanos (Grupo Mensageiros da Amizade 'Gruma'), Rua Guaranésia 164, Floresta, CEP 30000 Belo Horizonte, MG

2/17 **Benidorm**, Spain (Ken Warren) 85 1125
The Samaritans (Amigos Internacionales), Alameda 22, Benidorm (Alicante)

1/13 **Bloemfontein**, Republic of South Africa (Pam Williams) 83000
The Samaritans, 304/305 CNA Building, Maitland Street, Bloemfontein 9301 (Orange Free State), or POB 2201
Manned 18.00–23.00, week-ends also 15.00–18.00

1/3 **Bombay**, India (Sarah Dastoor) 379846
The Samaritans, Seva Niketan, Sir J. Jeejibhai Road, Byculla, Bombay 400008

1/12 **Boston**, USA (Shirley Karnovsky & Sally Casper) (617) 0220 & 536 2460
The Samaritans, 802 Boylston Street, MA 02199
Manned 00.00–24.00, visits 09.00–22.00

12/9 **Brasilia**, Brazil (Oyanarte Portilho) 243 3939
CVV-Samaritanos, Av.W5 Sul Q909 Mod.29, Brasilia DF

BRIDGETOWN, Barbados, WI – in preparation. Correspondents: Dr Jane Yeo, Veronda, Brownes Gap, Hustings, Christchurch & Sheila Hoad, 25 Blue Waters, Rockley, Christchurch

BRUSSELS, Belgium
(Independent of us: CHS, Rue St Georges 102, Box 20, 1050 Brussels; tel. (02) 648 4014)

BUDAPEST, Hungary – in preparation. Correspondent: Erika Meszaros, Jeszenek u. 66, 1171 Budapest XIV

(There is also Suicide Prevention, c/o Dr Miklos Kun, Keleti-Karoly u. 27, Budapest 1024; tel. 358 398)

BUENOS AIRES, Argentina (Alfredo Gazzano & Haydee Lange)
(Independent of us: Centro de Asistencia al Suicida, Casilla Correo 1603, Correo Central)

2/4 **Bulawayo**, Zimbabwe-Rhodesia (David Broomfield) 65000 & 65010
The Samaritans, POB 806

2/7 **Bunbury**, Western Australia (Jim Raynor) 097 21 1000
The Samaritans, 99 Victoria Street, Bunbury, WA 6230

1/34 **Busan**, South Korea (Dongsu Kim)
Saengmyung Eui Chunhwa, 48 1-ka Daechung-dong, Choongku, Busan 600

BYDGOSZCZ, Poland
(Independent of us, c/o Wladyslaw Sinkiewicz, Chodkiewicza 30; tel. 246/7/8)

1/28 **Cairo**, UAR (Emile Samaan)
The Befrienders, c/o 17 Koubbeh Street, Heliopolis

2/3 **Calcutta**, India (Vijayan Pavamani) 247 832
The Samaritans, 17 Road Street, Calcutta 700016

24/9 **Campina Grande**, Brazil – in preparation
CVV-Samaritanos

CAPE COD – see Falmouth

CARACAS, Venezuela – in preparation. Correspondent: Sra Glenys Rondon, Av.Fco. Solano, Res.Sansouci, Edif. El Pardillo, apto. 48, Chacaito

CHICAGO, USA – in preparation. Correspondent: Selina Reed, 5227 South University Drive, Chicago, Ill. 60615; tel. (312) 752 2274

1/15 **Colombo**, Sri Lanka (Nalini Ellawala & Sam Salviah) 92909
Sri Lanka Sumithrayo, 60B Horton Place, Colombo 7

1/22 **Curepe**, Trinidad, WI (Lucy Gabriel) 662 5172
Lifeline (The Befrienders of Trinidad and Tobago), Corner of Francis and Sellier Streets, Curepe; or POB 1224, Port of Spain

17/9 **Curitiba**, Brazil (Eloi Beraldo)
CVV-Samaritanos, POB 4144, CEP 80000 Curitiba, Paraná

DARWIN, Northern Territory, Australia – in abeyance

DEBRECEN, Hungary
(Independent of us, Suicide Prevention, Museum u. 4)

DELHI, India – see New Delhi

DERBY, Western Australia – in preparation

2/13 **East London**, Rep. of South Africa (Michael Barbour) 29028
The Samaritans, POB 1548, Eastern Province Building, Argyll Street

ÉVORA, Portugal – in preparation. Correspondent: Maria Helena Pedreza, Tapada do Ramalho, Talhao 4-1 esq., 7000 Évora

2/12 **Falmouth**, Mass., USA (Monica Dickens, Miriam Chader, Charles L. Hoffman & Dolores Patch) (617) 548 8900
The Samaritans of Cape Cod, Chamber of Commerce

Building, Academy Lane, Falmouth, MA 02541; & POB 65
Associate groups at Martha's Vineyard, tel. (617) 793 4100 and at Mid-Cape, tel. (617) 771 7770

FIJI – see Suva

9/9 **Foz do Iguaçu**, Brazil – in preparation

FREDERICTON, NB, Canada (Linda Beebe)
(Independent of us, Chimo Help Center, POB 1033, Fredericton E3B 5C2)

FUENGIROLA, Spain – in abeyance. Correspondent: Mrs Helen Scott, Apartado 174; tel. 863 060

1/8 **Gdansk**, Poland (Tadeusz Kielanowski) 31 00 00
Anonimowy Przyjaciel, ul. Piwna 36

GEORGETOWN, Guyana – in preparation. Correspondent: The Rev. Gilbert Harris, Transfiguration Vicarage, NE La Pénitence, Greater Georgetown

4/7 **Geraldton**, Western Australia (Margaret Harget) 099 21 4411
The Samaritans, 145 Marine Terrace, Geraldton, WA 6530
Manned 18.00–24.00

GILBERT & ELLICE ISLANDS – see Tarawa

14/9 **Goiânia**, Brazil (Jesús Oliveira) 223 4025
CVV-Samaritanos, Rua 72 No. 277, CEP 74000

1/18 **Göteborg**, Sweden (Greta Meyersberg) 112400 & 112422
Någon att tala med Samaritans, Västergatan 1A, 411 23 Göteborg

GOTHENBURG, Sweden – see Göteborg

GRANADA, WI – see St George's

5/6 **Greymouth**, New Zealand (Jewel Thompson) 6611
The Samaritans, 9 Herbert Street, Greymouth, South Island; or POB 448

GUAYAQUIL, Ecuador – in preparation. Correspondent: Sr Nicanor Marqués de la Plata, Casilla 3895

4/4 **Gwelo**, Zimbabwe-Rhodesia (Roy Rabey) 4040
The Samaritans, POB 89

HAIFA, Israel
(Independent of us; Ezrah Rishona Nafshit, Haifa)

HAITI – see Port-au-Prince

HARARI, Zimbabwe-Rhodesia: associate group of Salisbury

HAWAII – see Honolulu

HONG KONG – see Kowloon and Wanchai

HONOLULU, Hawaii, USA
Independent of us: Suicide and Crisis Center: Jean Lee, tel. 521 4555)

4/6 **Hutt Valley**, New Zealand (Jim Howcroft) 664 591 & 664 252
The Samaritans of Hutt Valley, 69 Woburn Road, Lower Hutt, North Island; or POB 27294, Wellington

2/11 **Ipoh**, West Malaysia (Leela Balasingam) 73405
The Befrienders, Servants' Quarters, behind the Anglican Church

ISTANBUL, Turkey – in abeyance

ITAIPU, Brazil – see Foz do Iguaçu

19/9 **Jacarei,** Brazil (Carlos Morães) 512 717
CVV-Samaritanos, Praça Tres Poderes 510, CEP 12300

JAFFA, Israel – see Tel-Aviv

JERUSALEM, Israel (Ruth Kaufmann) 02 69911
(Independent of us: ERAN, POB 8057)

5/9 **Jundiaí**, Brazil (Caio Jupert Fraga) 434 4037
CVV-Samaritanos, Rua Barao de Jundiaí 1090/s.6, Jundiaí, SP

3/7 **Kalgoorlie**, Western Australia (Esther Rohdnight) 090 21 4111
The Samaritans, POB 480, Kalgoorlie, WA 6430

2/15 **Kandy**, Sri Lanka (Raja Rajapakse)
Sri Lanka Sumithrayo, YMCA Building, Sangaraja Mawatha

KELOWNA, British Columbia, Canada (Joanne Wagner) 763 9191
(Independent of us: Crisis Line, POB 307)

KITA-KYUSHU, Japan
(Independent of us: branch of Inochi no Denwa. The Rev. Toru Akiyama, 1-8-1 Sutara, Wakamatsu-ku)

2/14 **Kitwe**, Zambia (Graham Piearce) 215 194
The Samaritans, Obote Avenue; or POB 793

1/2 **Kowloon**, Hong Kong (Andrew Tu) 3-370000 & 3-368888
The Samaritan Befrienders of Hong Kong, 45 Block 13, G/F, Lok Fu Estate

1/11 **Kuala Lumpur**, West Malaysia (David Muttu) 54144/5
The Befrienders, Sedia Bersahabat, 95 Jalan Templer, Petaling Jaya, Selangor

KUWAIT, Arabia – in preparation. Correspondent: Mrs H. Bidgood, POB 379; tel. 715 449

LAGOS, Nigeria – in preparation. Correspondent: Philip Warner, POB 7272, 4 Keffi Street, tel. 20143

LA PAZ, Bolivia – in preparation. Correspondent: Sra M. Carmena V. de Busch, Ed. Presidente Germann Busch, Plaza Isabel Católica

4/7 **Launceston**, Tasmania (Pat Igoe) 31 3355 & 39 1770
Life Link, POB 228, Launceston, Australia 7250

LENINGRAD, USSR
(Independent of us: Po Voprosam Semeinoi Zhizni, Ul. Rubinsteina 25; tel. 15 80 28)

LIMA, Peru – in preparation. Correspondent: Dr Lorenzo Loyola, Calle Jorge Valdeavellano 119; tel. 719 886

LJUBLJANA, Yugoslavia. Correspondent: Dr Onja Tekavčič, Ćegoranska 7, 61000 Ljubljana

LOBATSE, Botswana – in preparation. Correspondent: Jennifer Inger, POB 126, tel. 267

LOK FU – see Kowloon

LOS ANGELES, California, USA
(Independent of us: Suicide Prevention Center, 1041 S. Menlo Avenue, California 90006)

LOWER HUTT – see Hutt Valley

3/14 **Luanshya**, Zambia (Maurice Chwelwa) 2655
The Samaritans, POB 240

LUND, Sweden (Ninnie Sahlström)
(Independent of us: Kontakt-Tjänst, Stora Södergatan 39; tel. 110021)

4/14 **Lusaka**, Zambia (Denys Whitehead) 54968
The Samaritans, POB 2660

LUXEMBOURG, Luxembourg – in preparation. Correspondent: Dr Georges Müller, 35 Rue Victor Hugo, Esch-sur-Alzette

MACAU – in abeyance

MADRAS, India – in preparation. Correspondent: Vijayan Pavamani, 17 Royd Street, Calcutta 70016

MANILA, Philippines – in preparation

1/21 **Mar del Plata**, Argentina (Joaquin Peiró) 30 430
CVV-Samaritanos, Galeria de las Americas, San Martín 2634, local 48, 7600 Mar del Plata

MARTHA'S VINEYARD, Massachusetts, USA
Associate group of Falmouth, q.v.

MASCARELLAS, Zimbabwe-Rhodesia
Associate group of Salisbury q.v.

3/6 **Masterton**, New Zealand (Ken Daniels) 81259
YMCA Premises, Church Street, Masterton, North Island

MAURITIUS, Indian Ocean – see Beau Bassin

MEMPHIS, Tennessee, USA (Allan Battle)
(Independent of us: Suicide & Crisis Intervention Center, POB 4068, Tennessee 38104; tel. 901-525 1717 & 324 6669)

MEXICO CITY, Mexico – in preparation. Correspondent: Maria Sala de Gòmezgil, Instituto de Investigaciones Sociales, Torre de Humanidades 2, 7 piso, Ciudad Universitaria, Coyoacan 20, DF

1/24 **Montevideo**, Uruguay (Zelmira Martínez de Addis) 70 1024 & 40 6068
CVV-Samaritanos, Duvinioso Terra 1030 apto. 08

NAIROBI, Kenya – in preparation

1/14 **Ndola**, Zambia (Henry Machipishla) 4915
The Samaritans, Red Cross Centre, Dr Damie Street

1/33 **Nueva-Huila,** Colombia (L. G. Cortés) 26896 & 28437
CVV-Samaritanos, Carrera 5A No. 6–51

3/3 **New Delhi**, India (Kiran Sharma) 611918 & 618883
Sanjivini (The Befrienders), H-Block North, Defence Colony Flyover Shopping Complex, Jungpura side, New Delhi 110024

OKINAWA, Japan
(Independent of us: branch of Inochi no Denwa)

OPORTO, Portugal – in preparation. Correspondent: Belinda Maia, Rua Eng. Duarte Pacheco 186, Maia, Douro

ORLANDO, Florida, USA (Kathy Anderson)
(Independent of us: WE CARE, 610 Mariposa Street, Orlando, FL 32801; tel. 425 2624)

1/25 **Osaka**, Japan (Akira Nishihara) 06–251 4339
Suicide Prevention, 38 Sennen-cho, Minami-ku, Osaka, Japan 542

OTTAWA, Canada
(Independent of us: Distress Center, POB 2637, Station D, KTP 5W7; tel. 238 3311)

2/6 **Palmerston**, New Zealand (John Lloyd) 744-00
The Samaritans, 15 Amesbury Street; or POB 1963, Palmerston, North Island

1/27 **Paramaribo**, Surinam (Otmar Buyne) 99318
The Samaritans, H.D. Benjaminsstraat 16 & Akademische Ziekenhuis

1/16 **Paris**, France (Dorothy Ashworth) 723 8080
SOS Help, Paris Cedex 7; tel. 3207 75327
(Also, independent of us: Phénix, c/o Marie Madeleine Dautry, 225 Faubourg St Honoré, Paris 75008; tel. 924 2796)

PECS, Hungary
(Independent of us: Megyei Mentalhygieniai Intezet, Rakoczi ut. 2, 7601 Pecs 1; tel. 15 336)

3/11 **Penang**, Malaysia (Khoot Keat Siew) 363 987
The Befrienders, Counselling Centre, 360 Macalister Road

1/7 **Perth**, Western Australia (David Woodroffe) 09 381 5555 & 5725
The Samaritans, 60 Bagot Road, Subiaco, WA 6008
Telateen, same address; tel. 381 2500

2/5 **Peshawar**, Pakistan (Younis Sabir)
POB 28, Peshawar, North West Frontier Province

PETALING JAYA, Malaysia – see Kuala Lumpur

2/9 **Pinheiros**, Brazil (Walter Battaglia) 881 4119 & 64 1564
CVV-Samaritanos, Rua Henrique Schaumann 163, Pinheiros, CEP 05413 São Paulo, SP

PORT-AU-PRINCE, Haiti – in preparation. Correspondent: Sra S. Muñoz de Guarda, Correo San Enrique, Santiago, Chile

6/7 **Port Hedland**, Western Australia (John Watson) 091 72 1999
The Samaritans, POB 2113, South Hedland, WA 6722

PORT OF SPAIN, Trinidad – see Curepe

6/9 **Porto Alegre**, Brazil (Zélia Lacassagne) 25 0612
CVV-Samaritanos, Avenida Oswaldo Aranha 1092, conj. 07, CEP 90000 Porto Alegre, RS

3/12 **Providence**, RI, USA (Carolyn Benedict Drew) (401) 272 4044 & 4243
The Samaritans, 33 Chestnut Street, Providence, RI 02903

PUSAN, Korea – see Busan

QUITO, Ecuador – in preparation. Correspondent: Dra Carlota Felix, Ponce 109, Oficina 6

11/9 **Recife**, Brazil (Waldette Lacerda) 325 4109
CVV-Samaritanos, Rua dos Navigantes 1755, apto. 401, Boa Viagem, CEP 50000 Recife, PE

REYKJAVIK, Iceland – in preparation. Correspondent: Jon Bjarman, Haaleitisbraut 115, 105 Reykjavik

20/9 **Ribeirâo Prêto**, Brazil (A.K. González)
CVV-Samaritanos, Rua Wenceslau Bras 250, CEP 14100

Rio de Janeiro, Brazil (Normando Melo de Oliveira Dias) 252 5132

10/9 CVV-Samaritanos 1, Avenida Rio Branco 156, S/720, Rio de Janeiro, RJ; tel. 221 7723

13/9 CVV-Samaritanos 2, Rua do Bisp 86, Rio de Janeiro, RJ; tel. 248 7171

(Mr Dias is the Director of both Branches)

1/32 **Rome**, Italy (Elizabeth Wyatt) 501 1888

The Samaritans, Piazza San Sylvestro 8 (near GPO)

SACRAMENTO, California, USA (Bob Good) – Information Center about The Samaritans, 1525 Barnett Circle, Carmichael, CA 95608

SACUBVA, Zimbabwe-Rhodesia (Michael Zambesi) – associate group of Umtali, q.v.

1/23 **St Cloud**, Minnesota, USA (in abeyance). Correspondent: Lynne Lindemeier, The Samaritans, 2013 14th St North, St Cloud, MN 56301

ST GEORGE'S, Grenada, WI – in preparation. Correspondent: Archdeacon Huggins, The Cathedral

ST NOM LA BRETECHE, France (François Jelenques) 460 7543 & 749 7440

(Independent of us: Phénix, 1 Allée des Soleils, St Nom la Breteche 78860)

ST THOMAS, Virgin Islands, USA

(Independent of us: Hot Line, POB 696, St Thomas, 00801 USV)

1/4 **Salisbury**, Zimbabwe-Rhodesia (John Bamforth) 22000 & 20201

The Samaritans, POB UA 267, Union Avenue
(Same address for Denis Nelson, Secretary of the National Council of Samaritans)

SAN MATEO, California, USA (Charlotte Ross) (415) 349 HOPE & 573 2349
(Independent of us: Suicide Prevention Center, 274 W 20th Av., San Mateo, CA 94403)

SANTA ROSA, Brazil – in preparation. Correspondent: Sr R. Nonato de Britto, CVV-Samaritanos, Rua Jericho 109, Santa Rosa, CEP 58100, Campina Grande

SANTIAGO, Chile – in preparation. Correspondent: Sra Anne Bicheno, c/o UNESCO, Casilla 3187

4/9 **Santo André**, Brazil (Lorival Marcusso Blanco) 449 0332 & 0022
CVV-Samaritanos, Rua General Glicério 524, CEP 09000 Santo André, SP

21/9 **Santos**, Brazil (Rubens Petinati)
CVV-Samaritanos, Rua Evaristo Da Veiga 266, CEP 11100

22/9 **São Caetano**, Brazil (Lorival Marcusso Blanco) 449 0332 & 0022
c/o CVV-Samaritanos Santo André (q.v.)

7/9 **São José dos Campos**, Brazil (Mário Ferreira Vinhas) (0213) 21 4370
CVV-Samaritanos, Rua Tenente Nevio Baracho 201, CEP 12200, SP

1/9 **São Paulo**, Brazil (Rosa Maria Carleto) 34 4141
CVV-Samaritanos, Rua Abolição 411, CEP 01319

SAPPORO, Japan (Yoshinari Noda)
(Independent of us: Hokkaido Inochi no Denwa, 5-12 Sumikawa, Minami-ku, Sapporo, Hokkaido 061-21)

SCARBOROUGH, Ontario, Canada (Gurli Struwing) 291 2111
(Independent of us: Distress Center, POB 566, Postal Station A, M1K 5C5)

SENLIS, France (Eric Degremont) 164-453 2665
(Independent of us: Phénix, Place Gérard de Nerval, Senlis 60300)

SEOUL, Korea – in preparation. Correspondent: Sister Catherine, SHC, 3 Jongdong, Jungku, Seoul 1000

1/10 **Singapore** (Irene Jacob) 221 4444 & 221 2121
SOS – The Samaritans of Singapore, 591A New Bridge Road, Singapore 0208

SOFIA, Bulgaria – in preparation. Correspondent: Dr Georg Kotarov, 58b Buzludja Street, 1463 Sofia

SPLIT, Yugoslavia (Dr Petar Bokun)
(Independent of us: Vruča Linija, B. Santini 37, 58000 Split)

STAVANGER, Norway – in preparation. Correspondent: Finn Kolnes, Bethaniakjelleren, Waisenhusgate 39, 4000 Stavanger

SUVA, Fiji – in preparation

TARAWA, Gilbert & Ellice Islands – in preparation. Correspondent: Ann Heeley, King George V School, Bikenibeu

15/9 **Tatuape**, Brazil (D. Vallin)
CVV-Samaritanos, Rua Siria 67, CEP 03086

16/9 **Taubate**, Brazil (Paulo Pinto) 31 3571
CVV-Samaritanos, Rua Ubatuba S/N, CEP 12100

6/6 **Tauranga**, New Zealand (Walter Hurst) 81001
The Samaritans, POB Brooklyn 6309

TEL AVIV, Israel (Robin Lowey) 25 33 11
(Independent of us: ERAN, POB 33142)

TOKYO, Japan (Yukio Saito) 261 4629 & 5794
(Independent of us: Inochi no Denwa, c/o Tokyo Lutheran Center, 2-32 Fujimi 1-chome, Chiyoda-ku, Tokyo 102. The Director is also responsible for the Federation of Inochi no Denwa for the whole of Japan)

TRANSKEI, Southern Africa – see Umtata

TRINIDAD, WI – see Curepe

TRIVANDRUM, India – in preparation. Correspondent: Leela Tampi, 'Harshini' TC no. 15/1082, Voltas Lane, Vazhuthacaud, Trivandrum 695014, Kerala

3/4 **Umtali**, Zimbabwe-Rhodesia (Seymour Hutson) 63559
The Samaritans, 82 Second Street; or POB 133

UMTATA, Transkei – in preparation. Correspondent: Mrs Nontobeko Mafika, POB 126, Umtata 5100

VANCOUVER, British Columbia, Canada (Gary Mavis)
(Independent of us: Crisis Intervention and Suicide Prevention Center, 1946 West Broadway, V6J 1Z2)

VICTORIA, British Columbia, Canada (Anita Buckley)
(Independent of us: NEED Crisis Line, POB 5112 Station B, V8R 6N3)

1/19 **Vienna**, Austria (Maureen Agu) 73 33 74 & 73 03 553
The Befrienders, Seidlgasse 8/3, Wien 1030

VIRGIN ISLANDS, USA – see St Thomas

25/9 **Vitoria**, Brazil (Hilde de Oliveira)
CVV-Samaritanos, Rua E. Quadra 11 No. 14, Vila Vela, CEP 29000

2/2 **Wanchai**, Hong Kong (Anne Aston) 5-27 8484
The Samaritan Befrienders of Hong Kong, English-Speaking Branch, Sailors' and Soldiers' Home, 22 Hennessy Road, 3/F

WASHINGTON, DC, USA – in preparation. Correspondent: Lucy Murray-Brown, 3406 Garfield Street NW, Washington, DC 20007; tel. (202) 965 5876

1/6 **Wellington**, New Zealand (Les Freeman) 49-600
The Samaritans, Cathedral Building, Molesworth Street, Wellington, North Island; also POB 12044

List of contributors

DOMINIQUE ALESSANDRI is a Psychiatrist in Lyons, a member of Groupement d'Etudes et Prévention du Suicide and of Befrienders International

CHARLES BAGG, MA, MRCS, LRCP, MRCPsych, DPM is a Consultant Psychiatrist

LAURENCE BIGGS is Honorary Bursar of The Samaritans (Inc.)

JEAN BURT, MBE, MA is Joint General Secretary of The Samaritans (Inc.)

DAVID DAVIES, DM (Oxon), FRCP, FRCPsych is Medical Director of the Alcohol Education Centre at the Maudsley Hospital, London

GEORGE DAY, MA, MD is a Consultant to The Samaritans (Inc.)

JOHN ELDRID, AKC, Assistant Priest of St Stephen Walbrook, City of London, is Director of the London Central Branch of The Samaritans, a Vice-Chairman of The Samaritans (Inc.) and its Liaison with Befrienders International, and a Vice-President of the International Federation of Telephone Emergency Services

RICHARD FOX, MB, BS(Lond), MRCP, MRCPsych, DPM is Consultant Psychiatrist at the Bronx Psychiatric Center, New York, and Vice-President of the International Association for Suicide Prevention and Consultant Psychiatrist to The Samaritans (Inc.) and to Befrienders International

ROSEMARY HANSON is a Samaritan volunteer

DAVID MERRITT JACKSON is Honorary Publicity Consultant to The Samaritans (Inc.)

NUALA KELLY is a Samaritan volunteer

P. W. W. LEACH, MB, ChB is a Consultant Psychiatrist

IVOR H. MILLS, PhD, MD, FRCP is Professor of Medicine in the University of Cambridge

List of Contributors

COLIN MURRAY PARKES, MD, MRCPsych is an Honorary Consultant Psychiatrist

KENNETH RAWNSLEY, MB, ChB, FRCP, DPM is Professor of Psychiatry in the University of Wales

W. LINFORD REES, MD, BSc, FRCP, DPM is Professor of Psychiatry at St Bartholomew's Hospital, London

WILLIAM SARGANT, MA, MD, FRCP, DPM is a Consultant Psychiatrist at St Thomas' Hospital, London

GEORGE SPAUL, MB, BSc(Lond), MRCPsych, DPM is a Consultant Psychiatrist

ROY VINING, MB, BS is a medical practitioner and a Samaritan volunteer

H. J. WALTON, MB, PhD, FRCP, FRCPsych, DPM is Professor of Psychiatry at the University of Edinburgh

THE LATE REVD JOHN WILLIAMS was a Vice-Chairman of The Samaritans (Inc.)

MICHAEL YORKE, MA, Canon of Chelmsford, is a former Chairman of The Samaritans (Inc.)

Editor

CHAD VARAH, OBE, MA(Oxon), LLD(Leicester) is Rector of St Stephen Walbrook in the City of London, a Prebendary of St Paul's Cathedral, Founder of The Samaritans, President of the London Branch and Chairman of Befrienders International.

The Samaritans' Cassette Library

Samaritans in the British Isles can buy or borrow cassettes from their Regional Tape Librarian.

Samaritans elsewhere can address their requests to The Samaritans Inc., 17 Uxbridge Road, Slough, Berks SL1 1SN and these will be passed on to a suitable Tape Librarian. Neither Befrienders International nor The Samaritans Inc. keeps a supply of tapes.

All the recordings listed are confidential to The Samaritans and may be played only to Samaritan volunteers in good standing. They must on no account be used for family or other entertainment.

'Shorts' for preparation classes

No. 7 *The tongue-tied client* (or 'silent call') (about 15 minutes), plus *Suicidal thoughts* (about 15 minutes), which discusses ways of helping clients to reveal their suicidal thoughts and impulses. (Revised 1978.)

No. 24 *Advice dodging* (about 10 minutes) attempts to demonstrate how demands for advice and personal opinion can be parried.

No. 26 *Sexophony* (about 15 minutes) gives two contrasting responses to the aggressive sexual caller; useful also for informing prospective volunteers what they are letting themselves in for.

No. 27 *Fifteen pointers* (about 22 minutes) is a pencil-and-paper game relating to an insidious medical disease associated with a third of all fatal suicides.

No. 30 *I am the client* (about 24 minutes) attempts to envisage a client's emotional experience before, during and after his first encounter with a Samaritan volunteer.

For Samaritans taking preparation classes

No. 10 *Endogenous depressive illness* (about 30 minutes) is a MUST for anyone taking the class on 'Befriending the Client with Psychological Problems'.

No. 11 *Crisis* (about 30 minutes) is a bit sophisticated and psychiatric, but definite and most enlightening. Everything falls into a pattern. Good for study-groups.

No. 12 *Sex ahoy*! (about 40 minutes) is an amiable farrago intended to be helpful to those facing instructing preparation classes in 'Befriending Clients with Sexual Problems'.

No. 21 *Human behaviour* (about 36 minutes) is a 'non-psychiatric' study of human motivations and how they can get out of control.

No. 5 *A talk about talks* (revised 1975) (about 30 minutes) is a 'quarry' for branches' speaker's secretary. It discusses the content of differing Outside Talks and the choice and briefing of 'missionary' speakers.

No. 39 *The essence of befriending*. The befriending situation from the volunteer's point of view. Provocative.

No. 34 '*No, we are not doctors but –*' This is a useful talk for those who say we must never diagnose.

No. 38 *Referral too soon*: two contrasting role-plays, showing how to lose and how to sustain a client.

Special areas for small discussion groups

No. 40 *Sexual problems in adolescence* (35 minutes) covers an enormous amount of ground; boy–girl, girl–boy relationships, child–parent interactions, teenage–society conflict. With our increasing number of child clients, this talk is more than ever a MUST for all Leaders and Directors. (A new recording 1977 to replace No. 2).

No. 36 *Suicide* (32 minutes) (Weybridge workshop). Technically near-professional, it is a joy to listen to, and its contents are both illuminating and thought-provoking. A MUST for all In-service Study Groups.

No. 14 *Alcoholism* (about 35 minutes) is a lively and gripping survey, memorable and provocative.

No. 15 *Psychopathy* (about 50 minutes all told). Doris Odlum outlines the psychopathic personality; later Ian Lowry in role-play encounters a psychopath played by George Henshaw.

No. 16 *Drug addiction* (about 35 minutes) is a masterpiece of information and enlightenment. Gets the whole problem into perspective, and never flags.

No. 17 *Clients helpable and unhelpable* (about 55 minutes) is full of thumbnail accounts of clients of every variety; psychopaths, the endogenously depressed, the dispirited, the paranoid etc., and what can or cannot be done to help them.

No. 23 *Two contrasting phone calls* (about 15 minutes). A call from a distressed client is handled (a) by an inexperienced and somewhat insensitive volunteer; and (b) by one with greater empathy. The many subtle differences are worth detecting, and analysing in depth.

No. 31 *What Samaritans should know about VD* (about 30 minutes). This is a MUST for anyone who undertakes the Sexual Problem talks at Preparation Classes.

No. 41 *Bereavement.* Two extended and absorbing role-plays, (a) Embittered bereavement, and (b) bereavement accepted. Great depth.

No. 20 *Addiction to Samaritans.* A witty and good-humoured exposition with well-concealed sting. What is described so vividly does not apply to *you* of course, but you may be able to think of several volunteers whom the cap would fit.

No. 37 *Guess Wrong.* A three-choice role-play game used for training in USA. Splendidly enacted and amusingly different in approach from our own traditions.

No. 42 'BRENDA'

(a) *The Brenda experiment* is a 1976 role-play of scripts

included in 'house' edition of Chad Varah's 'Telephone Masturbators', performed by members of the Central London Branch.

(b) *Brenda's first five years* is a talk by Rosemary of Central London Branch with interludes of role-play. (See this book, p. 167.)

Long players for leisurely listening at home

Nos. 40, 12, 15 and 17 (see above).

No. 13 *Counselling a lesbian* (55 minutes) is a masterpiece of warm tactful handling, but inevitably slow-moving as it was role-play recorded at a large Swanwick conference. A MUST for all Directors and Leaders who may very well have to cope with this sort of situation.

No. 22 *The elderly client* (36 minutes) reveals many unexpected emotional problems encountered in old age; a bourne towards which (D.V.) we are all inexorably travelling.

No. 32 *Loughborough plums* (1976) Volume 1.

No. 33 *Loughborough plums* (1976) Volume 2.
York plums (1977) Volume 1.
York plums (1977) Volume 2.
York plums (1978).

No. 43 *Plenaries at York Conference (1978).*

(a) *Alcoholism* by Dr David Davies. (See this book, p. 139.) In 18½ minutes he gently refutes much that we have been taught and have accepted over the years, and replaces it with a much more logical picture. Possibly this talk should replace No. 14. And 'What it is like to be a compulsive Gambler' is an eye-opener to those of us who are puzzled (and impatient) with the inexplicable.

(b) *Marital Violence* by Dr J. Gayford, lasts an hour (but you would never notice it): gripping, instructive and enlightening.

Seminar 'plums' from York Conference (1978)

No. 44 (a) *Heresies and common sense:* provocative contributions by George Day, Mike Charman and Bob Withers.

(b) *Three cautionary tales.* A frank discussion of their client-catastrophes by David Evans, Jean Burt and Brenda Bridge, with comments by Richard Fox and Mike Charman.

No. 45 (a) *The press release* by John Curran, is a MUST for all Branch Publicity Officers, as is 'The Use of Radio' by Elizabeth Salisbury. Both classics.

(b) *What it is like to be a Suicidal Depressive* by Lynne of Dundee – a survivor's tale – is a real MUST for Preparation Classes, Training Officers, Leaders, Directors – the lot. Easily the best 15 minutes talk for years. Recording unfortunately sub-standard. (But see this book, p. 101.)

Organising 'Friends of The Samaritans' by Sylvia of Hereford, exemplifies how very rewarding a well-organised and well cared-for 'Friends' organisation can be.

More fuss about young people, a further fascinating instalment of last year's diatribe by Anthony Lawton.

Painless role-play by Maidstone is a unique A.B.C. for Branches still reluctant or resistant towards attempting role-play in Preparation Classes.